BOGART & BACALL

A LOVE STORY

BOOKS BY JOE HYAMS

THE WEEKEND GAMBLER'S HANDBOOK
(with Major A. Riddle)

MY LIFE WITH CLEOPATRA
(with Walter Wanger)

BOGIE

A FIELD OF BUTTERCUPS

ACCOMPLICES TO THE CRIME:
THE ARKANSAS PRISON SCANDAL
(with Tom Murton)

WINNING TACTICS FOR WEEKEND TENNIS
(with Tony Trabert)

MISLAID IN HOLLYWOOD

WINNING TACTICS FOR WEEKEND SINGLES
(with Pancho Gonzales)

BILLIE JEAN KING'S SECRETS OF WINNING TENNIS
(with Billie Jean King)

BOGART & BACALL

A LOVE STORY

Joe Hyams

David McKay Company, Inc. | New York

Bogart & Bacall: A Love Story
Copyright © 1975 by Joe Hyams
All rights reserved, including the right to reproduce this book,
or parts thereof, in any form, except for
the inclusion of brief quotations in a review.

Library of Congress Cataloging in Publication Data
Hyams, Joseph.
Bogart & Bacall.

Includes index.
1. Bogart, Humphrey, 1899–1957.
2. Bacall, Lauren, 1924–   I. Title.
PN2287.B48B88   791.43'028'0922 [B]   75–9842
ISBN 0–679–50549–0

Manufactured in the United States of America
Designed by The Etheredges

". . . all stories, if continued far enough, end in death and he is no true story teller who would keep that from you."
—ERNEST HEMINGWAY

"To die soon or die late matters nothing; to die badly or die well is the important point."
—SENECA

BOGART & BACALL

A LOVE STORY

PROLOGUE

"What's past is prologue."
—WILLIAM SHAKESPEARE: THE TEMPEST

Later Bogie would say that it was Betty's height that first impressed him, that and the way she moved with catlike grace. After being married to her for eleven years he would remark that of all the women he knew she had the most class. "A lot of broads in this town, but I married a lady with class," he would say of her admiringly in that distinctive voice of his that mated with hers so perfectly.

Even today, seeing her from a distance on a city street striding easily, with head thrown back, you would know why she interested him from the day they met, when she was only nineteen and he was forty-four. She was no ordinary girl then, just as today she is an extraordinary woman.

Many things would change in the nearly two decades since his death, but even today, when she is fifty, seen close up and without make-up, her face has not lost its distinctive line, but it is her eyes that rivet you. Feline, clear, gray, unwavering, penetrating, studying and sometimes mocking, making no attempt to hide the fact that they are evaluating, judging and

1

assessing you. And if you are found wanting or ordinary or dull they will shut you off.

But the most formidable thing about her today is her presence. She is never just anyplace, she dominates her surroundings, be they a party or a stage. She had immediate impact in the first film she made with Bogie, but success and maturity have added the element of charisma.

After Bogart's death in 1957 she would go through tortured times trying to find her place in life, seeking a replacement for the irreplaceable man who molded, shaped and made her into the woman she is today. Much of him rubbed off on her: the loyalty to old friends, the belief in morality and goodness, the dedication to being professional.

But not all that rubbed off is pleasant in a woman. The hard-boiled, sardonic attitude that was part of his character and hers, when she was young, is not always charming in an older woman. But it is as much a part of her as it was a part of him because they were, in the final analysis, mirror images of each other.

This book is not about Betty today, however. It is about the Betty Bacall of thirty years ago, when she first went to Hollywood as an unknown, a teen-ager, and fell in love with Humphrey Bogart, the most popular film star of his time. Mostly it is about the two people whose romance and marriage captured the imagination of people the world over and has endured beyond his death to become a legend in our time.

CHAPTER 1

"This is Duke Mantee, folks. He's the world-famous killer and he's hungry."
—THE PETRIFIED FOREST

There was a Blue Blood society in New York at the turn of the century and Humphrey DeForest Bogart's family was part of it. Humphrey's father, Dr. Belmont DeForest Bogart, was a third-generation American who could trace his family's ancestry back to 1500 through a long line of respectable Dutch burghers, and the Bogart's are included in each edition of Dau's New York Blue Book, from its first publication in 1907 until it was discontinued three decades later.

Dr. Bogart was a graduate of Phillips Academy, Andover, Massachusetts, and Columbia College of Physicians and Surgeons, New York. Humphrey's mother, Maude Humphrey, was also a third-generation American. She had studied art in Paris under James McNeill Whistler. By the time she was thirty she had become one of the foremost magazine illustrators of the day.

The Bogarts married relatively late in life—she was thirty-three and he was thirty-four—after a long courtship that began while he was still a medical student. He graduated from Columbia in 1896 and was licensed to practice medicine the following year. In

3

1898, after he had established a practice in New York, he and Miss Humphrey were wed.

In a family scrapbook there is a photograph of Dr. and Mrs. Bogart taken soon after their marriage. They were a handsome, if unevenly matched, couple. Dr. Bogart was five feet eleven inches tall, a foot taller than his petite wife.

In the faded photograph Dr. Bogart appears to have an athletic build, and on one of his large hands he wears a ruby ring rather than a wedding band. Humphrey inherited the shape of his face and his broad brow and piercing eyes from his father. Dr. Bogart looks somewhat younger than his bride, who was a dark-eyed brunette, with a delicate face and body to match and the imposing carriage that many small women possess.

What does not show in the photo is Maude's incisive wit, which discouraged many suitors but delighted her husband, who also had a sharp tongue. A chronic family problem was finding servants who would tolerate their employers' blistering sarcasm.

They were both politically conservative. He was a Republican and Presbyterian. She was a Tory and Episcopalian. Maude was, in addition, a leader in the early suffragette movement. She believed strongly in equal rights for women, not only at the polls but in the home.

Those were the days when an income tax was unthinkable, when John Jacob Astor could say, "A man who has a million dollars is as well off as if he were rich." The Bogarts were not rich by comparison with the Astors, Vanderbilts and others in their social strata, but they were well off by the ordinary standards of the day. Miss Humphrey earned as much as $40,000 a year illustrating stories for such publications as the *Delineator* and painting advertisements and magazine covers. Dr. Bogart had inherited money from his father, who had invented a process of lithographing on tin, and, in addition, averaged $20,000 a year from his practice.

Their combined income enabled them to live very well, particularly when one considers that in those days a couple could get a mahogany parlor table for $3.95, a brass-trimmed bed for $3.00, a sofa for $9.98. Corned beef sold for eight cents a pound and a good suit cost $10.65. The Bogarts had four servants: a cook at $5 a week, a laundress for $3.50 a week and two maids at $3.50 a week apiece.

The Bogart home, a three-story limestone house with bay windows and heavy decorations in bas relief, was at 245 West 103rd Street near Riverside Drive. At the turn of the century that area was a very fashionable thoroughfare lined with upper-class residences and the kind of shops that are now called boutiques. Their home was across the street from the old Hotel Marseilles, an elegant residential hotel that boasted among its permanent residents Sara Delano Roosevelt (FDR's mother) and the wealthy Rheingold brothers, founders of the beer company which carried their name.

Dr. Bogart conducted his medical practice from a mahogany-paneled, green-carpeted office on the first floor of the family home, and Mrs. Bogart did her art work in a third-floor studio. The nursery was also on the third floor, and a pigeon coop crowned the roof: raising pigeons was one of the Bogarts' hobbies. The doctor was also an ardent sailor, fisherman and a superb wing shot. A natural athlete, he had been first baseman on the Andover baseball team.

Because he was a doctor, the Bogarts were one of the few families on their block with a telephone. The house was heavy with tapestries, urns, potted palms, carved ceilings, rubber plants and classical statues holding light fixtures with alabaster shades. The parquet floors were covered with oriental rugs. The family also boasted a Gramophone, complete with horn and recordings of Caruso and dialect comedians on cylindrical wax records kept wrapped in cotton in small cartons.

In December 1899, Maude Bogart was in her ninth

month of pregnancy. The household was in the tumult customary at such times, as the mother-to-be busied herself with assembling a layette and decorating the baby's nursery—blue, because both she and the doctor wanted a boy.

The day before Christmas 1899 Maude Bogart went to the Keppel Gallery in midtown Manhattan, against the advice of her husband, to see a display of original drawings of the "Gibson Girl." On Christmas Eve she complained of pains, which Dr. Bogart at first attributed to overexertion. But soon she was unmistakably in labor, and he rushed outside to hail a hansom cab.

It was a wet, cold night with a light snow falling, and it took some time for the doctor and his anxious wife to get from their home to Sloan's Maternity Hospital in upper Manhattan. A few hours later, Mrs. Bogart gave birth to an eight-pound seven-ounce son—on Christmas Day, a fact Humphrey later lamented: "I never had a birthday of my own to celebrate," he used to complain. "I got cheated out of a birthday."

The Bogarts had often discussed a name for their firstborn if he was a boy. Mrs. Bogart persuaded her husband that he be named after her, but as a concession to him the child was given the middle name of DeForest.

One night when Humphrey was only a few months old Dr. Bogart proudly told friends after dinner at Lüchow's Restaurant on 14th Street over cigars and port that it was obvious from his son's firm grip that he would be a surgeon. The doctor took to stopping other physicians in the corridors at the Presbyterian Hospital, where he was a specialist in the Department of Heart and Lungs, to ask whether they thought Columbia or Yale was the better college for a future surgeon. It was soon decided between himself and Mrs. Bogart that young Humphrey would go to Yale.

The new baby caused little change in the family's routine. Dr. Bogart still held his office hours downstairs, while his wife worked in her upstairs studio with a skylight. It was here behind her locked door that she frequently endured anguishing migraine headaches. The doctor had his own cross to bear. Arthritic from birth, he took morphine—easily available to a doctor—and had become an addict who was constantly seeking "cures" for his narcotic habit. He managed to keep his addiction a secret from everyone but his wife. None of his children, patients or colleagues were aware of it. Humphrey only learned of it from his mother after his father's death.

Humphrey's airings were usually the responsibility of a young Irish maid who took him out in a high-wheeled carriage. But one afternoon, Mrs. Bogart took Humphrey to Central Park herself. While he was playing in his carriage she made a sketch of him. When they had returned home she worked over the sketch and sent it off to an advertising agency. It was bought by Mellins Baby Food for use in their ads and on their labels and soon became the most popular baby picture of the day. It made the infant Humphrey famous as the "Original Maude Humphrey Baby."

Each summer the Bogarts, like other well-to-do New York families, went through an elaborate ritual of departure for their summer home—in their case at Canandaigua Lake, one of New York's Finger Lakes. First the city house was thoroughly cleaned, a process that took days. On the day before departure the expressman and his big wagon called for the trunks. On the tumultuous morning of departure the family and servants assembled a mountain of bags, overcoats, umbrellas and sports gear and proceeded to the railroad station in two or three horse-drawn cabs.

When Humphrey was two years old the ritual was interrupted as the family was proceeding by Pullman car to their summer home. Mrs. Bogart, who was pregnant again, announced she was in labor. Doctor Bogart and his wife got off the train and found room in a boardinghouse where the doctor himself delivered his wife of a daughter who was christened Frances

7

(though always called Pat). The following year Mrs. Bogart gave birth to another daughter, Catherine Elizabeth, in a Presbyterian hospital.

Soon after Catherine was born, Humphrey became seriously ill with pneumonia. Thereafter, his mother was never quite convinced that he was not a sickly child. She wrote to a friend at the time, "He is a manly lad, but too delicate in health." As a result of her concern with Humphrey's health, Mrs. Bogart insisted that he be bundled warmly on his outings and often sat with Humphrey at mealtimes until he had finished all his vegetables. "That concern is about as close as my mother ever came to showing maternal emotion," Humphrey was to say many years later.

"I was brought up very unsentimentally, very straightforwardly; a kiss in our family was an event. Our mother and father didn't glug over my two sisters and me. They had too many things to do, and so did we. Anyway, we were mainly the responsibility of the servants.

"I can't say that I loved my mother, but I respected her. Ours was not the kind of affection that spills over or makes pretty pictures. If, when I was grown up, I sent my mother one of those Mother's Day telegrams or said it with flowers, she would have returned the gift to me, collect."

Although Humphrey had very little mothering as a child, Dr. Bogart was a strong paternal figure, although not overly sentimental either. A practical man, he gave Humphrey and his younger sister, Pat, a roulette set for Christmas one year and then played the game with them, saying he had intended for it to help them learn mathematics.

Dr. Bogart had high hopes for "making a man" of his young son and, whenever possible, took him away from the family home on camping or hunting trips. By the time Humphrey was eight he was an expert at sailing his own Great South Bay One Designer Sloop at Lake Canandaigua. His love of boats and the sailing fraternity was to remain with him all his life.

Although father and son had good times together, Bogie's parents often had terrible fights. "We kids would pull the covers around our ears to keep out the sound of fighting," Bogie once said. "Our home was kept together for the sake of the children and the sake of propriety."

A convivial man, Dr. Bogart liked socializing, but Mrs. Bogart, perhaps because of her migraines, was antisocial. Although the Bogarts had many invitations, she rarely went out of the house except when she was working. Humphrey later was to recall her as a snob and something of an anti-Semite, and Pat said their father couldn't keep a nurse for very long because Maude was jealous of any woman around him.

Most family arguments stemmed from one source —money. Dr. Bogart preferred hunting, fishing and sailing to medicine, and more and more the responsibility for the family finances rested on his wife.

Meanwhile, Humphrey was having problems of his own. "Part of his troubles came from his name— Humphrey," his sister Pat recalls. "It sounded sissy to a lot of kids, and Bogie was always in fights. Also, my mother liked to dress him in Little Lord Fauntleroy suits which she made herself."

His nickname was "Hump," and Pat was nicknamed "Bogie" because "our mother would never have permitted her son to be called anything but Humphrey."

"Bogie hated our mother even though she was soft on him," said Pat. "But he had a crush on my father, who was a real man's man. Our parents always disagreed about our care. Mother wanted to rule the roost but father wouldn't let her. She used to spank me and it hurt because she had such little hands they cut into me, but I only got one spanking from my father."

Apparently Humphrey got one memorable spanking from his father. When he was about ten years old he ran afoul of his father over an incident which his sister Pat has since forgotten. The event was, however, to leave a scar on Humphrey permanently.

9

"As I recall it," Pat said, "Humphrey did something which upset my father so much he hit him—the only time I can recall my father ever hitting him. He hit him in the mouth. I can still hear Humphrey howling with pain. My mother was furious and she screamed, 'If you ever touch him again, I'll kill you.'"

The blow damaged a nerve in Humphrey's upper lip. Although Dr. Bogart tried to patch it up, the damage was permanent. From then on Humphrey would have a scar and slight lisp.

Pat's recollection of the cause of Bogie's scar is at variance with many versions which Bogie himself gave. He was, presumably, embarrassed to talk about it, so he usually said the scar which had left him with a stiff upper lip was the result of a wartime wound. It seems likely that the true story was far less glamorous and interesting—and too painful a memory.

According to Pat, Humphrey "adored his baby sister Catherine [Catty], who was tall and slim with long legs, light brown hair and a rosebud mouth." Catty was also Maude Bogart's favorite, and when Humphrey and Pat went outside to play, Catty stayed in Maude's studio, sewing and designing clothes.

"We used to play in our backyard or in the streets of the neighborhood," Pat said. "We did naughty things like making faces at the neighbors' servants or people on the streets. And once or twice, we got picked up and brought home by the police because we were where we weren't supposed to be. My father had left directions that if we were ever in any trouble, we were to be brought directly home by the police, and because he was a prominent doctor, they kind of looked after us. I remember once being picked up by the back of the neck and being brought home because we were fighting with kids in another neighborhood."

Humphrey's closest childhood friend was William A. Brady, Jr., son of a next-door neighbor who had come to see Dr. Bogart complaining of a touch of ptomaine, that Victorian term used to cover a multitude of ailments ranging from indigestion to heart attack.

10

Mr. Brady, Sr., a big handsome man who later would play a key role in Humphrey's life, was one of the most fascinating promoters and showmen in America. Born in the Bowery of Irish immigrant parents, he had started his career at the age of seven shining shoes and selling newspapers. He had been a stage manager, actor, director and comedian and then a sports promoter. Most boxing managers consider themselves blessed if they can handle one heavyweight title holder. Mr. Brady had two—James L. (Jim) Corbett and James J. (Jim) Jeffries. One major Broadway hit is enough to win a producer a place in the *Who's Who of the Theater*. Brady produced nearly three hundred plays, including a dozen hits, and owned his own theater, The Playhouse, in New York.

Along the way he married two stars of the stage— Marie René and Grace George—and was father of another, Alice Brady, who was half a generation older than Humphrey. Bill, Jr., his son with Miss George, was Humphrey's age.

With young Bill Brady, Humphrey frequented Brooklyn's Orpheum Theatre, which offered movies and photographed bits of famous stage acts including Alice Lloyd, Eva Tanguay and James J. Morton. And they saw one of America's first color pictures, a 700-foot Kinemacolor feature starring Willie Collier, Raymond Hitchcock and Anna Held.

Humphrey fell in love with an English actress whose name he later forgot. Bill Brady and he used to go to the theater every matinee and sit in a box and watch the star, H. B. Warner, on stage and sometimes, in a very tense moment, yell, "Go to it, Harry." Then they would go backstage and ogle the leading lady. Sometimes Humphrey would help her into her coat and, as he recalled it, "shake all over."

Although Bill's father was in show business, it was on an "acceptable" level. Like all proper people of the time, the Bogarts were scornful of public entertainers who thrived on the attentions of the press. Dr. Bogart once told Humphrey that there were only three times

11

a gentleman's name appeared in the papers—when he was born, when he was married and when he died. Of course, one could glow quietly over certain kinds of publicity. For example, when Humphrey was ten years old, Dr. Bogart handed him a heavy, leather-bound volume. "Look through this for a familiar name," the doctor said. Humphrey found that his father had been given several paragraphs in *Who's Who in New York*.

"My father was very proud," Bogart later recalled, "but I think my mother was miffed. Her name wasn't in it."

Every Saturday afternoon Humphrey and young Bill Brady went on passes given them by Mr. Brady to one of the Broadway shows. In later years, when Humphrey was famous, he said that his notion of great acting came from these expeditions. By the time he was thirteen he had seen Laurette Taylor in *Peg O' My Heart*, Maude Adams as *Peter Pan*, Nazimova in *Bella Donna*. He recalled having seen Sarah Bernhardt at the Palace Theatre in a vaudeville act that featured in third place an English comic juggler named W. C. Fields.

Like all proper New York society children, Humphrey attended a private school, the Delancy School, where he remained until the fifth grade. Then he was enrolled at Trinity School, an old and select Episcopal institution for young gentlemen located on 91st Street near Amsterdam Avenue. He is listed on the records of Trinity as "a communicant of St. Michael's Church." He entered Trinity in September 1913, when he was not quite fourteen.

Every morning he walked to school outfitted in the proper attire: blue serge suit, including vest, white shirts with detachable collars, held on fore and aft by brass buttons, and, in winter, a Chesterfield overcoat with fly front and black velvet collar.

Trinity was run along the lines of a British boys' school. The day started at 9:00 A.M. with services in

12

the chapel. Latin, Greek and German were prominent in the curriculum, and there was a high premium on memorization of almost everything.

The head of the school, the rector, was Lawrence T. Cole, affectionately called Bunny Cole. A beneficent and compassionate gentleman, the rector always wore a black cassock, tied at his waist with a tasseled cord.

Years later Bogart was to recall one of many sessions in the rector's study.

"Herr Luther has reported you again," the headmaster said.

"Yes, sir."

"He complains that you started a riot in class this morning, and he's given you a failure in German."

"Yes, sir."

"Why?"

"I don't like German."

"Nor Herr Luther?"

"No, sir."

"Since you don't like German and you don't like English or history or economics, will you tell me if there's anything you do like, Master Bogart?"

"I like math, sir. Algebra."

"Why?"

"Because there's nothing theoretical about it—it's simply fact. You can do a problem and get your answer and then you prove the answer's right."

"But these riots! This endless flaunting of all authority. Why do you do these things?"

Humphrey didn't have an answer to that question then, though years later he was to volunteer one: "I always liked stirring up things, needling authority. Even in my childhood it gave me pleasure. I guess I inherited it from my parents. They needled everyone, including each other."

Humphrey's attendance at Trinity is still remembered by his classmates. Eric Hodgins, the writer, recalled that Humphrey wore a black derby hat day in and day out. "That made him stand out in the class,"

13

according to Mr. Hodgins, who never did figure out what significance the strange headgear had for young Humphrey.

"He was not a loner, and it was obvious from the way that Humphrey bore himself that he belonged to an 'in' group in school—though just what group was never clear," Mr. Hodgins says. "He was friendly but a bit distant—what would be described today as 'cool.'"

In those days at Trinity a lady's man was referred to as a "fusser." Although Humphrey did not win acclaim as the biggest "fusser" in his class, Mr. Hodgins remembers him as a contender for the title.

Humphrey apparently did barely satisfactory work at Trinity until 1916–17, when a case of scarlet fever caused him to repeat the eleventh grade. His average grade for that year was 70, just barely passing—but he graduated in September 1917.

Earlier in the year, Dr. Bogart had decided it was high time his son went away to the preparatory school he himself had attended, Phillips Academy at Andover, Massachusetts. In a letter to Dr. Alfred E. Stearns, the Academy's distinguished headmaster, Dr. Bogart wrote:

"I am anxious to send my boy of seventeen years, now at Trinity School in this city, to Andover next year," he wrote. "Will you kindly send catalogue concerning the school expenses, board, etc. As I have other children to consider it will be necessary to limit his expenses as much as possible.

"You will remember me as your teammate in baseball, also football, class of 1888. . . ."

By the end of summer Humphrey had been accepted at Andover. On September 12, 1917, Dr. Bogart wrote to Dr. Stearns saying, "Humphrey is a splendid fellow and very popular with everyone—he will do good work if placed with a boy who will not take his attention from the regular study periods. . . . May I ask that you take a personal interest

14

in the boy so that he will get started on the right path which will, I am sure, lead to a successful year."

From the very beginning Humphrey disliked Andover. There was no one at the train station to greet him. He found that he was expected to be on his own, and it took him a long time to find a wagon to haul his trunks to Taylor Hall, one of the newer dormitories, where he had been assigned a room on the second floor.

His room, number five, boasted a fireplace and was furnished with a steel cot, a small oak desk, a bureau, an oak armchair and a sizable closet. Happily, the single bathroom that serviced the other six occupants on the floor was next to his room.

Frederick M. Boyce, a physics teacher and the housemaster, lived on the ground floor with his wife and children. From the beginning "Freddie" made it plain that he would brook no shenanigans, and warned that there would be little time for anything other than study, anyway.

The other boys on the floor were cordial, but, to Humphrey's mind, bookworms. Charles Yardley Chittick, now a patent attorney in Boston, had the room across the hall. "If there's anything I remember about Humphrey in those days, it was his sullenness," Mr. Chittick says. "I got the impression that he was a very spoiled boy. When things didn't go his way he didn't like it a bit."

By Christmas vacation Humphrey was in difficulty at Andover, failing three of his five courses. When he went home he tried to avoid showing Dr. Bogart his report card, but it was Mrs. Bogart who was most upset. Dr. Bogart explained optimistically that it would take time for the boy to get adjusted, but she was insistent that his grades improve at once.

"If your marks don't improve measurably by the end of the next semester, we will withdraw you and put you to work," she threatened. On that note Humphrey returned to school.

15

The following month, on February 19, 1918, Dr. Stearns wrote Dr. Bogart that the faculty voted to put Humphrey on probation because "of the poor record which he has made this term . . . all of his teachers agree that he has good ability but that he has not exerted himself at all seriously during the current term; and that his low standing at the present time is due largely to that fact. It was also decided that his work in English should be readjusted, as he seems wholly unable at this time to meet the requirements of that particular course."

Dr. Stearns concluded with the warning that "if there is not an all-around improvement, we shall be compelled to require his withdrawal. I earnestly hope that such a catastrophe as this may be avoided."

Dr. Bogart instantly replied, saying that he and Mrs. Bogart would do everything in their power "to have the boy find himself. Humphrey is a good boy, with no bad habits, who simply has lost his head temporarily," he wrote. "The whole problem to my mind seems to be that the boy has given up his mind to sports and continuous correspondence with his girl friends. The harder the screws are put on, the better it will be for my son."

Apparently, Humphrey did not respond well to the "screws." On May 15, 1918, Dr. Stearns wrote: "To my great regret I am forced to advise you that Humphrey has failed to meet the terms of his probation and that it becomes necessary therefore for us to require his withdrawal from the school at this time. I was not present at the faculty meeting when this decision was reached; but I have learned from the boy's instructors that it was the unanimous opinion of those who are familiar with the situation that it would be unwise for Humphrey to remain here longer. I cannot tell you how deeply I regret our inability to make the boy realize the seriousness of the situation and put forth the effort required to avert this disaster.

"My experience, covering a good many years now, leads me to believe that Humphrey will profit greatly

16

by this seemingly unfortunate occurrence, and that it will tend to bring him to his senses as nothing else could do. I can only express the sincere hope that this will prove the turning point in the boy's life, and that from now on he will develop that serious purpose which he appears to have lacked thus far. . . ."

Two days later, in Dr. Bogart's absence "on business," Maude answered Dr. Stearns. "I am sending Humphrey $25.00 to come home at once," she wrote, adding, "Mr. Frank E. Kirby, a very prominent naval architect, and now building ships for the government, has promised to give Humphrey a job in his shipyard at once. I trust the boy will come to his senses and work. As Mr. Kirby has both brains and influence (he bought all the ships for the U.S. government the time of the Spanish-American War) I hope he can help Humphrey. . . ."

Years later, Bogart claimed that he was asked to leave Andover because of his "excessive high spirits" and "infractions of the rules."

Humphrey's homecoming was stormy. His father was quietly but deeply disappointed. It was becoming apparent that Humphrey would never go on to Yale and become a doctor.

Mrs. Bogart was harsh: "You've had every chance that could be given to you and you have failed—not only yourself but your parents," she said. "We don't intend to support you for the rest of your life. You're on your own from now on."

Humphrey moped about the house for several weeks before finding a solution to his problems. America was at war with Germany and he decided to enlist in the navy. Although barely of age, he had his parents' consent and blessings.

"The war was a big joke," Bogart said years later. "Death? What does death mean to a kid of eighteen? The idea of death starts getting to you only when you're older—when you read obituaries of famous people whose accomplishments have touched you, and when people of your own generation die. At

17

eighteen war was great stuff. Paris! French girls! Hot damn!"

He eventually was assigned to convoy duty aboard a troop transport—the *Leviathan*, formerly the S.S. *Vaterland*, Germany's largest passenger liner, which had been converted to a U.S. troop carrier.

He spent all of the next year aboard the *Leviathan*, shuttling troops back and forth between Hoboken, Brest and Liverpool. All told, Humphrey made between fifteen and twenty crossings aboard the *Leviathan* before the morning of November 11, 1918, when President Wilson announced that the Armistice had been signed.

Humphrey was almost twenty years old and had been in the navy for two years when he was finally given an honorable discharge. Later, he would say, "I was sorry that the war had not touched me mentally. I was still no nearer to an understanding of what I wanted to be or what I was."

The comment was revealing in light of the fact that at an age when most of his contemporaries were either at work or in college he was still drifting aimlessly without any real training for work or any idea of what he wanted to do with his life. So he went back to his third-floor room in the family brownstone. Although there was an Armistice between nations, there was no peace for Humphrey at home. His mother constantly belittled him, pointing out what he knew all too well himself—he had little education and no way of earning a living.

And he could not rely on his father for support. The doctor had taken to signing on as ship's doctor on freighters. Pat Bogart believes that the doctor was trying to escape from the constant marital squabbling at home and, with the children almost grown up, saw little reason to keep the family together.

Many years later Bogart was to say he believed his father left home whenever possible because his morphine addiction had become a problem; there was more morphine available without question to a ship's doctor than to a society physician. Although there is no corroborative evidence for this, Humphrey was the one left to listen to his mother's constant complaint about the men of the house who were good for nothing and willing to let her support the family.

During the next two years Humphrey made an indifferent attempt to join the business world. He worked for at least a year as a runner for the Wall Street investment house of S. W. Strauss & Co. Presumably it was no coincidence that the firm handled his parents' investments—it appeared that the Bogarts had not yet given up trying to help their son.

Those were the opening days of the Roaring Twenties. Maude Bogart and other suffragettes had secured the right to vote and were abandoning the last vestiges of Victorianism in dress, speech and thought. Women were discussing Freud over cigarettes (in long holders), drinking cocktails, bobbing their hair and wearing lipstick and rouge. A *New York Times* editorial lamented, "The American woman has lifted her skirts beyond any modest limitation."

The Eighteenth Amendment brought Prohibition, and with it the Jazz Age, complete with speak-easies, bathtub gin, bootleggers and gangsters machine-gunning one another down in broad daylight, just as in the movies Bogart was to make years later.

But Humphrey, brought up in propriety and the Victorian ethic that a man must work toward a future, felt guilty because he was working at a job without one. He constantly groused about being an errand boy to his friends, Bill, Jr., and Alice Brady.

One night Alice suggested that Humphrey see her father about a job. Bill, Sr., who was one of the top theatrical producers on Broadway, had decided to branch out into film production and was starting an independent movie company, World Films. Humphrey took Alice's advice and saw Brady, Sr., who hired him as an office boy with the promise that he would "give him a chance." Just what the "chance" would be was unspecified, but it promised more for the future than being an errand boy. Humphrey took the job.

Toward the end of a picture called *Life*, with Arlene Pretty and Rod LaRocque, Brady discharged the director and told Humphrey that this was his promised "chance"—he was to finish directing the picture. Although it seems unlikely today that an office boy be given the job of directing a film, the fact was that it was not uncommon at that time for most anyone to take over as a director. Not many films had been made, and there was little chance for anyone to learn the craft other than do it. Furthermore, since neither Miss Pretty nor Mr. LaRocque were big stars at the time, and the film budget was minimal, Mr. Brady was gambling very little.

Faced with the actors on set and a cameraman waiting for instructions, however, Humphrey was at a loss as to how to proceed. Brady, who had never directed a film himself, was forced to take charge.

Humphrey was not discouraged. He felt that although he hadn't made it as a director, he could write a better story than *Life*. He began drifting into Greenwich Village every afternoon, where he tried at least to look like a writer. After a few months he completed a story which he later described as "full of blood and guts; a pot-boiler to end all pot-boilers." He submitted the story to Mr. Brady, who said it had an interesting plot and passed it on to Jesse L. Lasky, who was then a top film producer. Mr. Lasky, in turn, gave it to his assistant Walter Wanger, who referred the story to the wastebasket. "It was awful," Mr. Wanger recalled, although years later, when he was a big Hollywood producer, Wanger would boast, "Bogart once wrote for me."

Despite Humphrey's failure as a director and writer, Mr. Brady still had a soft spot in his heart for the boy he had known since childhood. His own son had not shown any interest in the theater and it is not unlikely that he thought if Humphrey was involved in theater, Bill, Jr., might follow suit. So Brady made Humphrey stage manager of one of his plays at $50 a week. Then Mr. Brady's wife, actress Grace George, who was a top star on Broadway, suggested Humphrey manage her new play, *The Ruined Lady*, for the same salary.

Ironically, Humphrey had never sought a career of any kind in the theater, but now it was being handed to him, courtesy of his childhood friends. Later he would say he "owed it all" to the Bradys, although at the time it appeared that the debt would be minimal and they were merely acting out of friendship.

During the run of *The Ruined Lady*, Neil Hamilton, who was the juvenile lead, became ill. Brady required that the stage manager understudy all the male roles, so Humphrey was required to step in for Hamilton. A rehearsal was called, and on a Saturday afternoon Humphrey Bogart made his first professional appearance with just the cast as audience.

"It was awful," Bogart said years later. "I knew all the lines of all the parts because I'd heard them from out front about a thousand times. But I took one look at the emptiness where the audience would be that night and I couldn't remember anything."

Fortunately, Miss George also became ill before curtain time, so the play closed that night. Humphrey's debut was postponed.

Working for Brady was always exciting. One could never tell what the producer might do next. Often he would step in two days before an opening and tear the play to pieces. The actors would have to stay up all night putting the pieces back together.

One night in Atlantic City, Brady kicked Humphrey in the stomach. It was during the opening of a play called *Drifting*, starring Alice Brady. Mr. Brady hated long intermissions and sometimes arbitrarily shortened them by ringing the curtain back up himself. This particular night Brady brought the curtain up early enough to give the audience a good view of stagehands moving scenery. Bogart rang it down again. Brady, flushed with anger, caught his stage manager a good one in the midsection with his foot.

21

Humphrey bided his time. Later that evening, when the curtain was down and Mr. Brady was on stage making last-minute preparations for the next act, Bogart sent the curtain up. The set was a bar in Manchuria with only one white man, the bartender, in the scene. The rest were wild Manchurian natives —plus Mr. Brady, looking decidedly out of place. Brady was bewildered for a moment, then the fact that he had once been an actor came to his rescue. In a loud voice he asked for cigarettes. The bartender handed them to him. Brady threw a coin on the bar, stalked off stage and promptly fired Bogart. Humphrey, who had been fired and rehired with some regularity, gleefully departed, but was accepted back on the job the next day.

When the play opened at the Playhouse in Brooklyn, Brady, who had overheard Humphrey (then twenty-three years old) needling some of the actors about their easy jobs, said he was going to make an actor of him. He gave Bogart one line of dialogue.

The first time Humphrey trod the boards, Stuart Rose was in the audience with Humphrey's sister Pat, whom he was courting and would later marry. Dr. Bogart was in the audience, too, without Mrs. Bogart, who claimed to be "indisposed" on that night.

The opening was on Memorial Day evening, and Stuart, an officer in the National Guard, was in uniform, having just finished marching in a parade.

"Humphrey played a Japanese valet wearing a white jacket," recalls Mr. Rose. "He came on stage carrying a tray full of cocktails and had just one line to say, and he embarrassed me, he was so bad. But Dr. Bogart turned to me, put a hand on my knee and said, 'The boy is good, isn't he?' Of course, I said, 'Yes, he is.'"

Humphrey would later agree with Rose's assessment of his ability. "I was terrible," he said. "I don't remember what the line was I had to say, although I know it was only a few words, but I was so nervous that I just mumbled it. Luckily, since I was playing a Japanese, no one expected to understand me anyhow."

Despite Humphrey's unpromising stage debut, Mr. Brady still believed he had a future as an actor. Mr. Brady had once said there was one lesson he had learned from prize fighting and never forgot. It was always to go after the champion. Never waste time with second raters, he said. To that he added the admonition that if you did not know a champion when you saw one you did not belong in show business.

Apparently, Brady saw a champion in Humphrey because he seemed determined to make an actor of him, and Humphrey took the line of least resistance. He followed where Brady led. Bogart would later say he never had an acting lesson in his life; he learned how to act by acting, and he never believed in schools for acting such as the Actors Studio.

In any event, it is a matter of record that Brady next gave him a role as the juvenile in *Swifty*, starring Frances Howard (who later married Sam Goldwyn) and Neil Hamilton. This time his role was seventy "sides," or pages, long.

Brady taught young Humphrey a good deal. He gave what he called "What?" rehearsals in which he would sit in the back of the balcony listening to the actors on stage. When someone was inaudible in his lines, he would roar "What?" Bogart, slightly handicapped by his lisp, soon learned not to mumble.

There was one scene in which Humphrey had to rush downstairs with a gun and shout at Hamilton, "I'll kill you, I'll kill you, I'll kill you!" Mr. Brady sat in the pit watching the scene and making Bogart do it over and over again. Finally, as a devastating comment on Bogart's acting, he fell asleep—or pretended to.

Humphrey, furious, shoved Hamilton aside and went charging after Mr. Brady, who came roaring right back at him. Bill, Jr., and Hamilton caught Bogart and took him into the alley until he cooled off.

23

Bogart later recalled how his mother woke him up "swiftly" the morning after his acting debut by bringing the papers to his bedroom. Sitting on the edge of his bed, she rattled the papers before him. "I will read you the reviews," she said grimly. She chose Alexander Woollcott's notice first. " 'The young man who embodies the aforesaid sprig'—that's you, my boy —'is what is usually and mercifully described as inadequate.' "

It is remarkable that after such bad notices and unprofessional behavior anyone would offer Humphrey another role. But producer Rosalie Stewart had seen *Swifty*, which closed soon after it opened, and called Humphrey to say she had seen something in him. She offered him a $150.00-a-week part as a newspaperman in *Meet the Wife*, with Mary Boland and Clifton Webb. Again, Humphrey had not sought out the job, but it was offered to him and he accepted it without question. The show was to play at the Klaw Theater for thirty weeks, and Humphrey was on his way to being an actor without any real effort on his part, unlike most actors, who struggle for years to get a break.

After only three roles in the theater he had made it into a hit show—a remarkable leap to success. Even his mother was impressed with his good fortune, although she never became convinced that actors were socially acceptable. Dr. Bogart, however, was genuinely pleased that his son had finally found something for which he seemed to be fitted.

One night, a week before *Meet the Wife* was to close, Humphrey stayed too long at a party. At that evening's performance he blew his lines, causing Miss Boland to ad lib frantically for minutes while he leaned sweating against a wall, his eyes glazed. As the descending curtain's shadow reached his chin, Miss Boland turned on him in fury and announced, "Get this, Bogart—you'll never work in another play with me!"

But Humphrey kept working, alternating between

actor and stage manager until September 1, 1924, when he opened in *Nerves*, starring Kenneth MacKenna, Paul Kelly and a lovely blonde actress, Mary Philips. A war play, *Nerves* had the misfortune to be running opposite *What Price Glory*. It was on only a few weeks, but Bogart got favorable reviews from the critics.

"The notices gave me a badly swelled head," Bogart once said. "In one scene, while I was delivering a very dramatic speech, Mary Philips was supposed to walk away from me saying nothing. One night I noticed that she was putting a lot of *that* into her walk—so much so that the audience focused their attention on her instead of me," he said. "After the show I bawled her out plenty for stealing my scene. 'You can't do that,' I told her. 'That's my scene.' There was an amused twinkle in her eyes as she looked at me. 'Suppose you try to stop me,' she challenged. Well, I didn't try to stop her, because while I was talking, I suddenly became aware that here was a girl with whom I could very easily fall in love."

After the play closed, Bogart forgot about Mary Philips. He went back to work for Brady again as stage manager of a touring company of *Drifting*. A short time after the opening, Alice Brady, who was the star despite her fairly well advanced pregnancy, came unseasonably to her time on a Saturday night. By Monday morning another actress had to be found and coached to replace her. A talented, petite redhead named Helen Menken finally got the role, and Bogart was given the job of cueing her.

On her opening night Bogart, who had a complicated stage with eight sets to manage, had problems. Most of the slats fell down, some on Miss Menken. A fiercely articulate young woman who had been on stage since she was six, she turned loose a spate of fiery temper on Bogart. Later he said, "I guess I shouldn't have done it, but I booted her. She, in turn, belted me and ran to her dressing room to cry."

Nothing in Bogart's character at this time seems to

explain such action on his part other than his sister Pat's comment that "he had a terrible temper which he was never able to control." In any event, it is the first indication that he ever manhandled a woman, although, later, two of his three ex-wives would say that he roughed them up. It is worth noting, however, that he only fought physically with women to whom he was attracted.

After such an unpromising introduction Bogart began to court Miss Menken, who, although older than he and far more successful, seemed flattered by his attentions. Within a few weeks they decided they were in love, took out a marriage license, and commenced living together. But Humphrey was wary of the responsibility of supporting a wife. He had stumbled into his acting career, and undoubtedly felt that it could be lost as easily as it was found. Acting was too uncertain a career to plan on.

CHAPTER 2

The long arm of coincidence is a hackneyed phrase, and varying its form, endowing it with muscles, making it throw people about, and similar attempts at forcing situations only make matters worse. But people who believe in coincidence or fate may find it fascinating to consider that on almost the same day that Humphrey took out a marriage license for the first time, the woman who would be his fourth wife was being born in the same city.

Her name was Betty Joan Perske, born on September 16, 1924, the only child of Natalie Weinstein of Rumanian parentage, and William Perske, an Alsatian, then employed as a salesman of x-ray machines and general surgical equipment. Consider the irony here: Bogie had grown up in much the same neighborhood as a WASP with all the benefits of privilege, while Betty was to grow up in a Jewish household with family circumstances that were modest at best.

One can only speculate on what would have happened had Humphrey been walking on 103rd Street in 1924 and seen a baby being wheeled in a carriage and had been told that some nineteen years later the infant would become his wife.

Such speculation is fanciful, but it is a matter of certainty that during Betty's childhood in New York, there must have been many times when her path approached or almost crossed Humphrey's. He was to be in a total of seventeen plays and be married three times to actresses before Betty graduated from high school.

When Betty was three years old her father recalls taking her to a restaurant for dinner and being wheedled into ordering ice cream for dessert after he had first refused. When the ice cream appeared, Betty turned to him and said, "I get anything I want, Daddy."

Although the story is undoubtedly apocryphal, the fact is that as the only daughter of a young married couple Betty probably was as spoiled as family circumstances would permit, and in her mind, she probably did get everything she wanted.

In May of the year that Betty was three, Humphrey was cast as a Spanish osteopath in *Cradle Snatchers*. Alexander Woollcott, the most powerful critic of the day, who had given Humphrey a devastating review in *Drifting*, was to swallow his words in print and even quote the flattering opinion of Amy Leslie, the Chicago critic, who found Bogart beautiful. Miss Leslie wrote: "Humphrey Bogart created a furor as one of the hired lovers. He is young and handsome as Valentino, as dexterous and elegant in comedy as E. H. Sothern, and as graceful as any of our best romantic actors."

This lovely opinion sustained and nourished Humphrey, although he knew that Woollcott was a close friend of Helen Menken's. *Cradle Snatchers* was a hit, and his future looked reasonably secure but Humphrey was still reluctant to marry Helen, who was then the toast of Broadway in *Seventh Heaven*. She was more successful than he and had the larger income. He was afraid she might try to wear the pants in the family and he had seen enough of that in his own home. On the other hand, Helen was convinced that through her friendship with Woollcott she could help Humphrey's career.

Humphrey discussed the situation with young Bill Brady and Stuart Rose over a bottle of beer at a speak-easy. He added up the pluses and minuses. His friends listened sympathetically, agreeing that Helen was a strong woman who might also put career before marriage someday.

"But," Bill Brady warned, "you're in too deep now. If you don't marry her, you'll never get on the Broadway stage again. Alec will tar and feather you."

Humphrey undoubtedly recognized Brady's point, although it appeared to be a subtle blackmail. But, by then, Humphrey was hooked on acting—it was the only thing he could do to make a living. Although he probably would not get married to help his career, he might consider marriage rather than lose it. Also, he was very much a product of his times and upbringing. He had been living with Helen in an apartment at 43 East 25th Street and probably felt he "owed" her marriage. And, by then, he was too involved with her to see any honorable way out.

The marriage license they had taken out a few years earlier was still valid. In May 1926 they were married at the Gramercy Park Hotel in New York City, with Stuart Rose as best man. Both bride and groom signed the register as being twenty-six years old, although Miss Menken was actually at least three years Humphrey's senior.

The parents of the bride were deaf mutes, and the Reverend John Kent, who performed the service, was deaf. Mr. Rose recalled the wedding ceremony as "a macabre performance. The deaf minister read the service in a kind of sing-song and spelled it out in sign language." After the ceremony, Helen had hysterics and refused to see reporters gathered in the hotel lobby. "The whole thing was just too much for her," said Mr. Rose.

The marriage, which commenced on such a sour note, got worse instead of better. "We quarreled over the most inconsequential things, such as whether it would be right to feed the dog caviar when people were starving," Bogart said. "I contended the dog should eat hamburger and like it. She held out for caviar. What started out to be just a little difference of opinion would suddenly become a battle royal, with one or the other of us walking out in a fine rage."

They had been married only a few months when Humphrey's play closed. He landed another job as featured comedian in *Baby Mine*, a short-lived play starring Roscoe "Fatty" Arbuckle, who had been trying to fight his way back to popularity after a lurid Hollywood scandal involving a girl's death. The play lasted two weeks. Humphrey then went right into the cast of *Saturday's Children* when the star was taken ill in the middle of the Chicago run. He demanded that Helen accompany him to Chicago, but she wanted to try out for a new play. They separated, and although they tried to patch things up several times, they never succeeded. The final break came on April 2, 1927, at the Edgewater Beach Hotel when Miss Menken claimed Humphrey struck her in the face and body.

After a year and a half of marriage, during which they lived together only a few months, Miss Menken filed for divorce on the traditional grounds of cruelty. The old *New York Herald* story capsuled the divorce charges in its headline:

"HELEN MENKEN

"SUES FOR DIVORCE

"Wanted Home, Offered to Give Up Career; But Says Actor Husband Refused

"CHARGES HE BEAT HER.

"No Real *Seventh Heaven* with Humphrey Bogart."

Humphrey, then on Broadway in *Saturday's Children*, did not comment on the suit and Miss Menken waived alimony. Years later Humphrey would admit,

30

"I was to blame for the breakup of our marriage. I put my career first and my marriage second."

Humphrey was then twenty-seven years old. His improving talent and the vaguely Valentinoesque cast of his features had helped establish him as a juvenile lead. But he was not going to remain suitable for such roles much longer. Like most aging juveniles, he lived from day to day in the hope of a break—a role that would establish him as either a leading man or a heavy.

When he was not working, his life was one extended hangover. With Bill Brady, Jr., he was a familiar figure at dozens of speak-easies now almost forgotten— the Dizzy Club, the Hotsy Totsy, Chez Florence, Basque's, the Aquarium, Mario's, the Clamhouse, the Bandbox—all running wide open as Prohibition became more and more a joke.

It would be unfair to say that he and Brady supported these clubs, but they had running tabs at most and certainly would have been considered steady customers.

But although he drank a lot, it was at this time that he developed what Nunnally Johnson was later to describe as an "alcoholic thermostat," which enabled him to drink with pleasant and stimulating results, but never slopping over.

"Bogart just set his thermostat at noon, pumped in some Scotch and stayed at a nice even glow all day, automatically redosing as necessary," Johnson said. Bogart's system of drinking was to remain operative the rest of his life.

And always there were pretty girls around. Bogart never discussed his conquests, but years later he did admit to a friend in Hollywood that he and young Bill cut quite a swath among the Broadway chorus girls. "I had enough women by the time I was twenty-seven to know what I was looking for in a wife the next time I married," he said.

The following year the Perskes were divorced

and Betty's mother changed her name to Bacal, which has the same meaning in Rumanian (wine glass) as Weinstein does in German. Mrs. Bacal took a job as secretary in a firm of food brokers.

Betty regarded those young years as happy years. Freed of the nightly bickering with her husband, Mrs. Bacal was content to be alone with her daughter, whom she indulged as much as possible. She scrimped and saved and dressed Betty well and somehow even found money for ballet lessons. Even then, she talked of the future, when Betty would be "someone special."

Mrs. Bacal's plans were encouraged and partially financed by two of her brothers who were already successful in this country. Betty was sent to Highland Manor, a private girls' school at Tarrytown on the Hudson, New York, and spent the summers at Camp Cannihaw in Connecticut.

Just a few weeks after Betty celebrated her fourth birthday, Humphrey was married again, this time to Mary Philips, the girl he had been interested in during the run of *Nerves*. She was small, like Helen Menken and Maude Bogart, and, although not a beauty in the flashy vogue of the day, she was attractive, encouraging and understanding. She believed, as he did, that he had a future in the theater and she encouraged him to learn more about his profession. Their friends were all show-business people, and when Humphrey wasn't working—which was rare—he was seeing plays or talking about acting. Humphrey was twenty-eight, she was twenty-five.

Their marriage seemed to get off to a good start, and life was a wonderful merry-go-round for them with the brass ring always within reach. But in October 1929 the gay music had some sour notes. The *New York Times* reported to panic-stricken readers: "The second hurricane of liquidation within four days hit the stock market . . . it came suddenly, and violently. . . ."

The crash hit the films, already rocked by the advent of sound, particularly hard. Business slumped so badly that one theater offered two-for-one tickets and coupons entitling patrons to free Marcel permanent waves. Hollywood desperately needed leading men who could both act and talk. They frantically searched the ranks of Broadway players while trying to teach stars of the silent films how to talk.

Once again, Humphrey was to be handed a break on a silver platter. Stuart Rose, who had married Humphrey's sister Pat, was story editor of Fox Films, which owned that perennial film, *The Man Who Came Back*. Originally they had planned to cast silent-film stars Janet Gaynor and Charles Farrell in it but decided instead to use new actors in the hope of making new stars. They studio-tested almost every actor on Broadway, but the results were dismal. Stuart recommended that his studio test Humphrey. The result, according to Mr. Rose, was, "a very, very fine test."

With a contract and train tickets for Los Angeles in his pocket, Humphrey rushed home to ask Mary to quit her play and come with him. It was the first time he would be able to support her completely, and he was full of plans for going out to the Coast in style and living there in the grand manner. A $500-a-week actor when he worked on Broadway, his film contract called for him to be paid $750 a week, more than he had ever dreamed he would be earning.

But Mary, who was in a play, refused to go with him. She had a contract and, she said, her career was in New York. Since they were a "modern couple" though, they agreed that he was to date other girls while he was away, and she could go out with whom she liked. On that somewhat chilly note Humphrey left for Los Angeles, where he spent six weeks as a voice coach to Charles Farrell, who had been given the role after all. He then played a juvenile role in a film with Victor McLaglen and did a John Ford comedy starring Spencer Tracy, who had recently arrived from Broadway. Humphrey and Tracy were to begin their friendship on that picture.

33

In Humphrey's third film, a World War I aviation picture entitled *Body and Soul,* he played a flyer. Next, he had a small role in *Bad Sister,* in which Bette Davis made her film debut. He also played a cowboy in a Western and made a film with Joan Blondell in which he got tenth billing. He played a gangster for the first time in *Three on a Match,* starring Miss Blondell and, again, Bette Davis. Then, with the remarkable prescience that sometimes characterizes film producers, someone decided Humphrey had no future in movies. The decision was made on the basis of his stiff upper lip and slight lisp. Women would never go for him, so, after sixteen months, his contract was dropped.

His homecoming was less than triumphant. Mary confessed she had fallen in love with Roland Young, a small (5′ 6″) British actor, who was fifteen years older than Humphrey, whom she had met on tour. Since Mary had been honest with him—and he was not entirely blameless himself—Humphrey swallowed his ego, especially when Mary promised not to see Young again. Later Humphrey was to say he had learned a lesson—never to be separated from his wife again if he wanted to stay married.

With some difficulty he and Mary resumed their marriage, and Humphrey began doing the rounds, looking for work again, and finding very little. Broadway was experiencing its worst season. The depression was at its peak. Of 152 plays produced in 1933, fully 121 were flops.

Meanwhile, Dr. Bogart had fallen on hard times. He had lost most of his savings in the bank closings of 1933, and he and Maude had been obliged to move from the old Brownstone on 103rd Street to a modest apartment in Tudor City.

Neither Mary Philips nor Humphrey were working, and Humphrey was finally reduced to making eating money playing chess at the numerous "sportlands" on Sixth Avenue in the forties. For a bet of fifty cents a game he played all comers. Humphrey was both a

34

good chess player and hungry, and he won more than he lost. He soon landed a job at an arcade, where he sat in the window playing chess for a dollar a game. Most often he had only a doughnut and coffee for lunch.

The week after Betty's tenth birthday, Humphrey was working in the arcade when he got a message to come home immediately; his father was dying. Dr. Bogart died of a heart attack in Humphrey's arms two days later at the age of fifty-five. Years later Humphrey was to say he never forgot his father's death. "It was only in that moment that I realized how much I really loved and needed him and that I had never told him. Just before he died, I said, 'I love you, Father.' He heard me, because he looked at me and smiled. Then he died."

Dr. Bogart left a legacy of about $10,000 in debts, some $35,000 in uncollected fees, and the old-fashioned ruby ring he wore as a wedding band. Humphrey put the ring on, which he was to wear for the rest of his life, then went alone to Fresh Pond Crematory in Long Island, the only crematory in New York City at the time, to witness his father's burial.

Although he had never fallen back on his father for help, just the fact that the doctor was alive gave Humphrey a feeling of security. Now, without anyone to turn to, he was desperate. Mary Baker, who later became Humphrey's agent and was a close friend for many years, recalls Humphrey as being "worried about money for the first time in his life, and he didn't know which way to turn."

His acting career was at a standstill, but he kept doggedly on, determined to learn more about the craft which he had never sought but which was the only one he knew. With Mary, he sometimes stood in the wings or in the last row of plays, studying other actors searching for ways he could improve his own ability. Many nights he and Mary went to one of the all-night cafeterias in the Times Square area and sat at tables with friends, talking about acting and sharing a glass of hot water which they seasoned with ketchup, making a kind of soup which, they believed, gave them nourishment.

Gradually he learned. "There's been a lot of bunk written about acting," he was to say later. "But it isn't easy. You can't just make faces. If you make yourself feel the way the character would feel, your face will express the right things—if you're an actor. There are lots of things. How you walk. Try walking up to a door and opening it sometime on a stage. It isn't as simple as you think. You mustn't stand close to anyone on the stage. Two objects together become one object in the eye of the audience. Here's an actor's trick. Keep looking at somebody's hands. Pretty soon he'll feel like his arms are sixteen feet long. He'll fall apart trying to put them somewhere. You have to know what to do with your hands. All these things—you get to do them instinctively."

Bogart is remembered by an old friend of that time as "a well-behaved, agreeable, serious young man, but one who had no sense of direction." Eventually, setbacks and difficulty seemed to have provided him with it.

At about this time, soon after Betty's eleventh birthday, Mrs. Bacal scrimped together enough money to have a local photographer take some pictures of Betty which were put on file at the John Robert Powers Model Agency. Mrs. Bacal also brought Betty and the photos to the Conover Agency. (One of the partners in the agency at the time was a young Yale graduate and part-time model named Jerry Ford who, some thirty years later, would become President of the United States.) Conover, to his later regret, was to turn Betty down four times, because he had "too many like her already."

Mrs. Bacal's reason for trying to get Betty into modeling was practical. They needed the money. Also, Betty, as pictures taken at the time indicate, was a beautiful young girl with long brunette hair and lovely even features highlighted by the almond-shaped eyes which, later, were to become her trademark. Betty had some mild success as a model and was photographed in pre-teen wardrobes for many newspaper advertisements. Not only was she paid $10 an hour but, equally important, she was often able to get her school clothing at a discount from the companies and department stores that employed her.

Even then, Betty had begun to display the curious mixture of extreme aggressiveness, narcissism and exhibitionism that characterizes many actors, a fact her mother had not failed to notice.

Although Mrs. Bacal was ambitious for Betty, she was determined that her daughter finish high school before embarking on the acting career her mother had already decided would be hers.

Meanwhile, Humphrey's career took a turn for the better. He played a villain on Broadway in *Invitation to a Murder*. But the air of tough self-assurance that Bogart was to have in later years was conspicuous by its absence in those days. He was so tormented by self-doubt and financial concerns that his friends were worried that he might do violence to himself. Robert E. Sherwood, the playwright, who knew and liked Bogart, went so far as to write a small part as a football player especially for him in *The Petrified Forest*, starring Leslie Howard. The play's action takes place in a desolate inn and filling station on the broad highway from New York to the Pacific. The chatelaine of the oasis is an appealing child of nature, an impetuous French girl who, having married one of President Wilson's dreamy crusaders, found that she couldn't take it and returned to France. One day while she is reading the verse of François Villon, another vagabond troubadour appears—the dusty Mr. Howard, who is thumbing his way from horizon to horizon. They discuss philosophy and fall in love—she passionately; he with a desperate tranquillity. The situation is peacefully pathetic until a band of murderous criminals, armed with machine guns and other artillery and led by a Dillinger-like gunman, take charge and change the

37

play from an innocent pastoral into a wicked melodrama.

Producer Arthur Hopkins, who had seen Bogart months before playing his first role as a villain in *Invitation to a Murder*, thought he would be better for the gunman, Duke Mantee. Despite the objections of the playwright, Hopkins persisted and Sherwood finally arranged to have Humphrey read for him. Hopkins had been right.

"It was a big chance and he was mighty nervous," recalls Mary Baker, who was with Humphrey when he went for the reading.

Again, Humphrey stumbled into incredibly good luck. When Leslie Howard, who was the star, heard Humphrey's flat, world-weary voice coming from the stage at the audition, he said, "That's the man! I want him, and I'll work with him on the part."

The Petrified Forest played two weeks in Boston before opening in New York on January 7, 1935. Leslie Howard got critical raves, and Humphrey, as Duke Mantee, was reviewed favorably. For his role, Humphrey wore a three-day growth of beard. Mantee's whiskers became one of the most discussed features of the play. The *New York Post* reported that people who went to the box office asked for seats close enough to the stage to permit them to see Duke Mantee's beard.

Only one thing marred Humphrey's elation at his success: the tragic death of his boyhood friend Bill Brady, Jr., who was trapped in bed when his bungalow at Colt's Neck, New Jersey, caught fire. It was to be the second time in his life that Humphrey could remember crying.

At the funeral Humphrey saw his old friend and mentor, Bill Brady, Sr. Mr. Brady, who was then seventy-one, put his hand on Humphrey's shoulder and said he was glad that Bill had lived to see his best friend a success. "I always knew that one day you would be a great actor," Mr. Brady said. "I pray that I will live long enough to see that happen." (Mr.

Brady's wish was granted. He died in 1950 at the age of eighty-six, well after Humphrey had become a star.)

Humphrey made enough money from *The Petrified Forest* to pay off all his debts and his father's obligations and still have a thousand dollars in the bank in a fund that he called F.Y. money—money that gave him enough security to refuse a job he didn't want.

When Warners bought *Petrified Forest*, they signed Howard and optioned Humphrey for the film. When Bogart arrived in Hollywood—this time with his wife —he found that Edward G. Robinson had been chosen to play Mantee. Humphrey remembered that Leslie Howard had promised that if the play were made into a picture, Bogart would have his original role. He also remembered Howard was famous for keeping his promises.

He picked up the telephone and sent a cable to Scotland, where Howard was vacationing. Back to Warners came an ultimatum: Either Humphrey played the gangster or *Petrified Forest* would be made without Leslie Howard. Humphrey was signed by Warners.

Although he had a $400 a week contract with Warner's—a lot of money in those days—Humphrey remembered all too well his last Hollywood fiasco. He had seen too many Broadway actors "go Hollywood" only to have their contracts dropped. He and Mary lived modestly at the Garden of Allah, a group of thin-walled bungalows clustered around a pool on Sunset Boulevard. (The first time playwright Arthur Kober stayed in one of those villas he was awakened in the night by a sleepy voice saying, "Would you get me a drink of water, dear?" He got up, stumbled to the bathroom, and came back with a glass of water before he realized he was alone.)

The late Robert Benchley, the Garden's patron saint as well as one of America's top humorists, lived in Bungalow 20. Another beloved character was Ben the Bellhop, who had established a firm understanding with guests. Every time he came to a villa on an errand he received a drink as well as a tip.

There was twenty-four-hour bar service, and the Garden was the center of Hollywood's social activity. The Bogarts were soon right at home, enjoying a continuous party that floated spontaneously from one bungalow to another.

Humphrey drove to the Warners Studio in a battered Chevrolet and refused to admit that he was doing more than "just passing through" Hollywood. Jaik Rosenstein, then publicity and exploitation manager of Warner Brothers Theaters, recalls the day Humphrey came into his office to do a radio show.

"He was wearing a camel's-hair overcoat frayed at the cuffs and the collar," said Rosenstein. "I suggested that now that he was a star he should get himself a new coat. 'I've seen too many guys come here, make one picture and blow themselves to new Cadillacs and big houses,' Humphrey said. 'Then they end up in hock for the rest of their lives to the studio. I'm salting my money away for my F.Y. fund.'"

Because he was so forthright in interviews, Humphrey soon became the darling of the publicity department. The dizzy mechanics of publicity enchanted him and he started to drop into the studio publicity office to help the boys there invent stories about his background.

He soon learned that color rather than truth most often made news. With Geoffrey Homes, press agent on the film, he began to make up stories about himself: he had inherited a railroad station from obscure relatives in France; he once donned a beard and played a bull fiddle in a small orchestra to replace a beard-wearing, bull-fiddle playing pal who was ill; the studio gateman never recognized him; he was number one on a list of "The Ten Meanest Men in the World."

Despite his refusal to admit that he took his movie career seriously, Humphrey worked as hard as he was capable of on his role, and there are many people who

40

believe that his performance as Duke Mantee was his best. Certainly no one who saw *The Petrified Forest* is likely to forget the impact of his entrance into the dingy desert café.

Director Archie Mayo let Humphrey play Mantee as he had on the stage, which meant he did most of his acting while sitting in a chair holding a large rifle —a difficult feat since he had to get the characterization across without the usual help of movement. But he did have close-ups that gave him an opportunity to register heavily with the audience.

When the picture was released Humphrey was hailed as a coming new star. Richard Watts, Jr., critic for the *Herald Tribune*, wrote: " . . . once more Humphrey Bogart provides a brilliant picture of a subnormal, bewildered and sentimental killer."

Humphrey had finally graduated from the ranks of competent juveniles and was now recognized as a major actor. At the age of thirty-six he was about to enter a new stage of his life. Even his name was to change. From now on he would no longer be known as Humphrey. The press and public were soon to call him only Bogie, in the American style of giving nicknames to every star and politician considered truly important.

The public was also to discover that Humphrey Bogart in person was not detectably different from the tough, sardonic movie actor of the same name.

Humphrey was given a raise in salary to $650 a week and would soon go from picture to picture. He was on his way at last, just as Betty was ready to enter high school, two years sooner than the average school girl. Because the Bacals lived in a West Side Manhattan apartment, Betty was eligible to enroll at Julia Richman, a New York High School, then for girls only.

By this time Betty was certain that she was going to be an actress. And no one at Julia Richman doubted that that was her intention. Her English teacher, Mrs. Lilian Levy, remembers Betty making a declaration to that effect when she was twelve years old and it was reiterated many times later.

"I am going to Hollywood," Betty often said to Betty Kalb (now Mrs. Gene Barry), who was one of her best friends. "And I am going to Broadway," replied Betty Kalb. At Madison Square Garden one evening the two Bettys watched Helen Hayes and Tallulah Bankhead waving greetings across the arena and vowed that when they were famous they would do the same.

"I cut classes from time to time," Betty Bacall has said. "I wasn't ideally happy and I had my dreams, my acting. I cut to see Bette Davis in *Bad Sister* [in which Humphrey had a small part]. I was enamored of Bette Davis. Most of the heroes and heroines of my childhood were movie stars."

In Betty Kalb's opinion the romance with Humphrey Bogart was dimly foreshadowed one day in 1936 when the two girls went to see Davis and Bogart in *Marked Woman* at the 68th Street Theater. "I'm crazy about that man," thirteen-year-old Betty Bacal confided. "I love Davis but I should play opposite him."

Some months later when Miss Davis came to New York to promote a film, Betty Bacal and Betty Kalb waited four hours in the Gotham Hotel lobby for her, rode up in the elevator with her and followed her down a corridor just to hear her say, "I forgot the key, damn it."

Betty Bacal's adventures at Julia Richman have a curious parallel to Humphrey's at Phillips Academy. The administrative assistant of Julia Richman was to tell a *Life* reporter in 1945, "I've been here seventeen years, and when you graduate 800 girls a year, you only remember the very good ones and the very bad ones. I remember Betty Bacal very well."

Though in no way a confirmed juvenile delinquent, Betty is remembered as a chronic truant, a classroom cut-up, and a habitué of the soda fountain and booths of the Don Q. Pharmacy on Second Avenue, forbidden premises during school hours. It was there at about the age of thirteen that she and another friend, Joan Stanton (now wife of writer George Axelrod), smoked their first cigarette while sitting around drinking Cokes and eating Oreo cookies.

Sid Lefkowitz, owner of the Don Q., recalls Betty as "a normal kid, like everyone else. There was nothing extraordinary about her. She wasn't even very attractive."

This latter point is vehemently disputed by Joan Axelrod. "Betty was a ravishing beauty, but very tall, and in that era being tall was considered a great disadvantage because all the fellows our age were shorter."

Casual as she was about high school, Betty was not casual about her Saturday morning dramatic classes at Mrs. Dryer's School of Theater. "Betty knew what she wanted even then, and that was to be an actress," recalls Joan Axelrod.

After school, with her mother's encouragement, Betty continued to model girls' clothes for department store advertisements. Mrs. Bacal also saw to it that Betty dressed herself in simple good taste and helped her develop a talent for being well turned out on a meager budget.

"When I was a kid it was me and my mother against the world, and she was awfully good to me," Betty was to say later in a rare interview about her childhood.

While Betty was in her second year at Julia Richman, Humphrey and Mary Philips began having serious domestic problems. Although Mary had gone to Hollywood with him, she was restless while he was working. There was nothing for her to do in films. She felt her career was on Broadway.

When she got an offer to go back to New York to do *The Postman Always Rings Twice*, she accepted it. Bogart was furious.

"This is the first time I've really been able to support you," he said. "We could never afford to have

43

children before. Stay here and let's start a family. Anyway, the play isn't any good and you're wrong for it."

Mary was determined to return to New York, however, although Bogart was right. The play wasn't good and Mary was wrong for it, but she stayed on, looking for work.

While she was away, Humphrey met another girl, a hard-drinking, bosomy and petite blonde named Mayo Methot, who was in the process of getting her second divorce. The daughter of a sea captain on the Orient run and an Oregon newspaperwoman, Mayo had been in show business since she was a child and had appeared on Broadway in three plays. She made a reputation opposite George M. Cohan in *The Song and Dance Man*, and had feature roles in more than twenty films.

Although Mayo had been in the cast of *Marked Woman*, Bogart wasn't particularly interested in her until the night of the annual dinner of the Screen Actors Guild at the Biltmore Hotel in Los Angeles. Mayo was strikingly attractive in a flaming red dress with a conspicuous décolleté.

Bogart was sitting with a table of friends when he saw Mayo smile at him from the balcony. Suddenly, he remembered that she had been in a film with him. Tipsily he wrested the figure of a nude woman off a pillar and presented it to Mayo as an "Oscar for being the most beautiful woman in the room." They danced, and later that night after her date dropped her off at her apartment, Bogart came by for a drink. After that they saw each other frequently.

Bogart, who had loved sailing since the days at Lake Canandaigua, had gotten a good buy on a 36-foot cruiser that he kept at Newport Beach, where he joined the yacht club. Mayo also loved the sea, and they began spending their weekends on the boat. Finally, Mayo moved into the bungalow Humphrey had shared with Mary at the Garden of Allah Hotel on Sunset Boulevard.

When Mary returned from her trip to New York she was willing to forgive him his transgression—after all, she had committed one also—but she insisted he stop seeing Mayo. Humphrey refused to agree to her terms, and Mary said she was going back to New York to get a divorce.

Once again, Humphrey was in a bind. He had been living with Mayo and, belatedly, discovered she was jealous of every woman he had worked with in a film. Also, she showed the unmistakable signs of being an alcoholic. Later, he would say he didn't want to divorce Mary but he had already promised Mayo he would marry her. Twice before he had married women he had slept with over a period of time, and the pattern was established. He saw no way out of the trap he had set for himself and because of his notions of chivalry, he was soon on his way to the altar again.

In a rather prophetic interview, Humphrey explained to a fan magazine reporter one of the reasons he was marrying for the third time.

"I love a good fight. So does Mayo. We have some first-rate battles. Both of us are actors, so fights are easy to start. Actors always see the dramatic quality of a situation more easily than other people and can't resist dramatizing it further. For instance, I come in from a game of golf. Maybe I've been off my drive. I slump into my chair. 'Gosh, I feel low today,' I start. She nods meaningfully. 'Low, hmm, I see. You feel low. You come to see me and it makes you feel low. All the thrill has gone and . . . you feel low.' And we go right on from there. We both understand that one of the important things to master in marriage is the technique of the quarrel."

Humphrey married Mayo on August 20, 1938. He was thirty-eight; she was thirty-five. Their wedding night was a drunken debacle, and they had a fight which ended up with Humphrey spending the night with his agent's husband while Mayo spent the night with his agent, Mary Baker.

Humphrey bought a huge Spanish-style house on

Horn Avenue, over the Sunset Strip, complete with twenty-one finches, five canaries, four dogs, four cats, and a garden featuring sweet peas and petunias, which he tended himself. In such peaceful surroundings he and Mayo began to perfect the technique of the marital quarrel. Ironically, his career began to take a sharp upward turn.

The next year, Betty was fifteen and graduated from Julia Richman 459th out of a class of 884. *Spotlight*, the school yearbook for 1940, printed this capsule prophecy under her picture:

"Popular ways that win,
May your dreams of becoming an actress
Overflow the brim."

Two days after graduation, Betty, who was still studying ballet as well as drama, auditioned for Emil Diestal, head of the American Academy of Dramatic Arts, which had taken over several rooms in Carnegie Hall on 57th Street. In his notes Diestal recorded that Betty had a "pleasing personality, is intelligent and has a good sense of the dramatic." He went on to note, "She seems to know what she wants and where she is going." Diestal called her a "pretty child" who, "if she is interested," should grow up in the theater. Betty was accepted for the Academy's fall semester, and Mrs. Bacal borrowed money for the $500 tuition from a brother. Betty spent the summer as a counselor at Camp Cannihaw in Connecticut, where she had been for several previous summers, and started classes at the Academy on October 1, 1940, with about 150 other students including Jocelyn Brando (Marlon's sister), Nina Foch and Diana Dill, who was then going with a soda jerk named Kirk Douglas, whom she would later marry. Most of the students were about two years older than Betty.

The Academy had a traditional theater curriculum, including fencing, ballet, movement, speech and diction, as well as classes in acting. All classes were overlaid with a kind of Muzak—the sound of musicians continually practicing in the building.

46

Most of the students lunched at either a nearby Walgreen's drugstore, the Carnegie Delicatessen or, for an occasional treat, they went to Sardi's, which was then the most famous show-biz hangout. Nina Foch recalls that the cheapest lunch at Sardi's was canneloni. The restaurant also served the most delicious scones for dessert. "We used to order one plate of canneloni to share and then load up on the scones. We liked to go there because we could be seen by everybody."

Nina's recollection of Betty as a student is vague, but she remembers "she had a mother who was serious about pushing her."

Frances Letton, one of Betty's classmates and now associate director of the Academy, recalls Betty's performance in *Craig's Wife*, the exam-play given at the end of the season.

"She was very good," said Letton recently. "She not only had an instinct for comedy but a sense of comedy as well. The distinctive thing about her in those days was her vitality—she didn't have any hangups."

Admittance to the second year at the Academy was by invitation only. Betty got the invitation but refused it because, claims Letton, "I doubt she could afford the $500 tuition."

It is equally likely that the Bacals, mother and daughter, had decided it was time for Betty to start in earnest on her chosen profession. So she began a routine familiar to many other young acting hopefuls. She haunted producers' offices, and, among the huge, anonymous mob of young people trying to break into the theater, she became known as "the Windmill" because of her swinging walk and her long arms and legs.

After months of tramping around Times Square to no avail, Betty became discouraged and Mrs. Bacal annoyed. Betty's grandmother, who spoke little English, couldn't understand what was going on. "What do you do all day, child?" she once asked. "Why don't you get a good steady job and settle down?"

47

But Betty had no intention of settling down and was not interested in a steady job so, again, she decided to try modeling. A perfect size ten and the right height, 5′ 8½″, she lightened her hair and found a job modeling for David Crystal, a sportswear manufacturing house on Seventh Avenue. Her pay was $35 for a five-and-half-day week.

Other models who had previously worked for David Crystal and become actresses included Lucille Ball and a tall girl named Slim Hayes, who was to marry film director Howard Hawks and play an important role in Betty's future.

"We were getting ready for our fall season when Betty came to us in March 1941," recalls Morgan Fauth, designer for the clothing house. "We had ten other models and Betty was an all-around good type with a great figure, pretty face and personable manner." Her measurements at the time were: 34″ bust, 23″ waist, and 34″ hips.

Betty modeled dresses, coats and suits for fitting and showing purposes and spent most of her lunch hours trying to land a stage role. Nicknamed "Pinwheel" by the other models for her walk, she did well at David Crystal for almost a year until she was fired by Vincent Draddy, chairman of the house.

"She was a naturally funny girl," says Draddy. "Although she was a good model, she was really a comedienne and, I thought, better than Lucille Ball. But she was never serious about work and laughed all day long. She was constantly doing pantomimes of Katharine Hepburn and other actresses. One day I walked into the models' room and found her practicing a striptease, doing the whole thing very effectively without removing any of her clothes. That did it. I told the head model we had to put an end to this because Betty was an upsetting influence on the other girls. Instead of working, they were spending their time laughing at Betty."

Betty literally walked—or pinwheeled—a few blocks

up Seventh Avenue and got a job modeling evening gowns for another manufacturer. She did not last long at this job, either. "I wasted away missing my lunches, and the work was strenuous," she said recently. "Finally I gave it up and went in for ushering at the St. James Theater for $8 a week."

Her theory was that she would learn something by watching the actors, but about all she gained from the experience was a flattering tribute from theater critic George Jean Nathan who would later claim to be her "discoverer." In his 1942 nominations for "Best of the Year" in *Esquire Magazine*, he wrote: "The prettiest Theater Usher: the tall, slender blonde in the St. James Theater, right aisle, during the Gilbert and Sullivan engagement—by general agreement among the critics, but the bums are too dignified to admit it."

Bobsy Lovett, who was "on the aisle" with Betty, recalls her as being "pleasant, ladylike, lively and sometimes flighty. She used to do a great takeoff on Kate Hepburn saying 'Really, I do' from *The Philadelphia Story*."

Another of Betty's friends at the time told Francis Sill Wickware of *Life*, "People were never very nice to her. Betty learned to expect little from promises and never to expect something for nothing." A press agent once told her he would arrange to have her read for David O. Selznick at his office. On the strength of this, Betty rehearsed for days and took along a man to play opposite her. They waited for an hour and a half for the press agent to appear, then an hour more outside the office while Selznick settled sundry business affairs. Finally, Betty spoke up and reminded the press agent that she had been invited to read. "Oh, yes," he said and brought Betty into the office. "This is Betty Bacal, Mr. Selznick. Isn't she cute? Doesn't she remind you of K. T. Stevens?" Mr. Selznick agreed that she was cute and that closed the subject. Betty picked up her script and went home.

Betty was too busy with her career to have boyfriends, but she found time for occasional dates. One of the boys who dated her then was Ed "Duke" Gottlieb, now in the advertising business in Los Angeles.

"During the time Betty was a theater usher, I was at Harvard Law School, and whenever I'd get into New York, I would take her out.

"She was a knockout in those days with a laugh, delivery and a great sense of humor. I remember that we'd usually go out with other couples and we'd usually end up teasing her, telling her to give up the theater and get a job as a secretary, to do something constructive. There was no way to ruffle her. She was an actress, going to be an actress, and although she'd laugh good-naturedly and had a sunny disposition, she was like a bar of steel. She knew with a degree of certainty that she was going to make it."

One night Betty fixed up Ray Robinson, a friend of Gottlieb, with one of her friends. Robinson, now editor of *Seventeen* magazine, recalls the date clearly. "The girl she fixed me up with was a giant—she could suit up with Wilt Chamberlain—and we went to Sardi's where she kept waving so-called celebrities over to our table. Although it was Duke's first time there, and mine, too, we weren't so impressed by the surroundings as by the fact that her friends kept drinking and eating and we didn't have money to pay for it.

"At around 1:00 A.M. Ed and I adjourned to the men's room to go over our financial situation. The check came to thirty dollars and we had five dollars between us—enough for the tip. There was only one solution: for Betty, who knew Vincent Sardi, to sign an IOU and we'd pay it later. When we told Betty of our plight, she blurted out, 'It serves me right for going out with a couple of college sophomores.' But she told Sardi she'd sign the IOU. When we came out of the restaurant she was still so angry she couldn't see straight. 'Well, I hope you cheapskates are going to at least take us home by cab,' she snapped. Whereupon Ed and I started laughing. We had saved twenty cents out of our original capital for subway money, and when we told the girls that's how we were going home, they stormed off into the night—alone."

In the fall of 1941, aspiring actors and actresses were in the habit of congregating at Walgreen's drugstore in the Paramount Building on Broadway and 44th Street. The basement luncheonette had mirrors all around, good for checking one's appearance, and it was one of the few places in town where they could sit around over a five-cent cup of coffee and exchange information about upcoming casting calls. Among the group were Shelley Winters, Nick Conti, Betty and a girl who at the time was a friend of Leo Shull, an aspiring newspaperman who took notes on what he heard and learned about actors calls and casting and began to mimeograph a small sheet full of that information called *Actors' Cue*.

Shull left his paper around Walgreen's for anyone to pick up free of charge.

One morning Betty approached Shull. "Can I sell your paper for you?" she asked.

"Why not?"

Betty's eyes narrowed. "Can I keep half the money I get? I think I can sell it for twenty-five cents a copy."

"You got a deal," said Shull, who had been considering selling the paper after it was established.

Shull, who now publishes a successful paper called *Show Business,* recalls Betty as his first vendor. He remembers her as quite ordinary to look at but, he says, "She had chutzpah and that's ninety percent of it in this business. She was all over the place.

"She used to stand outside the theaters waiting for producers to come by. Then she'd buttonhole them, sell them a copy and hope they noticed her. Soon she began to sell out her copies of the paper and become a mine of information herself. She really got to be a reporter for me in time."

One of the producers who bought a copy of *Actors' Cues* from Betty was Max Gordon who, at the time,

51

had produced more Broadway hits than any other producer alive. Gordon recalls seeing Betty selling magazines on the street in front of Sardi's restaurant. "I told her, 'A pretty girl like you shouldn't be selling magazines. Come up and I'll give you a job.' "

Betty recalls the event as being slightly more dramatic. Her version: "I knew Max Gordon was casting a road company of *My Sister Eileen.* I chased him down the street, grabbed his arm and told him what an asset I'd be in the part of Eileen. Oh, it was a big speech I delivered—he'd never regret it and stuff like that.

"Fortunately he was in a good mood. He told me to come to a tryout at the theater at three that afternoon. I did nothing but shake until then. When I walked on to the stage I stayed over on the side where there was a chair to hang on to. Suddenly a voice from the dark pit out front told me to move to the center so they could get a good look at me. My knees clacked. I thought I'd pass out.

"They asked me if I could be ready to go the middle of December—called me up every day and gave me the big rush act. Then another girl got the part—some mother who kinda knew the ropes talked them into it. It was—oh, my biggest heartbreak in the theater."

Max Gordon was enough impressed by Betty's chutzpah and reading to give her a small speaking part in a play called *Franklin Street*, which the producer recalls as a play about acting school. Unhappily, *Franklin Street* folded after tryouts in Washington and Wilmington.

The folding of *Franklin Street* brought Betty's fortunes to an all-time low. She told a girl friend, "You know, things are just horrible. They can't possibly get any worse." She collected from unemployment insurance, gave part of her money to Mrs. Bacal, and contrived to get along on the balance, most of which went for clothes. Her eating was done mainly in Chock Full O'Nuts establishments. Occasionally one of her girlfriends would agree to go out for dinner with an admirer on the condition that he consent to feed Betty as well.

The Bacals, mother and daughter, and a sad-eyed cocker spaniel named Droopy, had moved several times in the past years and were then living in Greenwich Village in an apartment building at 75 Bank Street on the corner of Bleecker. The exterior of the building was unprepossessing; it was six stories high of yellow brick with dark orange brick marking each level. The interior was bland with institutional yellow walls and faded maroon carpeting over marble floors. The Bacals had one of the 88 studio apartments in the building which rented for $55 a month. None of Betty's dates at the time had ever picked her up at home. "I had the feeling that she wasn't too proud of the way she lived," one of them said.

Not long ago Betty was to recall those days: "I used to come home from pounding the pavements, turn on a sad symphony to make me even lower and sit there talking to that dog with the big sad eyes."

This low period of Betty's professional life coincided with a high in Humphrey's. In 1940, thanks to a fortuitous chain of circumstances, he got an important break. George Raft had been offered the role of a gangster in a picture called *High Sierra*. The Hollywood censors decreed that the gangster must die, because he had committed six killings. Raft refused to die in a film. Paul Muni turned it down because it had been offered first to Raft. James Cagney declined it, and so did Edward G. Robinson.

Jack Warner had no alternative but to heed the advice of Charles Einfeld, his publicity director, and assign the role to Bogart. When Mary Baker, Bogie's agent in partnership with Sam Jaffe, called to say the studio wanted him to do the film, Bogart said, "Sure. Where the hell's the script and when do I start?"

The script was delivered to him the following morning just as he was leaving for a weekend of sailing with the Coast Guard. A junior commander of Flotilla #21, Bogart attended weekly classes and stood watch

53

when called on to relieve enlisted personnel. It was a long weekend for him but he was ready for work, script memorized letter-perfect on Monday morning.

Although the film was an old-style gangster melodrama, Bogart brought to the part of the killer a psychopathic ferocity combined with appealing naïveté. In reviewing the picture, the *Herald Tribune*'s Howard Barnes wrote, "Humphrey Bogart was a perfect choice to play the role. Always a fine actor, he is particularly splendid as a farm boy turned outlaw, who is shocked and hurt when newspapers refer to him as a mad dog. His steady portrayal is what makes the melodrama more than merely exciting."

Bogart went to New York with Mayo to make some public appearances for the picture's opening. On the first day they found they literally could not leave the stage door—the street was jammed with Bogart fans. They had to move from the Algonquin Hotel and live in a dressing room in the theater to avoid the crowds.

But Warner still refused to believe that Bogart had any sex appeal. "He's a tough guy, not a lady's man," the studio head decreed.

Once again George Raft inadvertently furthered Bogart's career when he refused a role in *The Maltese Falcon* because he would not entrust his talent to an untried director named John Huston.

The Maltese Falcon, by Dashiel Hammett, was to establish a whole new genre of detective stories—cool, downplayed, explosively violent. The chief character, Sam Spade as played by Bogart, was an admirable but tragic anti-hero. In the story an arrogant private operative sends his partner out to trail a possible killer. The partner gets killed, and before the complex plot is unraveled there are two more murders, numerous sluggings, and a brutally realistic romance that culminates when the detective sends his lover to the penitentiary.

Bogart's chilling but somehow engaging characterization of the private eye was much the same as his gangster roles. His gravelly voice and intense manner were perfectly suited to the role of a private detective living by his wits, and Huston had him dominating nearly every scene. Bogart delivered such lines as, "Sorry, angel, I have a pressing date with a fat man," with an offhand nonchalance that made one aware of both his sex appeal and his disillusion with love.

The others in the film were also excellent. Sydney Greenstreet played the "Fat Man," head of an international gang, with bland villainy. Peter Lorre, who was to become one of Bogart's closest friends, played an effeminate scoundrel who was the Fat Man's shadow.

But it was Bogart who stole the show. Richard Shickel, in his discussion of Bogart in *The Stars*, summed up the appeal he had in such roles. "The central fact of his existence was loneliness shaded by desperation and accompanied by that special kind of unshaven squalor that is the mark of bachelorhood in a modern American city—unscraped dishes in the sink, rye whiskey in the file drawer of the desk, a magazine resting on an ottoman in front of a worn but comfortable easy chair commanding views of the television set and the bedroom of the pretty girl who lives across the airshaft and draws the shades carelessly when she undresses.

"His special knowledge was of the jungle of the city at night—which clubs the syndicate ran, which one-arm restaurants served good coffee, which hotels a whore could use, which streets were safe to walk on after midnight. It was this detailed knowledge that set Bogart apart from the ordinary lonely male; it was the rightness of the setting, mood and dialogue that established empathy with him."

When *The Maltese Falcon* was finished, Bogart and Mayo went to New York for a short vacation. Again they stayed at the Algonquin Hotel where they received a bill for breakage—a result of their quarreling—which they framed and hung over the mantel of their Hollywood home.

Meanwhile Betty had added an additional "l" to her

last name to keep it from rhyming with "crackle" and continued pounding the same pavement and visiting much the same theatrical offices which Bogie had haunted some twenty years earlier. If single-hearted devotion to getting ahead can accomplish anything, her progress was inevitable.

But while Bogie had stumbled into a career without seeking it, she was grateful to accept a $15-a-week role in *Johnny 2 x 4*, a play about a speak-easy which opened on a cold drizzly New York evening at the Longacre Theater on March 16, 1942. *New York Times* critic Brooks Atkinson described the play "as flat as the glass of beer that stood all night on the end table in the talking room . . . it is only a hack's dream."

Despite almost uniformly bad notices the play lasted 65 performances before folding in May. It is remembered now only for the fact that listed fourth from the bottom in the playbill's cast of sixty-six was one Betty Bacall who was making her Broadway debut. Once again, Betty was noticed by her co-workers, but this time it was not her walk that gained her attention, it was the talent she showed with her brief onstage appearance. The other girls in the cast voted for her as "the one most likely to succeed in the theater."

An actress who worked with her during this period was to say, "Betty was a Dead End kid, a kid off the streets. She's heard everything, seen everything, but it's not for her. You see her sitting and staring into space, dreaming—and she's dreaming of Betty Bacall."

World War II was in full swing by then, and gangster films were on the way out. As Alistair Cooke was to note about the period, "One gangster gunning down half a dozen men was pale stuff when Hitler was acting out scripts more brutal and obscene than anything dreamed of by Chicago's North Siders or the Warner Brothers."

For the wave of war films being produced in Hollywood James Cagney was too bouncy, Edward G.

Robinson was becoming too much of a father figure, and George Raft was too stylized to be pitted with any degree of realism against the Nazis. Bogart was the only Warner star who could conceivably outwit a Nazi and survive, because his basic character was more adaptable than that of the other members of the screen underworld.

As Cooke said, "He probably had no notion, in his endless strolls across the stage drawing rooms of the twenties, that he was being saved and soured by time to become the romantic, democratic answer to Hitler's New Order. Such calculations belong to social historians, not to their subjects. Not, certainly, to an actor who had his troubles with the bartender's tab and who was grateful to take any part for which his dark and glossy appearance qualified him. He was always content to nestle in the camouflage of any fictional type that came his way, provided the manager paid him and left him to himself; a very complex man, gentle at bottom and afraid to seem so."

Bogart who was then forty-one years old had made thirty films since *The Petrified Forest* and was then considered one of the top stars on the Warner Brothers lot. He had just signed to start a new picture, *Casablanca*, starring opposite Ingrid Bergman. His agents had negotiated a unique seven-year contract for him, calling for him to be paid $3,500 a week for forty weeks a year, and it was without options. The studio had to renew it every year, and as long as he could show up for work he would have to be paid.

When Bogart asked Warner how come he agreed to a no-option contract, the studio head explained, "Because nothing can happen to your face that will hurt it a bit."

Warner was telling the truth. Bogart's hangover-gray pallor, the lip drawn even tighter over his open mouth, sharp wrinkles around his eyes, and the whiskey-scarred voice all seemed to add to his appeal rather than detract from it.

When they started to make *Casablanca*, everyone

involved, including Bogart, Mike Curtiz, the director, the Epstein brothers who wrote it, and his co-star, Ingrid Bergman, thought the picture was going to be terrible. Nevertheless, Bogie worked with the same practiced professionalism he had brought to all his other pictures. *Casablanca* was keyed to the headlines of the day, portraying the intrigue between pro- and anti-fascist forces in North Africa before the Allied offensive. It was full of preposterous moments, but Bogart wrestled with the character of the soldier of fortune, Rick, a disillusioned democrat fighting the Axis long before the rest of his compatriots. As always, he used his own version of the Stanislavsky method to make the character seem real.

"You think it," he said. "If you think it, you'll look it. If you feel sorry, you'll look sorry." Playing a cool adventurer who was not going to tell a police interrogater (Claude Rains) why he came or what he was up to, he delivered lines which have since become classics:

"What is your nationality?"

"I'm a drunkard."

"Sam, I thought I told you not to play that song," he snapped at a nightclub pianist, and filmgoers today, as well as then, realized that here was a tough man who was vulnerable to love.

While Bogart was working on the film, Mayo was on the telephone to the set constantly. She was jealous of Ingrid Bergman, certain that Bogart was in love with her. She threatened to kill him if he left her. Believing the threat a real possibility, Sam Jaffe and Mary Baker took out a $100,000 policy on Bogie, insuring their firm against the financial catastrophe his death would cause.

After *Casablanca* Bogart starred with Raymond Massey in *Action in the North Atlantic*. As always he was in fine, mischievous form. One scene called for the stars' doubles to jump from the bridge of a burning tanker into the water below, which was aflame with oil.

"My double is braver than yours," Bogie said to Massey, who insisted that his double was the braver man.

The upshot of the argument was that both men did the stunt themselves. Massey burned his pants off and Bogie singed his eyebrows.

"The horrified reaction we got from the director and producer made it worthwhile," Massey told me. "Bogie was the star of the picture. If he had gotten hurt it would have cost Warners millions of dollars."

Although her career was also to take an upward swing, none of the critics paid any attention to Betty's performance in *Johnny 2 x 4*. An editor of *Harper's Bazaar* who was in the audience spotted her prowling gracefully into the speak-easy and saw in her the makings of a high-fashion model. Modeling again seemed the only solution, and Betty, who was then eighteen, started making the rounds of photographers' offices once more. Photographer Louise Dahl Wolfe was immediately impressed by her. "She's just about as smart as she can be," she said. "She has that wonderful yellow-green skin that's so good for color."

The editors of *Harper's* agreed, and soon Betty was working for the magazine on a regular basis. In December 1942—the same month that the Japanese attacked Pearl Harbor—Betty posed for Miss Dahl Wolfe with her hands in the pocket of a black outfit that made her look like a teen-age Mata Hari. She stood in front of a window with the legend "American Red Cross Blood for Servicemen." The session went smoothly. After it was over, the photographer confided that she thought the pictures might make the magazine's cover.

Some days later she telephoned to say Betty would be on the cover in March. To celebrate, Betty and her girlfriend went to the movies in Times Square. The picture they saw that night was *The Maltese Falcon*. The star was Humphrey Bogart.

CHAPTER 3

"You know how to whistle, don't you, Steve? You just put your lips together and blow."
—TO HAVE AND HAVE NOT

Like many would-be actresses, Betty entertained a secret hope that her picture on a national magazine cover would result in an interview for a theatrical job. She had no thought then of being in films: she had trained and was working toward a job on Broadway.

Meanwhile, in Hollywood, director Howard Hawks was faced with a problem. Warner Brothers had assigned him Humphrey Bogart as star of a film entitled *To Have and Have Not*, based on an Ernest Hemingway novel about students during a Cuban revolution. Hawks had gone down the list of contract players at the studio but there was no one, either new or established, who he felt would have the right chemistry to play opposite Bogart.

"Where the hell am I going to find the right girl?" he asked, Slim, his wife, over breakfast one morning in March 1942.

Slim, a 5′ 8½″ willowy blonde who, before marrying Hawks had been a top fashion model, was glancing over the current issue of *Harper's Bazaar* which had arrived with the morning mail. She looked up from the magazine at her husband. "Listen, sweets, you've always said you can take any girl and make a star of her. You've done it before. You'll do it again."

Slim was stating a fact well known in Hollywood. Her husband was famous for using unknown women with established male stars. He had given Rita Hayworth her first film break and had talked Carole Lombard into embarking on a new and highly successful career as a comedienne in *Twentieth Century*. Not coincidentally, the girls that Hawks liked resembled his wife somewhat in their casual, long-limbed type of good looks.

Slim pointed to a tawny blonde on the magazine cover wearing a Mata Hari costume in front of a window suggesting contributions to the Red Cross Blood Bank. "How about this girl?" she asked.

Hawks studied the cover photo noting the wide-set almond eyes, generous mouth and intelligent, almost insolent face. The girl was identified inside the magazine as "Betty Becall, young actress." The printer had misspelled her last name.

Hawks studied the photo carefully and agreed the girl was photogenic. He thought—but didn't say—that she bore more than a passing resemblance to his wife. A writer as well as a director, he had a type like Slim in mind when working on the script with screenwriter Jules Furthman and had even gone so far as to call the girl in the film Slim.

Later in the day he telephoned his secretary and asked her to find out something about "Betty Becall" —whether she had any acting experience and had any interest in testing for a film. Most important he wanted to know if there was any film on her in New York that he could see. The New York offices frequently tested models and young actresses to see if they had any qualifications for films.

Hawks' secretary misunderstood his instructions, however, and thinking Hawks wanted to see the girl, sent her a train ticket from New York to Los Angeles care of her model agency which, in turn, relayed the

ticket and message to Betty's uncle, Jacques Weinstein, a New York tax lawyer with a theatrical and
literary clientele.

Betty had just been offered a contract to appear as
"Miss Harper's Bazaar" in the Columbia musical picture *Cover Girl* and was on the point of signing. However, Uncle Jacques reasoned that she might have a
better opportunity in Hollywood as a potential actress
for Hawks than as a model for Columbia. At the very
least she might get a studio contract. These were the
days when unknowns were given contracts for $125 a
week and "groomed for stardom."

A brief family conference was arranged. Betty
agreed with her uncle, who said that in the Columbia
picture she would appear only a few moments on
screen as a model with perhaps only a line or two of
dialogue. Although there was only a slim chance that
Hawks would give her a role in a film (neither Betty
nor her uncle were aware of the title of the film or
the star), he would undoubtedly test her and then,
at least, she would have some film which could be
shown to other studios while she was in Hollywood.
Mrs. Bacal agreed, although she was nervous about
Betty being alone in Hollywood with all those
"wolves." She tried, in vain, to get a leave of absence
from her job so she could go with Betty but, in those
days, the train trip took three days and she could not
arrange for so much time off with her employers.

So it was decided that Betty was to go alone to
Hollywood but telephone home every night. Mother
and daughter spent the best part of two days shopping at S. Klein and a cut-rate Brooklyn store where
she bought her clothes for years. With much avuncu-
lar advice and motherly fretting, Betty was finally put
on the train from Grand Central in April 1943.

Betty was then just eighteen years old. Except for
brief stints at summer camp, she had never been
away from her mother for more than a few days. She
had only had walk-ons on Broadway and now she was
going to be interviewed by one of Hollywood's best-

known directors. Although in the past she had been able to hide her insecurities under a blanket of brashness, she was now truly on her own and frightened but, at the same time, exhilarated. She had never been afraid of a challenge and she was determined to accept whatever came her way and, good or bad, chalk it up to experience. As she was to tell a friend later, "Even if I didn't make it I could always go home where, let's face it, I wasn't leaving much of a career behind. I had nothing to lose and everything to gain."

Hawks had forgotten about Betty when, some weeks later, he learned from Warners New York offices she would be arriving at the Pasadena railroad station on the edge of Los Angeles. He checked with his secretary and learned of the mistake. He telephoned the Warner publicity department and asked them to arrange to have "the girl" picked up at the station.

The assignment fell to Leo Guild, a young press agent recently arrived from New York himself. Even now, some thirty years later, Guild remembers the day he picked up Betty at the terminal. "She was beautiful but, to my mind, too thin. But that's not what I remember best about the day. I'd gone out to get her in my own battered second-hand Chevrolet convertible and I was so embarrassed about the car that I spent most of the drive to the Beverly Hills Hotel where we had booked her apologizing for it. But she didn't seem concerned. She was too excited just to be in Hollywood. I waited outside the hotel for her to freshen up and then took her to Hawks' office at the studio."

On entering the hotel, Betty stepped into a scene that probably surpassed all of her fantasies about Hollywood. The Beverly Hills Hotel, then as well as now, is a sprawl of pink and green stucco set back on a 15½-acre site off Sunset Boulevard in the heart of a palm grove in the center of Beverly Hills. The lobby is quietly elegant and the head bell boy then as now is Johnny, whose face was famous from Philip

63

Morris cigarette advertisements. Film stars going to and from the Polo Lounge, the hotel's celebrated cocktail lounge, passed her on their way through the lobby. Orange and lemon trees and exotic tropical flowers nestled against the walls of her patio, which was larger than her living room in New York.

Although Betty was undoubtedly dismayed and timorous about going to see Hawks immediately after a three-day train trip, Guild was waiting outside in his car to drive her to the studio. She had just time enough to freshen up and run a brush through her long hair enough to get it shining.

Guild took the Coldwater Canyon route from Beverly Hills to Burbank, home of the Warner Studios, and pointed out the homes of the famous people as they passed by. One of the homes which Betty would later remember belonged to Edith Head, the Academy Award-winning designer who, some years later, would design clothes for one of Betty's films. Had Guild taken another route to the studios he would have passed in front of Hedy Lamarr's house, which Betty, in less than five years, would be living in herself.

Hawks was waiting for Betty in his office on the lot. His practiced eye immediately took in her wardrobe —neat and tasteful but inexpensive. She had, he would recall later, a beautiful face, but beautiful women were in great supply in those days when girls from all over the country were pouring into Hollywood hoping for a film break. Although Betty tried to give the impression of being calm, Hawks was aware she was nervous: her hands shook and she maintained one pose during most of their conversation—head down, greenish eyes lowered but looking up at him from a three-quarter profile. Automatically he checked this off as being the angle which photographers had told her was her best.

"I was not overly impressed with her at the first meeting," Hawks recalled. "But she was so eager that I told my secretary to get her a cab and send her over to three or four studios to see about work—and then have her come back to me. But Betty didn't want to do that. She wanted to go to work. *Now.* I told her that the women I used in pictures were not necessarily of any special age but they certainly did not have high nasal voices.

"You just couldn't read the lines," he said.

Betty's lip twitched and her skin suddenly became blotchy, a sign of nerves, Hawks noted.

"How do I change my voice?" she asked.

"I don't know," said Hawks. "But I can tell you how Walter Huston, the best actor I ever worked with, got his voice. You have to find out where your voice is coming from and then you have to practice to get it lower. You should get a board and put it over the top of a table or dresser so you can lean against it, prodding yourself in the stomach and speak from there. Just keep prodding yourself in the diaphragm. Then after you have control of yourself that way, read aloud from a book as though you were reading to an audience.

"And if I do that, will you teach me how to act?"

"No. But I'll try to teach you to non-act. First things first. When you've got your voice down, come see me again."

Hawks was intrigued enough by Betty's determined attitude and appearance, however, to arrange for her to draw enough money from the studio paymaster to pay her hotel bill for a month. He also gave her some pocket money and then dismissed her.

Betty telephoned her mother that night and pleaded with her to join her in Hollywood. Within the week Mrs. Bacal arrived with Droopy, the cocker spaniel. Mother and daughter moved to a small furnished apartment in Hollywood where they could keep expenses down. Meanwhile, Betty spent hours every day doing as Hawks suggested—trying to lower her voice. She rented a car and drove alone to the beach alongside the Pacific to lonely places and shouted until she was hoarse, always trying to bring her voice up from the diaphragm. Mrs. Bacal cooked for them on a hot plate and encouraged her daughter to keep trying.

Mother and daughter had the same goal: to get Betty started in Hollywood. One afternoon Betty telephoned Nina Foch, who had been in her class at the American Academy of Dramatic Arts and who was already on her way in films. Miss Foch went over to see Betty and her mother. "I had the definite feeling that they were making a concerted effort to start Betty on her career. When they found out I couldn't do anything for them they shrugged me off."

Three weeks after her first meeting with Hawks Betty was back in his office. "Hello," she said in a very deep voice.

"I had to admire her," said Hawks. "She hadn't gone out or done anything for three weeks other than work on her voice. She was no longer talking from her throat but her diaphragm, but I told her she was going to have to work on the voice constantly until, eventually, it became part of her.

"I had a hunch then that I might be able to do something with her because she was so willing to work. That's part of the game, being willing to take instructions and direction and to work. I had just the germ of an idea of what could be done with her, and as a director, it was part of my job to find and develop new talent."

Hawks considered putting Betty under personal contract, but first he wanted to see how she was with people. So he invited her to his home for an informal Saturday night party. Hawks has since forgotten who the guests were but he recalls a "handful of stars, some top writers, a director or two and one or two writers." Most of the men were married and had brought their wives, most of whom looked on Betty as a predatory female and competition not only because she was beautiful but because she was young. Although some of the men were intrigued by Betty, she was too nervous and too much aware of being on display to relax. And she was overly conscious that in this gathering of celebrities she had no stature. It was a cruel test for Betty, who didn't feel she belonged. Everyone else seemed to be having a good time, and many of the guests, including the host, were drinking and Betty didn't drink.

When the party was over, Hawks, who had had a few drinks, found he would have to take Betty home, a circumstance which displeased him.

"What's the matter?" he asked Betty testily in his car. "Couldn't you get somebody to offer you a ride?"

"I don't get along too well with men."

"Are you nice to them?"

"I try to be," said Betty.

Hawks thought for a moment. Finally he said, "Don't be nice the next time. Try insulting them and see whether maybe you do a little bit better."

The following Saturday night Betty was a guest at another party at Hawks' home. When the party ended she went over to Hawks. "I've got a ride home." There was a grin on her face.

"Good for you. What did you do?"

"I did what you told me to do. I insulted a man. I asked him where he got his tie. He said, 'Why do you want to know?' I said, 'So I can tell other people not to go there.'"

Hawks was delighted. "Who was the man?"

"Clark Gable."

That night Hawks lay awake in bed tossing and turning, unable to sleep. And then the idea that had been in the back of his mind began to take shape. With Betty's new deep voice, her sultry looks and almost masculine quality to her character, she reminded him of Marlene Dietrich. He would use Betty's raw material and shape it into another Dietrich.

The following morning he suggested to writer Jules Furthman that he change the character of the girl, Slim, and make her insolent—but people would like it.

"Like Dietrich?" asked Furthman.

"Like Dietrich," said Hawks.

Furthman caught onto the idea at once and began working on developing the new character.

At lunch later that week in the studio commissary the director saw Humphrey Bogart sitting alone at a table.

"How's the script coming, Howard?" Bogart asked.

"We're working on it," said Hawks noncommittally.

"I've heard you're planning to use a new girl in the film."

Hawks decided to tease Bogie's interest a little. "I'm going to try something," he said. "I'm going to try and make a girl as insolent as you are."

Bogie grinned. "Fat chance of that."

Hawks matched the actor's grin. "I've got a better than fat chance. The new girl you've heard about. We're writing a part for her now and I'll tell you one thing: in every scene you play with her, she's going to walk out and leave you with egg on your face."

"Want to bet on it?" There was challenge in Bogie's voice.

"I'll bet," said Hawks, who knew that Bogie would now be curious about the new girl which would make it easier to sell him on her as a co-star even though she was an unknown.

Meanwhile, Hawks, who had been working steadily with Betty, discovered that she had one major fault. She was afraid to try things because of her inexperience; she had never played a scene with anybody except in acting classes. So, one afternoon, he gave her a scene to study and asked her to read it with a Spanish accent.

"I don't know a Spanish accent," she murmured.

"I didn't ask whether you know one. I said, 'I want one now.' "

Betty tried to read the lines but her accent was so deplorable that Hawks was soon doubled up with laughter. "Get fifty dollars from my secretary," he said. "Then get somebody to teach you a Spanish accent."

Within a week Betty was back with a passable Spanish accent.

"I've changed my mind," said Hawks. "We've decided now to make her a Swedish girl."

All told, he had Betty do six different language accents over a period of two months.

"I wanted her to get over her fear of trying to do new things because of her inexperience," Hawks said. "She learned the accents and she found out it didn't hurt her to be laughed at and she could do anything she set her mind to. I'll say this for her—she'd try anything. At the same time she was learning poise."

Hawks, wise in the way of studio politics and machinations, suspected that, at the last moment, he would probably be assigned a contract star for the role opposite Bogie, but he felt that Betty could bring a quality to the role that none of the contract actresses had. He also knew it would be a fight to get the studio to agree to an unknown unless they were excited by her and felt they could profit from her. That meant that he needed to get the studio to consider putting her under contract, and the first stage in this process was for them to test her.

Studio executives, aware that Hawks was working with Betty, soon became curious about her and since the director had a reputation as a latter-day Pygmalion, Jack L. Warner, the studio head, gave instructions that Betty was to be tested. Everything was working out according to Hawks' plan.

Screen tests in those days were usually little longer than three or four minutes, and the routine was for an established star to read lines with the newcomer. Not only did the test consist of the brief scene but also close shots of profile, full face, and three-quarter face.

Charles Drake, one of the most handsome and promising contract players on the lot, was assigned to do the test with Betty. The scene they were to do was from *Claudia*, a comedy, and it was a standard used for most females being tested.

69

Hawks had wanted Betty to test in a scene from his film and wanted to direct the test himself. But he was overruled by Warner, who insisted on the established routine with another contract director in charge.

The test was not especially noteworthy. Betty was too nervous and although she had some flair for comedy, she was not comfortable with the strange director. Warner was not particularly impressed, but Hawks was still convinced that in the right scene with the proper lines Betty would be good. He decided to back his faith in Betty with his own money and put her under personal contract at $150 a week— half of what she had been earning in New York as a model. And he kept after Furthman to work on the character of the girl in the film. But old pro that he was, the director decided to hedge his bet and had two scripts written; one in which the girl didn't have much of a part and the other with the new character.

Charles Feldman, Hawks' agent, who would later become a producer, read the latter script and told Hawks, "My God, that's a hell of a part. Who are you going to use for the girl?"

"That kid from New York," said Hawks.

"For Chrissake, you can't use her," said Feldman vehemently.

Hawks was not willing to admit to himself—or to the studio—that he had been wrong about Betty. By then he had spent more than three months working with her and he was convinced that with the proper training and direction she would be perfect for the role he had in mind. It was a challenge, and Hawks— a former automobile racer—was accustomed to accepting and besting challenges.

Determined to prove that he was right, he started on a rigorous program to develop Betty's character. He had started working with her voice. Next he determined to develop her ego.

"Ego is important to everyone, but especially to a woman," he said. "When an established female star comes through a door, she is secure in the belief that

70

every man in the room wants to lay her," he said. "But a girl who is just beginning in films entering through the same door just stands there frightened. Therefore I had a set procedure when I started working with a new girl.

"Each day I spoke with a few people on the lot—grips, wardrobe people, lighting technicians, people who usually worked on my films—and asked them to go up to Betty and say something complimentary about the way she looked or was dressed. And I asked some of the male workers to whistle at her when she walked by.

"I recall once walking to the studio commissary with her for lunch when some men whistled and, at first, she was nervous and kind of slouched over, sort of hurrying up her pace. Then I saw her smile—that kind of secret smile that women have when they know they are appreciated—and she relaxed, tossed her head back and became very animated, proud that I noticed how the men reacted to her." The director also began to help Betty develop the attitude that was later to become her trademark. One of the first things he taught her was to slow down, to study people and situations before speaking.

"When you look at a man, study him so that he wonders what the hell you're thinking," he told her. "And when you speak, always use your film voice; keep it low and husky. A man hearing that voice will think all kinds of interesting things: how many bedrooms, how many bottles of gin did it take to get that voice."

A few days later Betty told him that in the past when she went into stores, salesgirls wouldn't even turn around to look at her. But when she spoke in her husky voice they paid attention because the voice had so much authority in it.

In Hawks' view the voice and attitude were integral parts of the personality he wanted to develop. His model for Betty was still Dietrich, and he arranged to have Dietrich's movie *The Blue Angel*, screened

71

for Betty. Later, he told her that he wanted her to adopt some of "that character."

Betty was young, pliable, eager to learn and she had faith in Hawks. For the first nine months she was in Hollywood she commuted from the apartment she shared in Hollywood with her mother to Hawks' office almost every day in a beat-up four-year-old Plymouth coupe.

There is no record of her dating anyone at the studio during that time, although it is certain she had many offers. She was determined to "make it" her way, unlike many other young actresses who, on arriving in Hollywood, played the social game and tried to go to the right parties hoping to make an impression on an important producer or director. Eating and drinking together, going to the bull fights in Tijuana and week-ending with important people were emphasized much more in Hollywood than in most places.

Of course there were the legends of actresses who had affairs with important studio people who, in return for favors granted, would push their careers. Betty was undoubtedly aware of the stories—they were common gossip at the studio—but she kept to herself.

"Betty was a loner," said one actor who tried unsuccessfully to date her. "She stayed by herself most of the time and, as I remember it, she even brought her own lunch so she wouldn't have to go to the commissary alone. Once or twice, when I talked with her, all she was interested in was acting. Nothing turns a fellow off more than a lovely young thing who has such an immense determination to succeed."

"It was a lonely life," Betty was to say later. "All I did was study and work and try to develop myself into what Hawks wanted."

Hawks couldn't teach Betty the quick repartee and snappy lines that went with the character he was developing—that would only come with time and experience—but he knew that he could write the proper lines into the script and he felt Betty could deliver them with his guidance.

Finally, Hawks was really certain he could get the performance he required from Betty and, to prove it, he decided to screen test her again and direct the test himself. The studio reluctantly gave him permission. There was only one problem. He needed a test that would use all of Betty's pluses in less than three minutes, and he didn't have such a scene in the film. He knew that Betty was at her best and most comfortable when she was lazing around, leaning against something, and he planned to make use of this. So he wrote a scene himself and decided to test Betty alone.

In the test which Hawks directed himself, Betty leans against a door and says to Hawks, who is off camera, "You know how to whistle, don't you? You just put your lips together and blow." He also included some shots of Betty at her best angles—a three-quarter shot in which her head was slightly down and she was looking up.

When Hawks showed Feldman the test, the agent said, "My God, she's great. You'd better use her." Jack L. Warner was equally impressed and offered to buy half of Betty's contract but Hawks declined the offer. He was now gambling for higher stakes. He would make Betty a star, first, and then discuss her contract with the head of the studio.

Although it was not yet confirmed that she would have the role opposite Bogart, there was no doubt that, at the very least, she would have some part in the film, and the various departments of the studio were alerted to begin their processing routines.

Now, for the first time since she had arrived in Hollywood, Betty was dazedly involved in big-studio routine. Although never an ugly duckling, the various departments at the studio seemed determined to make her into a swan. Every morning for weeks she reported at 6:00 A.M. to the make-up department where her hair was washed then dried, after which a

73

half-dozen stylists experimented with her hair. Make-up artists tried to widen her eyes, then narrow them, then highlight them. All of this was opposed by Betty, who, having been a model, already thought she knew what make-up looked best on her. She complained to Hawks, saying that she thought he wanted her as she was. That was why he had signed her.

Hawks laughed and said the make-up people had a job to do, too, but he finally gave strict instructions that they could try anything they wanted except shave her eyebrows, cut her hair or cap her teeth without his express approval.

Betty also spent many afternoons in the studio publicity department where hundreds of first names were tried with Bacall. The studio did not like Betty as a first name and she was determined to keep her own last name. Finally, she chose the name Lauren in memory of a maternal grandparent. The studio publicity department interviewed her for hours before preparing a two-page biography which would describe her as "arresting rather than beautiful" and note that she had "long, lithe legs, curves in the right places and the proper proportions." There was only one slight inaccuracy in the biography. Betty was identified as "the daughter of parents who trace their American ancestry back several generations." It was wartime, and the studio felt compelled to make everyone 100 percent American.

By the end of November, Hawks had a first-draft shooting script prepared and approved by the studio, which also approved Betty for the leading lady. There was only one stumbling block ahead: Bogart had the right to approve of his female star. Would he accept an unknown?

CHAPTER 4

*"I think this is the beginning of a beauti-
ful friendship."*
—CASABLANCA

In 1943 Bogart was the king on the Warner lot thanks
to the success of two of his most recent films: *The
Maltese Falcon* and *Casablanca,* for which he had
received an Academy Award nomination. Audiences
watching Bogart play his tender, understated love
scenes with Ingrid Bergman against the tinkly background of "As Time Goes By" were suddenly aware
of a quality—very much a part of his own character—
that had never before come through so clearly on the
screen. "They saw an approximation to the melan-
choly man whose wryness was the mask of an incor-
ruptibility he mocked," Alistair Cooke wrote. Warner
finally began to think of Bogart as a romantic leading
man.

Then forty-four years old, Bogart had been married
for six years to Mayo. Soon after their marriage he
and Mayo became known to the press as "The Battling Bogarts," and their home had a sign out front:
Sluggy Hollow. Their 36-foot cruiser was called
Sluggy, after his pet name for her. Even their Scottie
dog was named Sluggy.

Jaik Rosenstein, who was present at the inception of

mily disputes, recalls that they could start otice or seeming provocation. "Mayo always he gave up her career when she married Bogart d constantly taunted him with that fact," he said. "She was a bitterly unhappy woman who demeaned Bogie's success and, to put him down, used to call him, 'that cheap little ham actor.'"

The fact is that Mayo had never been a star. She had always been a featured player. In 1937 she made only one film, *Marked Woman*, the picture in which she and Bogart first met. In 1938 she made two B films, two more in 1939 but only one in 1940. While Bogart's career soared, hers plummeted, and since marrying Bogart she had let herself go physically and gained weight. Never a beauty, she had turned into a short and dumpy character actress, but she resented the fact that Bogart never insisted she be given a small role in any of his films.

She resented this unwillingness on his part just as she resented his success, and he resented her right back. They both expressed their resentment in public, in bars and nightclubs at the top of their voices.

Parties at Sluggy Hollow might start off quietly enough, but usually they disintegrated into a battle. Not infrequently the guests, infected with the Bogarts' brawling, joined in the fray, and more than one party ended in a free-for-all.

At a New Year's Eve party at their home, attended by James Thurber, Elliot Nugent, Louis Broomfield and other celebrities, the martial spirit was such that one bespectacled guest challenged another: "Let's fight with our glasses on." Thurber was so fascinated that he sent the Bogarts a window-sized cartoon of the fracas inscribed "Jolly Times—1939" that Bogart hung over the bar next to the Algonquin Hotel bill for breakage.

It is a cliché in psychology that people frequently choose a partner in marriage who has characteristics that they admire but lack themselves. Bogart was a realist. He knew the men he played so well on the

76

screen were far removed from his own characteristics but he recognized the value of his new image as a "tough guy" and Mayo enhanced the image. She was truly tough; a tiger who would take on anyone in a fight. It is probable that Mayo's primary role in Bogart's life during the early years of their marriage was to fortify his image.

Sometimes when he and Mayo were in the midst of one of their brawls, she would suddenly pick up her highball and heave it at him. Bogart never bothered to duck, but would sit calmly in his chair while the glass whizzed uncomfortably close to his face. "Mayo's a lousy shot," he would explain to guests as the glass shattered behind his head. "I live dangerously. I'm colorful. But Sluggy's crazy about me because she knows I'm braver than George Raft or Edward G. Robinson."

Instead of trying to hush stories about his militant marital life, Bogart related funny anecdotes to anyone who interviewed him. He told reporter George Frazier about the night he and Mayo were emerging from "21" in Manhattan and were besieged by autograph hounds.

"In his anxiety to get away, Bogart slammed a taxi door just as his wife was about to step in," Frazier reported. "The awareness that she was surrounded by a gibbering mob of her husband's admirers increased her anger. 'That cheap little ham actor,' she screamed, going on in such a vein for two or three minutes. The kids listened in awe. Finally, one youngster closed his autograph book and turned to his companion to say, in a voice quivering with admiration, 'Gee, she's even tougher than he is.'"

Undoubtedly Bogart enjoyed some of his noisy arguments with Mayo. He was, after all, an actor, and actors traditionally seem to thrive on drama in their domestic lives. But there was probably more to it than just that. Howard Hawks once asked Bogie if he could get an erection without first having had a battle with Mayo. Bogie looked at Hawks a moment and said, "You know, I guess you're right. I probably couldn't."

Mayo was able to drink most men under the table, a feat Bogart greatly admired. However, though his "thermostat" didn't fail him, he had changed during their marriage from a moderate drinker to a steady and capacious one.

Mayo, however, did not believe in moderation. She could and did drink until she was unable to stand, and Bogie claimed she did her best to get him to increase his consumption. "She got me drinking and kept me drinking because that was the only way she felt she could keep me," he once said: the only time he ever said anything critical about Mayo in an interview.

It would be unfair to assume that Bogart's marital life was an unending battle and that Mayo was only a fiery-tempered drunken shrew. She had been remarkably kind to Bogart's mother and sister Frances Rose (Pat), who came to Hollywood and moved to an apartment near them in 1935. Pat described the two Mrs. Bogarts as being "alike as two peas in a pod. Mayo was very small and a spitfire, just like my mother. They loved each other." Bogart had, by then, made peace with his mother, who was ill and nursed by Mayo until her death in 1940 at the age of seventy-five.

Bogart's other sister, Catherine, had died in 1937 at the age of thirty-three. "She was a victim of a speakeasy era," Bogart explained to friends. "She burned the candle at both ends, then decided to burn it in the middle." The record shows that Catherine died on the operating table of a ruptured appendix. Excessive drinking had weakened her resistance, the medical history said.

Mayo was also responsible for getting Bogart a business manager, "Morgan Maree, who wisely invested Bogie's money (he earned $3,500 a week, forty weeks a year) and saw to it the Bogarts lived on a budget.

An item on that budget was for a carpenter named

Graham who was on constant call. His job was to repair any damage the Bogarts might have inflicted on a host's home or in their own. Graham had a supply of twelve doors of various shapes and sizes in the cellar of the Bogarts' home on Horn Avenue above the Sunset Strip.

One day Jaik Rosenstein attempted to play mediator in a Bogart family dispute. During a friendly chat in Bogie's studio dressing room, he told the actor that when Mayo began needling him he should ignore it, let it go in one ear and out the other.

"That would never work in a million years," Bogart answered.

Rosenstein said he ought to try it. Bogart shook his head, meanwhile finishing his make-up at the dressing table. He adjusted the snap brim of his hat in the mirror and started out for the sound stage, with Rosenstein following.

Suddenly Bogart stopped and turned around. "I want to explain something that you apparently don't understand," Bogart said. "My wife is an actress. She's a clever actress. It just so happens that she's not working right now. But even when an actress isn't working, she's got to have scenes to play. And in this case I've got to give her the cues."

Bogart's gallant defense of Mayo was in keeping with his character. Despite his newly acquired tough guy image, he was still a gentleman, the product of his background and early training. Although the public was not aware of it, he was, behind the façade, still a beautiful and loving man. He was, however, becoming disenchanted with Mayo's excesses and privately he told a friend that he didn't know what he was going to do about her.

"She's my responsibility," he said. "But she needs help and I don't know how to get it for her because she won't accept it. Least of all from me."

Bogart continued to maintain his equanimity and patience under circumstances far more trying than any script demanded. "He got so used to bottles being

79

thrown at him at home that the violence of a movie fight scene seemed tame to him," says Mary Baker.

"During the early forties Bogart would come to Warner Brothers with bags under his eyes a Redcap couldn't have hefted." recalls actor Pat O'Moore, an actor friend of Bogart's. "I stayed with him sometimes at a hotel when Mayo would kick him out of the house. Every morning he would light a cigarette on awakening, order orange juice and coffee. Then we'd go down to the car and he'd be sick for a few minutes. After he vomitted, we'd go to the studio and he'd have more coffee. Then he'd be all right."

Bogart revealed none of this tempestuous life before the cameras, but consistently turned in smooth, underplayed, professional characterizations in pictures not always worthy of his talent.

Although king of the Warner lot, Bogie was not a king in his home. Mayo was becoming more difficult every day. "She would love him one moment, and in the next breath, she would try to kill him," Pat O'Moore said.

From an attractive blonde, Mayo had become blowsy. Her face was now puffy, her skin scaly. Although she was a good cook, she stopped eating and drank almost constantly.

Bogart finally persuaded her to go to a physician who reported she was an alcoholic and suggested psychiatry. The psychiatrist diagnosed her as a paranoid and schizophrenic and warned Bogart that she was capable of violence to herself or someone else. He recommended psychotherapy in a rest home, but Mayo flatly refused.

After this disheartening report, Bogart was despondent. He had known of Mayo's alcohol problem when they were married, but it was only during the last couple of years that she had let her drinking get out of control. She was always drunk when he came home, and try as he might, there was no way to keep liquor from her. If he hid the bottles, she ordered more from local liquor stores, and as fast as he cut off her charge

80

accounts there, she opened new ones. After all, she was Mrs. Humphrey Bogart and tradesmen were eager to get her business.

He was only too well aware of her violent temper; she had once stabbed him with a knife in a fit of jealousy because he had been to the Finlandia Baths with a friend. In Mayo's view the baths were little more than whorehouses, and nothing could convince her to the contrary. Only the hasty intervention of Mary Baker kept the stabbing incident out of the newspapers.

Mayo had also threatened to shoot him on more than one occasion and, lately, she had been talking more and more about suicide. One morning shortly before *Casablanca* was finished, Jaik Rosenstein got a telephone call from the Warner police chief, Whitey Blaine. "Bogie's wife attempted suicide last night," the chief said. "You'd better get over there, see what the problem is and hush it up if you can."

When Rosenstein arrived at the house Bogart let him in. "Did she really try to kill herself?" the press agent asked.

"Well, she cut her wrists, but not very deep," Bogart said.

Rosenstein sent Bogart off to the studio, then called to Mayo, who came downstairs weeping, with clumsy bandages on her wrists. She put her arms around Rosenstein and sobbed, "Oh, I don't know what I'm going to do. I know he's running around on me."

Rosenstein told Mayo that her jealousy was natural enough but that she was overplaying it. Bogart was not interested in any other woman, but he soon might be if his home life didn't improve. It was a prophesy eerily accurate.

Despite Mayo's fears, Bogart was not a lady's man. He had married the three women with whom he had had extensive affairs, and there was no woman at the time who interested him. Like most film stars, opportunity for affairs was thrust at him almost daily, but although he had ceased loving Mayo, he respected her

81

too much to cheat on her. Nevertheless Mayo continually accused him of having affairs and was jealous of every woman in his films.

When he was working she had begun to telephone the set almost hourly ostensibly to say "hello" but, he knew, she was really checking up on him.

The tempestuous lovemaking which formerly characterized the ending of most of their quarrels had given way to endless bickering and recriminations with Mayo. More often than not she passed out in a drunken stupor as soon as they got to bed.

He felt pity for Mayo—a major step in the transition from love to dislike—and he felt guilty about leaving her although he must have been aware, as were all of his friends, that his marriage had run its course. But as an old-fashioned man with old-fashioned virtues he planned to stick it out and hope for a miracle or for something to happen.

The fuse of a midlife marital explosion was there. It only remained for someone to come along to light it.

CHAPTER 5

Although Betty knew that Hawks was preparing her for a role in a Bogart film, she had no idea it was *the* starring role as his leading woman. When Hawks told her that he wanted her to meet Bogart, Betty's reaction was less than enthusiastic.

"I had always believed everything I saw on the screen and I believed those 'dese, dem and dose' routines he always gave out with his characterizations," she said. "When I first went out to Hollywood I was walking on stars. I had visions of playing opposite Charles Boyer and Tyrone Power or some other leading man. But when Hawks said it was to be Bogart, I was disappointed and thought, 'How awful to be in a picture with that mug; that illiterate. He mustn't have a brain in his head. He won't be able to think or talk about anything.' "

The meeting, arranged on the set of *Conflict*, in which Bogart was starring as a man who killed his wife and inadvertently gives himself away, was hasty. Introductions were made, some small talk attempted, and then Bogart was called back before the cameras.

Later, Bogie would say of his first reaction to Betty

—the girl Hawks had promised would rival him in insolence—"She's a very long girl."

Betty must have been put off by his height, too. Bogie was shorter than he appeared on screen. A shade over 5′9″, he would have been only an inch or so taller than Betty if she was not wearing high heels.

The disparity between their ages must have been stunningly apparent to each of them. Off screen and without make-up, Bogie's face was seamed and lined, a map of the hard life he had lived by the time he was forty-four. Betty's extreme youth—she was nineteen at the time—must have been a minus factor from Bogie's point of view. Even as a young man, he never liked young women, according to his sister Pat. His first wife was his senior, and his second and third wives were nearly his age. But Betty, who had grown up fatherless during most of her childhood, no doubt found older men attractive.

If they talked for any length of time, they must instantly have been aware that their attitudes toward life were sharply divergent. Bogart was a cynic in contrast with Betty who was an innocent and an optimist. He had grown up with all the advantages of wealth, education and a WASP background, while Betty was a Jewish girl from the Bronx. These two people prove the truth of the old saw that opposites attract.

Bogart approved of Betty as his co-star and was, apparently, sufficiently impressed by her so that he suggested to Charles Drake, who was starring with him, that he invite Betty to drop by the set again. It was Drake who had made Betty's first screen test.

Drake says, "Bogie and I had been friendly until Betty came to the set to visit me, and then he took an almost violent dislike to me. The picture with her hadn't even started yet, but I think he was already interested in her."

Betty was interested enough in Bogie to come back to the set once more—this time to see him and not Drake. But there was no time for them to really get acquainted: Bogie and Mayo were committed to make a USO tour in Europe and Africa and left before Christmas for several weeks.

In the interim, Betty went back to her daily routine, working with the wardrobe, make-up and publicity departments at the studio and attending constant sessions with Hawks, who was preparing her for the film.

She had moved with her mother to a small furnished apartment in an unglamorous section of Beverly Hills, a few blocks from the Beverly Wilshire Hotel. There were no servants, and Betty generally got her own breakfast, since she had to be at the studio by eight o'clock. Mrs. Bacal cooked dinner in the evenings and Betty helped with the dishes. She made occasional appearances in the clubs along the Strip, where she drank almost nothing, smoked a great deal and danced conservatively, either leaving the floor or collapsing with mirth when she got involved with partners who liked elaborate steps. Her favorite expression at the time was "mad." She did "mad" scenes, smoked like "mad" and told friends she would soon go "mad" if the cigarette shortage didn't let up.

If she thought about Bogart at all, it was probably only fleetingly and with apprehension. He was not only the star of the picture but he was also one of the top stars in Hollywood, and she would have to do her best to be able to even register on the screen in a scene with him. She was undoubtedly aware that she had the kind of break that made the Hollywood legend so universal, but it is doubtful that she considered herself a Cinderella. She had worked hard all of her life and no one had ever given her anything for nothing before.

The first cast reading for *To Have and Have Not* was held on March 6, 1944, on Stage 16 of the Warner Brothers lot in Burbank, California. The sound stage was as cavernous and gloomy as a wharfside warehouse. The film set, the interior of a shabby hotel, thrown up in a distant corner, was bathed in a glare of blue-white light coming from a battery of huge arc lamps manned by a dozen hairy union men tinkering stolidly with electrical cables and fuse boxes. Occasionally they peered down in boredom from the steel bridgework on which they perched.

A photograph taken at the time shows the cast of the movie gathered in a corner of the sound stage around both sides of a long wooden table littered with the props of early morning workers everywhere: cups of coffee, white packets of sugar and small pitchers of milk; half-empty boxes of Danish pastry and donuts, napkins; ashtrays smoldering with half-finished butts trailing a haze of smoke. There is a profusion of scripts on the table, each bound in a red cover and stamped because of wartime restrictions, "Save Film."

In the photograph, director Howard Hawks sits, back to the camera, facing the stars of the film, Humphrey Bogart and Lauren Bacall. Bogart, in open-necked shirt with sleeves rolled to just below the elbows, is apparently pointing out something to Bacall who is seated next to him. There is a look of real authority about Bogart, with shirt sleeves rolled up, that was in sharp contrast to the fresh innocence of Bacall, who is wearing a tailored suit with white blouse which makes her look like a teen-ager—she was nineteen at the time. A cascade of brown hair frames her Slavic face, which is tilted down, while, at the same time, she is looking up at Bogart with wide, almond-shaped eyes. He is truly a veteran of the Hollywood jungle, while it has been almost exactly a year to the day since her arrival in Hollywood, and this is her first film.

The two stars are flanked by songwriter-actor Hoagy Carmichael, Walter Brennan and Dolores Moran, opposite them is Hawks; seated to his left is script girl Meta Wilde; actor Dan Seymour is on his right.

One celebrated person avoided being photographed because of his inherent shyness. This was author William Faulkner, who had been brought in by Hawks

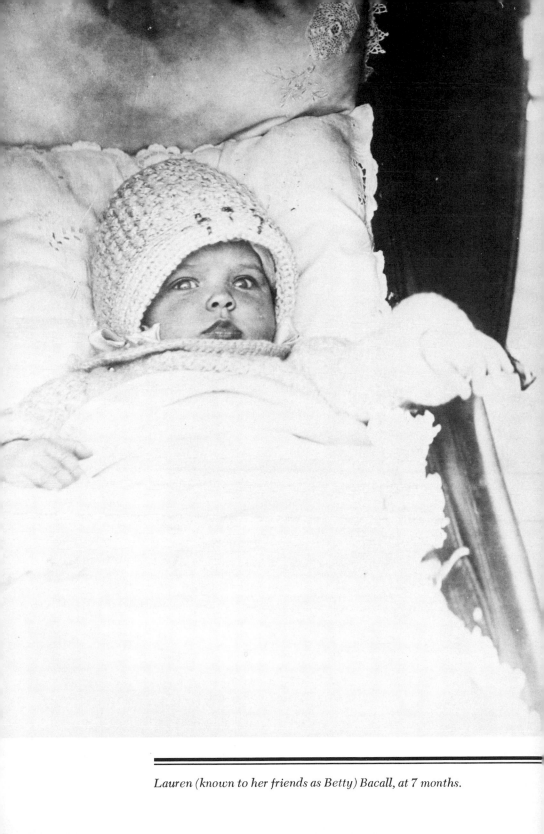

Lauren (known to her friends as Betty) Bacall, at 7 months.

ABOVE: *Lauren Bacall, at 5½ years.*

OPPOSITE: *Lauren Bacall, at 10 years.*
This is Betty's first professional photo.
She was a juvenile model for
the John Robert Powers Agency, and
this photo was on file at the agency.

BELOW: *Lauren's first leg art. At Highland Park Manor, the private girls' school at Tarrytown-on-the-Hudson, 9-year-old Betty posed for her mother one Sunday in a new coat and hat Mrs. Bacal had brought with her. She remembers spilling chocolate malted milk down the front of the coat the first night she wore it and trying to clean the stains off with a bottle of toilet water.*

OPPOSITE LEFT: *Betty was 12 years old when she graduated from Highland Park Manor. At the time her desire to be the "old-fashioned" type drove her mother to distraction. Betty designed the dress, and in her hair she wore a large, dramatic white bow—another of her inspirations. In the photo with her is her school chum Helen Blackwell. The class prophecy read that Betty "would grow up to break men's hearts."*

OPPOSITE RIGHT: *Lauren Bacall, at 13. Betty was a "senior" at Camp Cannihaw in Connecticut. The pleased grin is due to the fact that she had just won the swimming competition for camp seniors. One of her duties was to take care of the younger campers.*

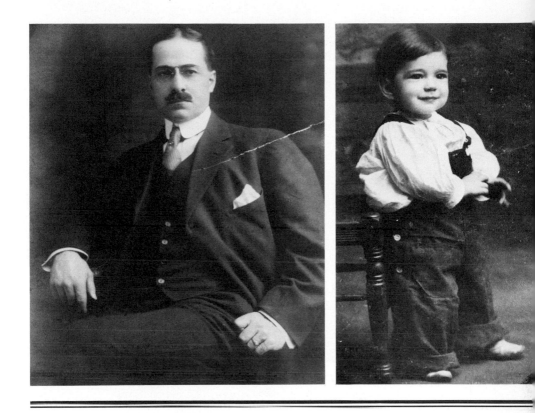

OPPOSITE: *Maude Humphrey and 4-month-old son, Humphrey.*

ABOVE LEFT: *Dr. Belmont DeForest Bogart, Humphrey's father. He wears the ruby ring that Humphrey inherited and wore for the rest of his life.*

ABOVE RIGHT: *Bogie around 3 years old.*

RIGHT: *Bogie in the U.S. Navy, which he joined after flunking out of preparatory school at 18.*

OPPOSITE PAGE: *Humphrey Bogart, Mary Phillips (who became his second wife), and Paul Kelly in* NERVES, *produced on Broadway in 1923.*

Bogart and Mayo Methot,
his third wife, on their wedding day in the
den of their Hollywood home,
"Sluggy Hollow," 1938.

This photo was taken on May 22, 1945, at Betty and Bogie's wedding
at the beautiful Malabar Farms home of author Louis Bromfield.
L TO R: *Bromfield, Bogart, Mrs. Bromfield, Natalie Bacal
(the bride's mother), Bacall, George Hawkins (Bromfield's secretary), and
Municipal Judge Herbert L. Schettler, who officiated at the ceremony.*

ABOVE: *Wedding day. Betty and Bogie with Judge Schettler.*

OPPOSITE TOP: *Betty and Bogie's first picture together,* TO HAVE AND HAVE NOT, *1945 (Warner Brothers).* L TO R: *Dan Seymour, Aldo Naldi, Lauren Bacall, Bogart, Sheldon Leonard. (Vitagraph Inc.)*

OPPOSITE BOTTOM: TO HAVE AND HAVE NOT. L TO R: *Dolores Moran, Bogart, Marcel Dalio, Lauren Bacall, Dan Seymour, Sheldon Leonard. (Vitagraph Inc.)*

ABOVE: *Bogie and Betty in a studio still.*

BELOW: *A publicity photo of Lauren Bacall probably taken in 1944 prior to her starring with Bogie in* TO HAVE AND HAVE NOT.

OPPOSITE: *A publicity still from* THE BIG SLEEP, *1946. (Museum of Modern Art Film Stills Archive)*

*A rare photo of Bogie,
shirtless,
taken on holiday in
Palm Springs.*

and the studio to rewrite Furthman's script. A tiny gray-haired man, one of America's most distinguished novelists, Faulkner was paid only $300 a week for his chores compared with Furthman who was a $3,000-a-week writer. But Faulkner had been having problems because of his excessive drinking. He was broke and accepted the assignment, which called for him to write the script, with the understanding that he would get a bonus if the stayed on the wagon. He wrote three pages a day, and these were filmed while he worked on the next three pages, a practice that would be unthinkable today when computers tell the director how much time he may take for a certain scene. But in 1944 films were still being made at a leisurely pace, and *To Have and Have Not* had a shooting schedule of almost three months. Today it would have been made as a TV Movie of the Week in less than a month.

The film as rewritten by Faulkner and Furthman bore little resemblance to the original Hemingway story but it had all the elements of *Casablanca*—a rough-and-ready American expatriate surrounded by French war politics, a sentimental piano player and a beautiful girl. The action takes place on the French-owned West Indies island of Martinique, with Bogart playing the owner of a motorboat which he rents to prospective fishermen. Betty played a "young woman with a past" who was stranded without funds on the island. As usual, Bogart's character was tough and taciturn and he approached his romance with Betty without frills, as straight as a shot of raw whiskey. Hawks surrounded the barely adequate story with a *Casablanca* mood and turned the whole thing over to his stars—100 minutes of Bogart-meets-girl, with a dash of war added to give it a taste of danger.

It was a convivial set. With the exception of Betty, almost everyone on the film knew everyone else. Most of the actors and crew had worked with Bogie or Hawks before on other films. Sid Hickox, the cameraman who would receive an Academy Award nomination for his work on the film, had photographed other pictures with Bogie and his wife, Mayo Methot. Script girl Meta Wilde, who lived with Faulkner, had worked with Bogie on half a dozen other films and was assigned to help Betty with her dialogue and cue her from the sidelines.

Then, as now, films were made out of continuity; all scenes made in one location are filmed at one time to avoid frequent and expensive moves and time-consuming camera setups.

On the fourth day of shooting, Bogie and Betty had their first scene together, which was also Betty's first appearance on the screen.

It was a simple scene, but Hawks wanted Betty to make an impact and he had tailored the scene for her. It was the scene he had used as her final screen test. It was filmed on the sound stage in a set designed as the hallway of the seedy hotel in Martinique where much of the film's action takes place.

The scene called for Bogie, accompanied by Gerard, the hotel proprietor (played by Marcel Dalio) to stop by the door of his room and start to unlock it when the door on the opposite side of the corridor opens and Betty, wearing a simple black and white checked suit, comes out with an unlighted cigarette in her hand.

She sees Gerard first and asks, "Have you got a match?"

Gerard searches his pockets and turns to Bogie, who has been doing the same. "I think I've got some in here," Bogie says and opens the door to his room. He enters, followed by Gerard.

Betty pauses in the doorway, leaning against the door sill, and looks into the room while Bogie opens the drawer of a table. He looks at Betty as he takes out a box of matches and tosses the box to her.

"Here you are," he says.

Betty catches the box, extracts a match, lights a cigarette, closes the box and tosses it back to him and says, "Thanks," and leaves.

The entire scene called for Betty to say a total of six

words and be on camera for less than a minute. But, she said later, "I was so scared I was shaking like a leaf and I kept dropping the matches. When I tried to light the cigarette my hand was shaking so I couldn't get the flame to meet the cigarette. Bogie started kidding me out of my nervousness and helping me. Pretty soon everything was easy and I relaxed. It was as if I'd known him always."

Mickey Seltzer, who worked in the studio publicity department, was on set watching the scene. "The electricity between them was not to be believed," she says. "It was so tangible you could feel it in the air. I knew something was going to come of it."

At that moment, however, Bogie and Betty merely had a mentor-student relationship which helped her get through her "debut" on the film. But after a few days it became apparent that Bogie had more than just a professional interest in Betty. Experienced observers noted this by the things he didn't do as well as the things that he did.

Usually when an actor is not in a scene he leaves the set, but when Betty had scenes without him, Bogie would sit in his camp chair and watch her. Later, she would sit down next to him and, over a cup of coffee, they would talk over the scene with Bogie occasionally giving her suggestions.

By the end of the first couple of weeks of filming, Betty was sitting on the set watching Bogie, and sometimes they would disappear into his or her trailer for long talks.

At lunch breaks, cast and crew frequently went together to the studio commissary where a subtle caste system was in force. Stars usually sat on one side of the room, while crew and featured players sat on another. On the stars' side, there were tables large enough to seat a group of six as well as tables for two.

At first, Betty and Bogie joined Hawks and some of the other stars of the film. But by the end of the week they began to sit at a table by themselves. After lunch they would leave the commissary together and ride the bicycles, used by actors for transportation on the lot, through the studio streets.

By the start of the second month of filming they were driving together—usually with a third party as "the beard"—to Lakeside Golf Club for lunch, in either a studio limousine or Betty's battered Plymouth coupe. Bogie's lunch there invariably consisted of a bottle or two of beer, two eggs over light, crisp bacon, toast and black coffee. Sometimes he and Betty would share a martini and a few puffs on the same cigarette.

Bogart soon began to display the light side of his character. Dan Seymour remembers the day when Bogie borrowed a set of handcuffs from Scottie, the film's prop man, and handcuffed Betty to her dressing room just before a lunch break. He then went to lunch at Lakeside but after a few minutes sent Scottie back to the studio with the keys.

"When Betty joined us at lunch her eyes were blazing," said Seymour. " 'I ought to kill you,' she told him, but she was laughing."

Bruce Bennett, a former Olympic decathlon champion who played Tarzan in an early film and was a Warner star, recalls seeing Bogie and Bacall on the grass in front of the sound stage one day during the second or third week of shooting. "Bogart couldn't keep his hands off of Betty, and I remember her saying, 'Bogie, for Chrissake, take it easy. If anyone ever gets a picture of us here, it'll be in every paper in the country.' "

Despite such public display of affection there were no published reports of their romance. "Set romances" were generally accepted by members of the film community, and there was a gentlemen's agreement among the Hollywood gossip columnists that romances involving married stars were not to be reported unless a divorce was announced.

Meanwhile, Hawks was delighted. He had made Betty into the character she played in the film, the essence of Bogieness. Not only was it believable that

90

the character Bogie played would fall for her but Bogie was also falling for her personally. The director had structured their love affair inadvertently while structuring the movie. Life was imitating art, and what appeared on the film each day was sensational.

Every day after work, the previous day's film, or "rushes," was screened for the director, the cameraman and, occasionally, the stars. Hawks had refused to let the studio executives attend screenings; his reputation as a director and starmaker was so formidable that it was easy to convince them to wait until the film was completed and then they could see it all. Bogie preferred not to see the rushes. He had enough faith in the director to rely on his judgment for the character he played. Betty was excluded from viewing the rushes. Hawks didn't want her to become self-conscious or overly concerned with her make-up, wardrobe or camera angles. She accepted the dictum without argument after first asking Bogie if he thought Hawks was right. "He's the director, baby," Bogie said. "He knows what he wants and what he's doing."

Thanks to Hawks' guidance, Betty was giving a novel, effective and daring (for that time) interpretation of sex which, the director knew, would appeal to audiences. Her performance was in such contrast to the usual wishy-washy movie heroine that audiences would be shocked and delighted. Mostly she suggested an old-time high school chum who has gone on the town and seems to enjoy it. Tough most of the time, coy never.

Betty was creating her effects with fairly obvious devices, some intuitive and some built into her performance by the director. The most conspicuous device —for which she would later be tagged "The Look"— was an insinuating pose with her head bent forward a bit so that her rather Slavic eyes gazed obliquely and suggestively at whomever she was talking to.

Betty would later say "The Look" was an accident. "I was so nervous at first that I held my head down

91

hoping people wouldn't notice I was shaking, and then I raised my eyes but not my face when they spoke to me."

Soon, Hawks was asking her to give Bogie "The Look" in scenes. There was something cool about that look and it became part of Bacall's attitude in the film.

Like most good directors, Hawks was not merely content with the actors' lines; he was also trying to establish the right attitudes for them, and he was lucky enough to strike the right attitude for Betty right off—as a female Bogie—and then make the most of it.

Simple scenes were written which highlighted her husky, underslung voice which was ideal for the double entendre and which made even her simplest remarks sound like jungle mating cries. For example, in one scene she embraces Bogie for the first time and remarks, after some tentative osculation, "It's better when you help." The line would bring the house down with laughter.

Hawks worked just as hard establishing the proper relationship and attitude for Bogie. Asked why he took care of Walter Brennan, who played the drunk in the film, Bogie answered: "He takes care of me." That answer described their entire relationship.

If Bogie was aware, as he must have been, that Betty was stealing the picture from him, he never showed any concern. He was falling in love with her and he wanted her to be good.

Hawks intended to keep a competitive edge to their relationship on screen, however, because that was part of their relationship in the film. One day he told Bogie, "Just because you're falling for this girl don't give her the best of it. Try to take an occasional scene away from her and see if she can stand up to you." Bogie did as he was instructed, but Betty stood up to him because she had Hawks to help her with her lines and delivery.

However, Hawks allowed Betty some leeway of her

own. Time and again he let her decide for herself about how to play a scene, and she based her decision on how she would handle the situation in real life. One of the most successful scenes in the picture was to be of her own invention. After a highly charged few minutes with Bogart, late at night in a cheap hotel room, the script called for her to reluctantly retire to her own quarters. At this point in the shooting, Betty complained: "God, I'm dumb." "Why?" asked Hawks. "Well, if I had any sense, I'd go back in after that guy." She did.

By the middle of April—six weeks after the film started—Mary Baker was to observe that Betty courted Bogie as much as he courted her. Bogie was, after all, one of the top stars in Hollywood, which made him a glamorous as well as exciting person. Despite his gruff exterior and screen image he was cultured and well read, not at all the "dese, dem and dose" character she had first believed him to be.

Bogie was surprisingly well read, and not merely in the best-sellers but in the classics as well. He had a good knowledge of American history and Greek mythology. He could and did quote from Plato, Emerson, Pope and many English dramatists and he could quote more than a thousand lines from Shakespeare.

The twenty-five year difference in their ages also worked to his advantage. Betty had grown up without a father, and Bogie was not only a father figure but he was tender and loving. His age gave him the experience and compassion that men of her own age could not possibly attain.

In the beginning of their affair Betty would probably have settled for being just Bogie's mistress, but he introduced a new note for her: ambition. He did not want her as a mistress; he wanted her as a wife. And he promised her that it would happen, that it was all over between Mayo and him, that it was only a matter of time before they were divorced. She believed him because she was naïve and because she wanted to believe him. She wanted to believe that the

93

poor Jewish girl from the Bronx could actually see her fairy tale come true, could actually be not only a movie star but the wife of the top movie star in Hollywood.

Betty knew he was falling in love with her and she encouraged him, even though she was putting herself in a position in which she would probably get hurt, but she trusted Bogart not to hurt her. He was, she knew, a gentleman not only by breeding but instinct.

"I think Bogie fell in love with Betty because she *was* the girl in the film, the exact opposite of the girl he was married to," said Hawks.

In truth, Betty had become the character she played so well on the screen, a sort of masculine-feminine girl who approaches a man with his own technique. She presented Bogie with a provocative, slightly mocking mirror image of himself and she offered him the blunt familiar honesty of the man's world, admitting without euphemism to being interested in sex. She was able to give him the security of feeling covered so far as his sex reputation was concerned. He could only be flattered that such a beautiful young girl found him exciting.

Unlike most actresses, who are so narcissistic the only love affair which they are capable of having is with a mirror, Betty gave herself completely to Bogart without restriction, emotional holds, or problems. She was also able to be one of the fellows—to follow where he led—in a graceful subtle way. She knew he loved boats and she had thrown herself wholeheartedly into learning how to sail a Dyer Dink and, within a few weeks, was proficient at it. She cared little about appearing inexperienced before him on the water or clumsy or soaking wet. She merely wanted to do the things that pleased him.

"He was enchanted by her," said Pat O'Moore. "Little wonder. Betty was fresh and, despite her attitude, she was still very much of an innocent. He was fascinated by this unformed thing which he could

94

mold into the perfect wife, and that's what Betty wanted—to be his wife."

Toward the middle of the second month of production, Mickey Seltzer became an almost daily visitor on the set. "Bogie and Betty had such beautiful chemistry going then that I used to find any excuse I could just to see them playing scenes together," she said.

"Off the set Bogie used to kid her along and she would give it right back to him. But even in this badinage you knew that what they were saying to each other was not what they were really saying."

Hawks found himself in the position of directing their love affair as well as their love scenes. One day he heard Bogie talking in front of Betty in a disparaging manner about Jews. The director noticed that Betty excused herself and, with a flushed face, walked away.

"I thought you were interested in Betty," Hawks said.

"Very interested," said Bogie.

"If I were you, I'd shut up about Jews."

Bogie turned pale. "Oh, my God, I didn't know she was Jewish."

"Well, she is."

"Oh, Lord," said Bogie. "What'll I do?"

"Well," said Hawks. "Why don't you play it off as a joke and ask her doesn't she ever get mad, as though you've been kidding all the time."

On another occasion, Hawks advised Betty, "If you're really serious about Bogie, don't ever fight with him. He's married to a girl he fights with all the time and he's not really a fighter. He just fights when he's attacked. So, never, never fight with him and you'll probably get along. That's the best way to handle him because it's something he doesn't know."

Hawks later recalled, "I think Bacall realized that intuitively anyway, and no matter what Bogie said or did she never fought with him."

One can only guess at Bogart's inner conflict dur-

95

ing those days. He was falling in love with Betty, who was light-hearted and gay, but he was married to Mayo, who was like a weight around his throat. After the day's filming was finished, he and Betty went their separate ways; Betty to the small furnished apartment in Hollywood she shared with her mother, and Bogie to the big home he lived in with Mayo, who was becoming increasingly difficult. Whenever he started a new picture her hostility increased. She resented the fact that she was home all day "with nothing to do and no one to see." By then, she had alienated most of their friends and she spent the day drinking.

"If it wasn't for you, I'd have been a big star," she often wailed. "I gave up everything for you, you've given up nothing for me." And then the battle would start.

Now, instead of fighting back, Bogie would more often than not get up and leave the room. Occasionally he would even leave the house, then telephone Betty from a pay phone and ask if he could drop by her apartment "to visit and talk" for a few minutes.

Betty, whose salary remained at $150.00 a week, was still living with Mrs. Bacal and Droopy, the cocker spaniel, in a small furnished apartment only about a five-minute drive from Bogie's home. Although Betty occasionally went out, she was usually at home—waiting for Bogie's call. He had gotten into the habit of telephoning her most every night, usually from a downstairs room of his home while Mayo was upstairs.

On those occasions when he came to visit, Mrs. Bacal would busy herself in her bedroom or the kitchen or go out for a walk with Droopy, leaving Betty to offer Bogie a martini and sympathy.

Soon Bogie was avoiding going home at night, and Betty acquired the nickname among his friends of "The Cast." "When he wasn't going home, we'd tell Mayo he was out with 'the cast,'" Mary Baker said.

The first assistant director on the picture had become a good friend of theirs, and Bogie and Betty often had dinner at his home or someone else's in order to avoid being seen in public.

There were very few small restaurants in Hollywood where they could go, so they often drove out to the beach, ordered hamburgers at a drive-in, and ate in the car in one of the parking spaces overlooking the Pacific. Sometimes they just walked hand-in-hand along the beach in their bare feet, laughing and giggling like two teen-agers.

Bogart and Betty lived dangerously during this period of their courtship, which Bacall has described as "our flirtatious period."

Bogie was spending a lot more time than was his custom with "The Cast," and he had taken to going to the Yacht Harbor alone on the weekends. Even under the best of circumstances Mayo was jealous and suspicious, and Bogart's new routine put her on guard.

She knew that one of the few places he could go without attracting undue attention was to the Yacht Harbor, where the *Sluggy* was moored. So one Saturday afternoon Mayo went to the harbor to check on Bogie, who said he was going to the *Sluggy* to do some repair work. Betty, who was aboard, saw Mayo first, tumbled off a bunk, and hid in the head. Mayo came on board and settled down to wait for Bogart. Betty waited her out for half an hour until Bogart returned, satisfied Mayo that he was indeed alone, and took her off the boat.

Often Bogie and Betty drove to Newport Yacht Harbor where the *Sluggy* was anchored, and there, over a meal prepared by Bogie on the boat's camp stove, they would spend hours on the fantail under the stars talking about the day when, eventually, Bogie would be free to ask Betty to marry him.

During this time, Bogie never made disparaging remarks about Mayo. "He was still loyal to her but he was torn. Their marriage was over and he knew it, but she was still his responsibility," Betty said later.

Betty was patient, aware that time was on her side,

but like an infatuated schoolgirl, she one day sat on the set doodling on a piece of paper "Betty Bogart, Betty Bacall Bogart, Betty B. Bogart."

It was apparent to Bogie's friends that this was not just a "fling" with Betty; Bogie meant it. When Pat O'Moore asked Bogie if he planned to divorce Mayo, Bogie's answer was, "I don't want to break this marriage up, but I like Betty's youth, her animal-like behavior, and don't-give-a-damn attitude."

At Newport Yacht Harbor, where the *Sluggy* was moored, Betty was called "Ladder Legs." "She had long, thin legs, and she could step on board carrying a bowl of ice without using the ladder," Pat O'Moore said.

O'Moore and his wife, Zelda, frequently "chaperoned" Bogie and Betty at the harbor because the club members' wives took a dim view of any romantic escapades in the belief that if they countenanced such activities for one member, other husbands might take this encouragement to use their boats for a rendezvous.

One night Bogie and Betty spent the night aboard the *Sluggy* tied up alongside the yacht club dock. The next morning there was an uproar among the wives of some of the club executives when he and Betty came on deck. It was apparent that they had spent the night aboard. The executives held an impromptu meeting and, encouraged by their wives, decided such "scandalous behavior" should be punished. But while the meeting was being held, Pat O'Moore got wind of it and he and Zelda slipped over to the *Sluggy* and went below. When the executives returned to ask for Bogie's resignation they were greeted by Pat and Zelda in pajamas and yawning conspicuously. The committee members, satisfied in the belief that Bogie and Betty had been chaperoned, stayed on board just long enough to have a drink and laugh at the misunderstanding.

An enterprising fan-magazine reporter got wind of the story and called Mayo to check on "divorce rumors," mentioning Betty as "the other woman."

When Bogart came home that night he was faced with an irate wife who demanded "the truth" and, in the same breath, threatened to kill him before she would let him go. Luckily, she passed out before she could do any damage.

Bogart, who was filled with remorse and pity for Mayo and was also feeling guilty because he had not told her about Betty himself, stayed home that night. The next morning, Mayo awakened before him and locked him inside the bathroom. She stood outside the door with a gun in hand, threatening to kill him if he tried to leave for the studio.

When Bogie failed to arrive on time, as was his habit, the studio dispatched Jaik Rosenstein to the Bogart house to see if anything was the matter. It took Rosenstein two hours to convince Mayo to let Bogie leave for work. When he did leave he took with him a small suitcase filled with personal belongings, fully intending to move into his dressing room at the studio.

But Mayo was frantic, and friends convinced Bogart that if he didn't go back to her she would probably kill herself, or Betty, or him—or all three. He returned home, but it was an impossible situation.

Mayo was finally aware that after years of being jealous of other women one had finally come along who threatened to destroy their marriage, while Bogart was beset by guilts and fear of what Mayo might do to herself or Betty. He was torn apart by his loyalty to Mayo and her dependence on him and his love for Betty, whom he saw on the set every day.

What made Bogart feel even worse was that Betty was understanding. She said she knew how he felt about Mayo, and she would stop seeing him if that's what he wanted. But that wasn't what Bogart wanted. He wanted Betty and was determined to have her. But they agreed not to see each other until he and Mayo resolved their marriage problems. For the last week of *To Have and Have Not* Bogie and Betty worked together during the day but he went home at night to face Mayo and battles which he had come to dread.

The press had begun to telephone the studio publicity department demanding to know the status of Bogart's marriage. "I used to go tripping the light fantastic all around the truth," recalls Mickey Seltzer. "But it was a pretty impossible job to explain some of the rumors and things like, how come Bogie has a black eye?"

A few days after *To Have and Have Not* was completed, on May 10, Bogart and Mayo went to the *Sluggy* for a weekend to try to solve their problems. At two the following morning Pat O'Moore got a telephone call from Bogart.

"I've left Mayo," he said. "Call Betty and ask her to come and get me on Highway 101. I'm walking to town."

O'Moore who did not drive, telephoned Betty, who drove up the highway at 4:00 A.M. looking for Bogart. "Suddenly I saw this figure in rope-soled shoes plodding down the road," said Betty.

When she stopped the car, Bogie got in. His first words to her were, "My God, how I need you."

CHAPTER 6

"You're good, awful good."
—THE BIG SLEEP

Despite Bogie's professed need for Betty, he felt Mayo needed him more. "We had some good years together and I just hate to throw them away," he told a friend. "I owe it to Mayo to give our marriage every chance."

The principal reason he was so unwilling to make a commitment to Betty was the twenty-five year difference in their ages. "I don't know how the hell I got mixed up with a nineteen-year-old girl," he confided to his childhood friend, Lee Gershwin, at a party.

So, once again he told Betty he was going to try to make a go of his marriage and he would have to stop seeing her—for both their sakes. Again, Betty was understanding. She would do anything he wished.

The separation was made easier by the fact that they would not be seeing each other daily on the set. Bogie was scheduled to make another film for Warners, but he refused, saying he was tired and needed a rest. The studio promptly suspended him. For weeks Bogie moped around the big house on Horn Drive. He repaired the bird cages, lengthened the dog-run, trimmed roses, puttered around the garden, did odd plumbing chores and tried to give the illusion of being a typical suburban husband on vacation at home with his wife. But Mayo, thinking she had won him back, promptly reverted to the bottle and tablets.

Again Bogie began to call Betty, who said she was still waiting—if and when he wanted to see her.

Once again Bogie left Mayo to return to the studio and Betty who had already begun to work some changes in his life. She had convinced him that his drinking was a habit which Mayo encouraged and supported. Now that he had Betty he no longer needed an escape from reality. He promised Betty that he would cut down on his drinking—a promise he was to keep during the run of the picture while they were together.

Although Betty was being hailed as a "new star" on the lot, *To Have and Have Not* had not been released, so she was still unknown to the public. Her salary for *The Big Sleep* was only $250 a week, $50 less than she made as a model when she left New York. Although she had posed for studio publicity pictures in some pretty fancy garments, she had an unusually small wardrobe with no furs or jewelry.

Her scale of living had not improved since coming to Hollywood and she was too proud to accept any financial help from Bogart, although she did allow him to occasionally buy the groceries she prepared for their evening meals. Usually they dined in the apartment with Betty, who had learned the European style of cooking from her mother, laboring over a small two-burner stove with a tiny oven, preparing special dishes such as soufflés and creamed cauliflower for Bogie, who actually preferred a more basic diet such as roast beef, steak, chops and hamburger.

Bogie had promised Mayo that he would not embarrass her in the community by flaunting Betty publicly, so they rarely went out to night spots. All of Bogie's friends were aware of the separation, however, and Bogie proudly took Betty to meet them, usually at their homes.

Peter Lorre, who had been a friend of Bogie's since they worked together in *Casablanca*, became one of Betty's biggest boosters.

One night when Bogie confided to Lorre that he was not certain marriage to a girl as young as Betty would work, Lorre advised him: "So. What's the difference? It's better to have five good years than none at all."

Bogie also took Betty to meet his sister Pat at her apartment. "I've brought you another sister to replace Catty," he said, referring to their sister who had died in 1936.

Later, she would say, "Humphrey loved Catty, who was tall and slender and had a short waist and long legs like Betty. In fact, they looked very much alike. And I think that was one of the reasons he fell in love with Betty."

Their romance had still not yet received any publicity because in those days Warners was able to bring pressure to bear on most reporters; threat of being barred from the lot was enough to bring the local newsmen in line. The gossip columnists avoided mention of the romance not only because of the unwritten code but because of the possibilities of a lawsuit. Betty would have had a libel suit if charged in print with having broken up a marriage, and Bogie could also have charged that the publicity broke up his marriage.

Mayo was not above going to the press herself, however. Weeping, she tried to enlist the help of Louella O. Parsons, the most powerful Hollywood gossip columnist, as a go-between. Miss Parsons kept the call confidential on the promise that when a divorce action was filed she would be given the news in advance. Miss Parsons then called Bogart, who told her that he was in love with Betty and wanted to marry her but there was still details to be worked out with Mayo. In exchange for Miss Parsons' confidence, he also promised to give her an exclusive.

Such promises of confidentiality are part of a columnist's stock in trade and such deals were one of the reasons that Miss Parsons often got "scoops" on the break-up of many Hollywood marriages.

Immediately *The Big Sleep* began, Bogie and Betty resumed their mentor-student relationship. During a love scene with Betty, Bogie recalled something he had seen Lynn Fontanne do on stage—she ran her hand up the side of an actor's face and gave it a slight slap. "A very tantalizing thing to do," he said. Betty tried it and it worked.

Whenever he had comments or criticism for Betty he would take her aside or tell her in the privacy of her dressing room. Betty recalls one scene in which the doorbell rang in the enormous mansion where she lived in the film. She had to answer the door. They had a few run-throughs and just before the take Bogie took her to one side.

"You've been walking to the door like a model," he said. "You must always realize in a scene that you have just come from someplace else. Ask yourself: What was I doing before? Was I filing my nails? Combing my hair? You should have an attitude when you walk to the door."

"I never forgot his advice," said Betty. "Ever since then, whenever I've had to play a scene, I've always thought, 'What was I doing before this?' It couldn't be simpler, but most people never think of it."

For the first time during their relationship, Betty and Bogie were able to let themselves go, at least on set, and they were as playful as school children much of the time. Some of their humor was, to say the least, corny. They had a routine involving Joe Miller jokes which broke them up and were practiced at most every opportunity. The routine went like this:

BOGART: Do your eyes bother you?
BETTY: No.
BOGART: They bother me.

BOGIE: Swell day for the race.
BETTY: What race?
BOGIE: Human race.

BETTY: Know who's in the hospital?
BOGIE: Who?
BETTY: Sick people.

BOGIE: Didja hear what the ceiling said to the wall?
BETTY: No.
BOGIE: Hold me up, I'm plastered.

Hawks, who had engineered the romance and quarterbacked it from the beginning, was suddenly odd man out. "They were so much in love it was hard to get any real cooperation for me," he recalled. "Actually I was so mad about their attitudes that I had to cut two or three scenes because they would have been just too difficult to film. Betty wasn't by any manner of means a skilled actress yet, and it required a lot of work to get from her what I wanted. And Bogie had lost some of his ability to help her as he did in the first picture because he was now so involved with her."

But Hawks was not averse to taking advantage of their involvement. One of the most tender scenes—understated as always—is when Bogart tells Betty she's "Good, awful good," and the audience knows he really loves her.

Later in October, while *The Big Sleep* was still in the early stages of production, *To Have and Have Not* was released in New York. It received excellent reviews and Betty was hailed as an important new star. Writers devoted columns of space analyzing "The Look" and discussing her "cohesive physiognomy," meaning her face, which photographed perfectly from all angles. (The writers were unaware that Hawks rarely photographed her full face.) Walter Winchell, the most influential columnist of the day, in a rare gesture on his part, wrote a full column of praise about Betty tagging her as "The Bacall of the Wild."

Time magazine was to say of her: "Lauren Bacall has cinema personality to burn, and she burns both ends against an unusually little middle. Her personality is compounded partly of percolated Davis, Garbo, West, Dietrich, Harlow and Glenda Farrell, but more

105

than enough of it is completely new to the screen. She has a javelin-like vitality, a born dancer's eloquence in movement, a fierce female shrewdness and a special sweet-sourness. With these faculties plus a stone-crushing self-confidence and a trombone voice, she manages to get across the toughest girl a piously regenerate Hollywood has dreamed of in a long, long while—Her lines have been neatly tailored to her talents. . . . Besides good lines, there are good situations and songs for Newcomer Bacall. She does a wickedly good job of sizing up male prospects in a low bar, growls a *louche* song more suggestively than anyone in cinema has dared since Mae West in *She Done Him Wrong* (1933)." (*Time* neglected to mention that Betty only mouthed the lyrics to the song. The singing voice was Andy Williams'.)

When Marlene Dietrich saw the film in New York she telephoned Hawks and said, "You SOB, that's me twenty years ago."

Warner Brothers was ebullient. A rival studio offered $75,000 for Betty's services in a new film and her career seemed assured. There seemed to be some truth, after all, to the Cinderella myth. Betty now had the Prince, but the Wicked Stepmother still had an emotional hold on him.

Just before Christmas 1944, Mayo telephoned Bogie and pleaded with him to come home, to try again. "You'll see, I've changed," she said. "Let's just give it one more try, for old times' sake. You owe me that much."

When Bogie refused to come home Mayo threatened to kill herself, saying that without him she could not and would not continue living. Once again friends prevailed.

"I came into make-up one morning and Bogie was waiting to tell me he had gone back to Mayo," Betty said later. " 'I had to go back,' he told me. 'I wouldn't throw a dog out in the street in her condition. I have to give her every chance.' So he went back, and I cried my heart out. What else was there to do?"

106

Bogart gave Mayo a diamond and ruby ring for a Christmas present. Again they went to Newport and aboard the *Sluggy* to talk things over. Again he started to walk back to town on Highway 101 and was picked up by Betty.

Bogie had finally decided that it was over with Mayo. True to his promise, he called Louella Parsons to say that Mayo had agreed to a divorce. "I believe it's the right thing to do," he said. "I have told Mayo I am not coming home. She can have anything she wants if she will let me go—and I believe she is too sensible to want to hold me after six years of continual battling."

Miss Parsons wrote that the Bogarts were having marriage problems but carefully avoided any suggestion that there was another woman involved.

Betty was to describe Christmas 1944 as one of the best times of her life. "I had everything I wanted. I had Bogie."

Bogart's Christmas present to Betty was a gold whistle inscribed, "If you want anything, just whistle."

The Big Sleep was completed on January 12, 1945. After Hawks showed a rough cut to Jack Warner in a studio projection room, Warner was so enthusiastic that he bought Betty's contract from Hawks, who would later say, "I felt I had done as much as I could with Betty. I didn't feel I could keep on doing the stuff she did best and ought to do. She was not an actress. She was a personality."

Not only was Betty to get a large cash bonus but her film salary was increased. Her first job for the studio, however, was to go to New York to do personal appearances for *To Have and Have Not* and promote *The Big Sleep*, which was to be rushed into release. Meanwhile Warners began to tout Betty as "The Look" in what was probably the biggest publicity build-up in the studio's history.

But first, Betty and Bogie went to Palm Springs for a few weeks' rest. Bogie played golf while Betty watched and tooled around in a golf cart with him.

He chased balls and watched while she took lessons at the elegant Racquet Club where, later, they lunched on cold crab and lobster with Charles Farrell, the silent-screen star Bogie had coached on his first abortive visit to Hollywood. After retiring from films, Farrell had founded the Racquet Club, which was the place for *the* Hollywood crowd in Palm Springs.

For the first time they were able to go out together in public without fear of publicity. Wearing casual sports clothes, they strolled hand in hand down the desert town's main street, pausing from time to time to ogle the paintings on display at sidewalk art galleries. Every night they dined at a different restaurant or at the home of friends from Hollywood.

Soon it was time for Betty to return to Hollywood to pack and prepare for what Bogie termed her "triumphal homecoming" to New York. In the interim, Bogie decided to spend a few days visiting his old friend, novelist Louis Bromfield, who had a 600-acre working farm named Malabar near Mansfield, Ohio. Bromfield, who had won a Pulitzer Prize in 1926, had also written several best-selling novels which were turned into films, including *The Rains Came* and *Mrs. Parkington.* (He sold film rights to the latter for $60,000 on the basis of a one-paragraph synopsis before the book was even written.)

Bogart had often brought Mayo to Malabar for visits but their last visit there ended disastrously when she started a battle with him. Ellen Bromfield Geld, daughter of the novelist, recalled, "One of my mother's favorite Venetian lamps went whizzing past Bogie's ear, and in an instant the entire room exploded into a cyclone of books, ashtrays, whiskey bottles and all imaginable items that could be lifted, swung and hurled."

Despite the carnage, Bogie was still a welcome guest at Malabar, where life was always exciting with lots of stimulating company in the thirty-room main house. Bogie rarely sat down to a meal with less than eighteen people, including the author's family and other guests. He ate of the best quality food fresh from the garden, dairy or hen house. He slept late in the mornings while the author did his literary work. Afternoons were spent walking in the woods, with Bromfield talking about life and farming—the author was one of the world's foremost experts on agronomy. Evenings were spent drinking—but not too heavily. Bogie remembered his promise to Betty. He missed Betty and telephoned her in Hollywood three times a day, sometimes more. Finally, they made a date to meet in New York on February 1st.

Before leaving Malabar, Bogie asked Bromfield if he would object if he and Betty had a quiet wedding ceremony at the farm when his divorce was final. "Just let me know a couple of days in advance and I'll arrange everything," was the reply.

Bogie arrived in New York a day ahead of Betty and, after fortifying himself with a little hair of the dog, simultaneously announced to the press from his Gotham Hotel suite his impending divorce from Mayo and his engagement to Betty.

"Sure, Mayo and I used to fight like hell," Bogart told columnist Inez Robb. "Frankly, and offhand, I'm not the easiest guy in the world to live with. But I can't say that I think fighting is an extra added attraction in any marriage. I don't want to end my life punch drunk and walking on my heels.

"And you might say that my engagement to Baby has nothing to do with this divorce. That was arranged a long, long time ago and has nothing to do with Baby. She's a swell kid, and I'm afraid I've made it kinda tough for her by shooting off my big face the way I have. I've probably loused up everything."

Bogart's reference to Betty as "Baby" was instantly picked up by the press, although he had rarely called her "Baby" before. Later, the Bogarts would both resent the appellation, probably because it made such obvious note of the fact that he was old enough to be her father.

International News Service sent Miss Robb's story out on their vast newspaper syndicate on January 31, 1945. In Los Angeles the story was headlined: "Bogart Discloses Plan to Marry Bacall, Actor Says His Wife Has Agreed to Give Him Divorce."

Meanwhile, Betty, accompanied by Droopy, the cocker spaniel, left Hollywood and entrained for New York with a brief stopover in Philadelphia, where *To Have and Have Not* was breaking all records.

When Betty arrived at Grand Central Station she found a large crowd waiting just to see her. "I've never encountered anything like Grand Central the morning I arrived here," she told a reporter for the *New York Herald Tribune*. "I never saw so many people in my life—it looked as though they were hanging from the ceiling. And then the reporters and photographers began asking me questions and taking pictures."

Perched atop her baggage in a typical cheesecake shot, carrying her cocker spaniel and chain smoking, she parried questions with the ease of a full-fledged star. Told that Bogie had said they were engaged, she said, "That's the first I've heard of any formal engagement." Asked if she was going to marry Bogie, she quipped, "He'll have to ask me first."

The press delayed Betty at the terminal past the time she had agreed to meet Bogie at the hotel. When she telephoned him to explain the delay, Bogart was furious. "You actresses are all alike," he scolded. "Your career comes above everything else."

Betty rushed to the hotel and Bogart's suite. When she walked in the door he started to cry. "He didn't think I would come," she said later.

By this time the balance of their relationship had begun to change. Bogart was no longer the pursued, he was the pursuer. He was well aware of the difference in their ages and he undoubtedly wondered what such a young and desirable woman as Betty saw in him. Although a world-famous star, he was, in his own view, not especially handsome or desirable, and, in his private moments, he probably did not consider himself a great lover.

Also, Betty was an actress. Bogart's past experiences with actresses had not been encouraging. They were more career- than marriage-oriented. He probably felt that now that Betty seemed to have a big career in sight she might well decide she did not need him. His premature announcement of their engagement to the press was most likely his way of boxing her in.

During her New York visit Betty made a record of some sort by giving sixty-two interviews in seven days, and managed to say practically nothing in any of them. The art of gracefully saying nothing is a considerable accomplishment and, as *Life* was to note, "In spite of her tender years and the strain of her first trip as a budding star and the piquant state of her relationship with Bogie, she acquitted herself very well indeed."

One of the interviewers was Betty Leibowitz, a *New York Herald Tribune* reporter who had been one of Betty's classmates at Julia Richman. Miss Leibowitz recalled Betty at Julia Richman as being, "a little bit better-looking than most, tall, thin and a trifle awkward.

"The Lauren Bacall of today has not changed much in actual physical appearance, but in her mental attitude she has. She is a poised young woman who seems to know exactly what she is going to do and how she is going to do it."

To her surprise Betty learned that she was a heroine at her old alumnus. Her picture was displayed prominently in the Guidance Office.

She was also a heroine to the public. Unable to leave the Gotham without being attacked by autograph and souvenir seekers, she spent a large part of her time with Bogie in the comparative seclusion of the exclusive "21" club, where she lunched with people like Clifton Webb, the celebrated playwright-director-wit George S. Kaufman and playwright Moss

Hart, who told her, "You'd better retire right now. You'll never top the reviews you got for your first picture."

She also met many of Bogie's old friends from the theatrical and newspaper world. He took her to the celebrated Bleeck's Artists and Writers Club, the hangout for newspaper people next door to the *New York Herald Tribune*, where she was taught to play the match game with old-timers such as Stanley Walker, one-time managing editor of the *Tribune*, and drama critics Howard Barnes and John Chapman.

She took it all in stride, enjoying her newfound celebrity and keeping herself in the background.

One of the big surprises which Bogie had during the visit was Betty's attitude toward the theater. He wanted to see the hit plays because there wasn't time enough for the others. But Betty insisted on seeing two plays which were definitely not hits.

"Why do you want to waste your time on those plays?" Bogie asked.

He soon learned the reason. Two of Betty's girl friends from her early days on Broadway were in the shows and she wanted to say hello to them and show off her man.

There was only one complication during their New York stay. Bogie received telephone calls from his lawyer saying that the publicity was making Mayo angry. She was being difficult about signing the out-of-court settlement. Bogie then began to refuse to allow any pictures to be taken of himself and Betty. After one was snapped at a party for Navy veterans, he went to the Navy public relations office and had the offending picture barred from publication.

But it was too late to stop the publicity. The press was determined to celebrate the romance, which was paralleled in the public's interest only by the Simpson-Windsor nuptials.

Soon after Betty and Bogie returned by train to Hollywood and the Garden of Allah, Bogart signed the out-of-court settlement that ended his marriage

112

with Mayo. That night he ran into Mary Philips, his second wife, at LaRue's Restaurant on the Sunset Strip.

"He was despondent and miserable," said Miss Philips, then married to Kenneth MacKenna, a story editor for MGM. "The end of the marriage bothered him even though he felt he was doing the right thing."

To cheer up Bogart, Mrs. MacKenna told him she wanted to give him a gift—two china dogs that had once belonged to his mother. "He cried," Mrs. Mac-Kenna said.

Bogart was divorced from Mayo on May 10, 1945. The hearing was in private and the decree sealed. As part of the divorce settlement Bogart gave Mayo a large sum of money plus ownership of one of the two Safeway Stores in which he had invested. He didn't contest the divorce, which was granted on the common Hollywood grounds of "great mental suffering." In the usual Hollywood tradition, Mayo told the press "Bogie and I are the best of friends. He is a very nice guy. It was a very nice marriage."

Simultaneously with the news that Mayo's divorce had gone through came a request from Chicago that Bogie attend the "I Am an American Day" celebration. "Meet me in Chicago," he told Betty. "I've got a job to do there. Then we'll go on to Louis Bromfield's farm and get married. Might as well kill two birds with one stone."

It was not the most romantic proposal a young girl could imagine but it was just what Betty had wanted and worked so hard for. Although she had not put any pressure on Bogart, she had allowed herself to be courted knowing that he was married, and she had played the role of "the other woman" in a consummate manner. She made no demands on Bogart nor did she threaten to end their relationship if he did not divorce Mayo. But her very willingness to go along with him was in such sharp contrast to Mayo's threats and violence that her undemanding acceptance became an activity in itself.

113

It had been almost a year from the day they had first met, and Betty had made the metamorphosis from a brash Broadway hopeful into a full-fledged movie star—she had jumped within weeks from twenty-fourth to sixth place in popularity among all Warner Brothers stars. She had also changed from a girl who "never had much success with men" into a sultry siren who had been courted and was now about to marry one of the most famous film actors of the time.

CHAPTER 7

"Play it, Sam."
—CASABLANCA

On May 2, 1945, eleven days after Bogart's divorce from Mayo was final, Judge Herb Schettler of the Mansfield, Ohio, Municipal Court nervously fingered the Phi Beta Kappa Key chained to his vest as he drove up the winding driveway past the small lake to the large white main house of novelist Louis Bromfield's Malabar Farm. A month earlier, Bromfield's secretary-manager, George Hawkins, had visited the judge in his chambers and asked him if he would officiate at the wedding of Humphrey Bogart and Lauren Bacall. Judge Schettler was delighted. It would be the biggest wedding of his career and would undoubtedly put Mansfield on the map. "But," Hawkins warned him, "the wedding must be kept a secret. There must be no leaks to the press."

The judge kept his part of the bargain. Two weeks before the wedding he and six friends had gone ice fishing in Canada. During the weeks of drinking, fishing and horseplay, Judge Schettler had told his companions nothing of the movie stars he was scheduled to marry the day after he returned home. But, when he got off the train from Toronto, one of his fishing partners' wives confronted him with the news. "I understand you're going to marry Humphrey Bogart and Lauren Bacall tomorrow at Malabar Farm." Warner Brothers had no intention of letting the most celebrated lovers since Wallis Simpson and the Duke of Windsor get married without publicity. They alerted the press, and within hours newsmen from all over the nation began to converge on Mansfield.

Meanwhile, Bogie, Betty and Mrs. Bacal had gone from New York to Chicago, changed trains, and continued on to Mansfield. Mrs. Bacal had come along because twenty-year-old Betty had to have a parent's signature to get a marriage license.

It was almost midnight when they arrived in Mansfield, a small town of about 50,000 population. The Bromfields were on hand to greet them and drive them to Malabar. Betty was so excited and nervous that she could not go to sleep, so Bromfield took her on a tour of the huge house with its half a dozen sitting rooms decorated in striking combinations of gray and yellow, red, green and white. Telephones and typewriters were in every bedroom, with one exception. Bromfield explained that he and his wife slept in a room in which neither a telephone nor a typewriter was permitted.

Betty and Bogie played a game of Ping-Pong in the much-used game room. Bogie lost. The score was 21 to 10. He instantly challenged Betty to a pool game which he won.

Betty and her mother shared a guest room and Bogie slept in another wing of the house. The next morning they were up at six to drive from the farm to the old red-brick County Courthouse in downtown Mansfield, where Judge Schettler met them. The probate judge waived the five-day period for the license, and Betty told him that she was a resident of Lucas, Ohio. In order to get married in Ohio, one party is supposed to be a resident of the state. Betty and Bogart then went to Mansfield General Hospital for a quick blood test. When the results were phoned

116

to the courthouse and the license issued, the party returned hastily to Malabar Farm, where the press had already converged.

Judge Schettler pushed his way through the reporters, cameramen and a barrage of questions:

"Do you have a license?"

"What kind of ceremony will you perform?"

"You mean you wrote the ceremony yourself?"

"What kind of judge are you?"

The questions penetrated the judge's thin skin, but he kept his temper as did Bogie and Betty, who posed for photos and answered questions. Betty declined only one request. She refused to lift her skirts for photographers who wanted a leg shot.

The sun shone brilliantly over the white buildings and green gardens of Malabar Farm, where the ceremony was to be held in the great central hall. A huge recessed window at one end caused the whole breathtaking exterior landscape to appear part of the room. There were also flowers banked in the window.

The ceremony began promptly at eleven to the strains of the "Bridal Chorus" from *Lohengrin* by Wagner, played at the piano by Hope Bromfield, the author's teen-age daughter. George Hawkins brought Betty on his arm down a flight of stairs to a landing and then into the central hall where Bogie, with best man Bromfield beside him, stood on a tigerskin bagged by the author some years before in India.

Betty wore a rose-beige doeskin suit with brown accessories which she had bought on a hasty shopping trip with Bogart just before leaving New York. A contemporary account by a fashion writer also noted: "The top of the two-piece costume buttoned down the front. Neckline of the bodice was accented with a dark brown chiffon scarf. The sleeves were full and long, closing at the wrists with tight bands. The belted waist line was of brown and the skirt straight and narrow.

"Miss Bacall, without headdress, wore her hair softly waved. Her brown heel-less pumps were of

117

perforated gabardine trimmed with matching faille bows. Jewelry worn by the bride was a yellow gold bracelet with the inscription 'Betty Bacall' and a gold whistle attached.

"She wore two pure white Aculeate orchids. Carrying out the old tradition, 'Something old, something new, something borrowed and something blue,' Miss Bacall wore her jewelry, which was old, her wedding suit, which was new—she borrowed a lace handkerchief from Mrs. Bromfield and the embroidered 'Betty Bacall' on her slip was in blue stitching."

Bogart's wardrobe did not get such complete coverage from the press. He wore a gray tweed suit, black elevator shoes (Betty was not wearing high heels), a maroon tie, and white carnation in his lapel. Bromfield, who usually greeted houseguests in overalls and manure-covered boots, wore a smart blue suit. Before the wedding Bromfield had been reminded strongly by Hawkins to, for Christ's sake, button his fly.

The press, who had been asked to wait outside during the ceremony, attempted to invade the house, and some went so far as to climb to a transom in the hope of getting a picture. But their attempts were thwarted by security guards.

It was a brief ceremony—less than three minutes long—and Betty had to shift her chrysoberyl engagement ring from her left to right hand to make room for the linked gold wedding band that matched the one Bogart wore.

The ceremony was almost brought to a standstill—by laughter—when one of Bromfield's half-dozen boxer dogs waddled in and lay across the judge's feet.

But Judge Schettler ignored the dog and proceeded: "I charge you to remember that love and loyalty alone will serve as the foundation of an enduring and happy home. . . . Your life will be full of peace and happiness and the home which you are establishing will last through every vicissitude. . . . You will, Humphrey Bogart, have Betty Joan Bacall to be your wedded wife? You will love her . . ."

The rings were exchanged and they were married. Bogart's face was tear-stained when he kissed the bride. "He cries at weddings," Betty was to say later. "He's really very cute about it. Really, I think the words get to him."

After the ceremony Bogie, who was sipping a martini while Betty sipped wine, solemnly told the judge: "I feel more married today than I did the other three times."

He soon regained his sense of humor. When a reporter asked Betty if she was going to continue her movie career or stay home and nurse a family, Bogie answered for her. "A lot of people would like to know that, including Warner Brothers."

Betty and Bogie spent their first night as man and wife in a large bedroom suite at Malabar. The following morning they entrained from Mansfield for Chicago, where they changed trains and went on to Hollywood. Their honeymoon consisted of the two days spent on the train. They had meals brought into their sleeper.

They arrived in Hollywood without fanfare—Warners had not been apprised of their arrival—and went directly to a luxurious duplex "villa" at the Garden of Allah, where they planned to live until they found a house.

On their first night home, Bogie gave Betty a surprise wedding gift, a full-length mink coat. She carefully spread it out on the floor of their hotel living room suite, took off her shoes and slowly, luxuriously walked over it, saying, "I've always wanted to walk on mink."

Bogie was delighted.

CHAPTER 8

"Before I found you I was finished."
—THE TWO MRS. CARROLLS

Most Hollywood people assumed that Betty married Bogie because the marriage would bolster her career and he would give her the financial security she never had. There was considerably more speculation about why Bogie married Betty, with the consensus being that it was a late-in-life infatuation on his part which would soon dissipate. "It'll never last," the cynics said.

Bogie's friends, however, knew why he wanted Betty for his wife. Despite his screen image, Bogie was an insecure man; he needed the constant bolstering that Betty offered. "He was her god, and she accepted everything he said as if it were carved on stone," said one of his good friends. They complemented each other in many important ways. Bogie supplied the background, heritage and experience that Betty sorely lacked. She brought to him a complete understanding and sympathy, a passionate and genuine love that was relaxing rather than demanding, a lively, curious and youthful spirit and a sense of practicality.

As a boy, Bogie had always admired "old-fashioned women," and Betty was exactly what he sought. He realized that her screen image was a false front; she wanted a home, children and a good marriage more than a career. Betty was not, in any sense, a typical starlet-swinger. She was as puritanical as he and, although young and beautiful, she was not and never had been a flirt.

It is ironic that their screen personalities were almost as identical as their real personalities. They both hid behind their public façades because, in reality, they were "squares" who wanted little more from life than a warm and fulfilling relationship. While their fans, imagining them as symbolic of a new type of romantic couple, lived vicariously through them, the reality was that Bogie and Betty wanted nothing more than the very ordinary life most of their fans wanted to escape.

Even before their marriage Betty had begun to work some changes in Bogart's life. While married to Mayo he had very nearly, by his own admission, become an alcoholic. Mayo would match him drink for drink and then taunt him to take more than he could handle. But Betty drank rarely, perhaps a glass or two of wine with meals, and there was no need for him to compete with her. During the year of their courtship Bogie began to nurse two Scotches with a moderate dash of soda all evening. And he cut down on his lunchtime drinking.

Although they had lived together for part of that year of courtship, the real beginning of their relationship was to occur now that they were married and back in Hollywood.

Eleven days after their wedding they returned to Warner Brothers to work in different pictures: Betty in *Confidential Agent*, opposite Charles Boyer, and Bogie in *The Two Mrs. Carrolls*, opposite Barbara Stanwyck.

Their arrival on the lot caused a stir with the press, who were on hand to photograph the newlyweds. Everyone from stars to grips and laborers offered them congratulations. Jack L. Warner had a wedding gift for Betty. During *The Big Sleep* she was loaned a handsome black Chrysler convertible coupe, which belonged to the studio, to drive while on the lot. At the end of each day, she returned home in her own five-year-old jalopy. The car was her wedding present from the studio head.

While they were working together at the studio, their lives soon fell into a comfortable and practiced routine. At 5:30 A.M. of every working day a small leather-covered bedside travel alarm, a wedding present from a fan, buzzed on the night table next to their bed. Bogie turned off the alarm, kissed Betty on the cheek. While she pulled her thoughts together, he did some quick calisthenics—knee bends and limbering up exercises—then dashed into his bath and shaved and showered while Betty performed her morning ablutions.

Promptly at 5:45 they left their bungalow for the fifteen-minute drive to the studio, usually in Betty's new car, with Bogie driving. They rarely spoke as the car parted the morning mist that inevitably hung over Laurel Canyon at that hour. They had learned that before coffee it was best to refrain from conversation. But Bogie usually smoked a cigarette during the drive; the first of the two packs of cigarettes he would smoke during a day.

After arriving at Warner Brothers punctually at six, Bogie escorted Betty to the make-up department for her picture, kissed her good-bye, and then went down the hall for his own make-up. There was usually coffee and fresh donuts in the make-up department. If there was time, Bogie would walk down the hallway, ceramic coffee cup in hand, to visit Betty, who was usually under the dryer, and give her a kiss.

"We were absolutely wild about each other," Betty said. "When I was away from Bogie for even three or four hours I couldn't wait for the moment I saw him again, and he felt the same way about me."

Whenever schedules permitted they lunched together. If there was time, they drove to the nearby Lakeside Golf Club where they usually ate alone. If time was short, they met in the studio commissary or in one of their dressing rooms where food was delivered.

At the end of the day, whoever was finished first would wait for the other so they could drive home together.

At night, dinner was usually prepared by May, a cook who had been with Bogie during his marriage to Mayo, and served in the living room where they watched the evening news as they dined, they sat on opposite ends of a couch studying and learning lines for the next day. Because they had to rise so early they were usually in bed by 9:30 or 10:00.

About once a week they dined out—usually at LaRue's Restaurant on the Sunset Strip. They sat in the first booth, which became known as the Bogart booth. Unless they had an early morning call, they usually stopped for at least one dance at the Mocambo, a popular Strip nightclub. Whenever Emil Coleman, the orchestra leader, saw them enter he signaled his musicians to play "That Old Black Magic," which the Bogarts considered "our song." Oblivious to all eyes in the place, they invariably danced to it.

Immediately after the Stanwyck film, Bogart went into *Dead Reckoning* at Columbia Studios, a whodunit in which he played an ex-paratrooper who regretfully discovers that Lizabeth Scott is a murderess.

While Bogie was at the studio, Betty remained home and began to decorate their bungalow which, like all the villas at the Garden of Allah, was done in a Spanish motif with a tiled Spanish kitchen, colored tiles on the bathroom walls featuring blue peacocks. She particularly disliked the dining room, which had green walls. Betty started her redecorating project there. She painted the ceiling and walls of the dining room black and hung black curtains over the window overlooking the pool, she set three black candles on the dining room table. The effect was, to say the least, dramatic, but Betty liked it and Bogie made no comment.

One of their first dinner guests was Jaik Rosenstein, the Warner press agent who had since become Hedda Hopper's assistant, or "leg man." Rosenstein, who had known Betty since she first arrived in Hollywood, was to write about the dinner: "Betty was now quite different from that eager, fresh-eyed young thing. When I came in she was attired in a black hostess robe that trailed slightly on the floor and she was completely dignified. Her greeting was restrained and formal. Marriage to Bogie had changed her from a starlet into a grand dame."

Other friends noticed that Betty was changing, too. She was beginning to reach out, to experiment, and to find a new image for herself as a woman. She was preparing herself to be what she would later become —one of Hollywood's top hostesses—but it would be a long process of trial and error before she finally was to achieve the proper attitude and approach.

Meanwhile, Bogie, who had never wanted children before, was anxious to have a family with Betty and had started taking hormone treatments. As a result of the treatments, all of his hair except for one sideburn and one eyebrow had fallen out in patches.

Because he was nearly bald he negotiated a new contract with Jack L. Warner in a ten-minute telephone conversation leaving his salary to be negotiated. Mary Baker was present at the first meeting with the studio head with her partner, Sam Jaffe. Jaffe tentatively suggested a salary of $125,000. Mr. Warner smiled. Jaffe hastily concluded the meeting. Outside Warner's door, Mary asked Jaffe why he didn't finish the negotiations. "Warner was smiling when we mentioned $125,000," Jaffe said. "I think we ought to ask for more money." "How much more?" Mary asked. "Enough to at least make him frown," said Jaffe.

Weeks later, when Bogie went to sign the contract, he was wearing an ill-fitting toupee. Warner, who had heard rumors that Bogart was going bald, eyed the toupee suspiciously but said nothing. Later, however, he telephoned Mary Baker to ask if the rumors were true. Mary admitted they were. Warner was in a panic. "Good God!" he said. "Some leading man I've signed up! He has hardly a hair on his head."

The hair began to grow back as it had fallen out—in patches. Warner had his star again, but with a most unusual contract. The brief conversation between actor and studio head had become a ninety-page legal document that guaranteed, among other things, that Bogart was to do one picture a year for $200,000 (a sum that had made Warner frown). Bogart could reject two out of three stories submitted to him, but he either took the third or furnished the studio with his own story. He could turn down any director he didn't like with the exception of five whom he had approved when he signed the contract: William Wilder, William Wyler, Edward Dmytryk, John Huston and John Ford. He also was allowed to do one outside film for himself each year. The contract was to run for fifteen years, guaranteeing him $3,000,-000 and the right to do outside films.

It also specified that Bogart was to receive $1,000 a week for living expenses when on location; he was to be given round-trip tickets from Los Angeles to all locations for his family and one other person of his choosing, usually a hairdresser-secretary who handled his "rug" (toupee), answered mail, and mixed drinks. He had approval of all publicity releases on his pictures and the right to approve all photographs taken of him before release to the press—again, the toupee, which he hated, was his main concern.

There were other inclusions tailored to his personal taste: he was to quit work at 6:00 P.M. daily (thus allowing himself time for a drink after work before going home), and there was a paragraph devoted to the size and furnishings of his dressing rooms at the studio and on location, with a mention that each was to be equipped with a refrigerator.

125

"Whenever we'd move or change locations, the thing of importance was not the script or costume, but 'Where the hell's the refrigerator?' " said Bob Schiffler, Bogie's sailing companion and make-up man.

Bogie had the right to select his own make-up man, and whenever Schiffler was available he went on Bogart's pictures. "I told him many times he didn't need make-up," Schiffler said. "He was never concerned about his looks but he liked to have me around and I liked to be with him."

Bogart had achieved a position of real financial eminence at the studio commensurate with his box-office value. After nine suspensions at Warners—taken because he held out for better parts—he was on his way professionally to being what he had been privately all along: his own man.

He expressed this view over lunch at the Lakeside Golf Club to reporter Philip K. Scheur of the *Los Angeles Times*. "When I was coming up, the studio used me as a threat to the top boys: Muni, Raft, Cagney and Robinson," he told Scheur. "When Muni, Cagney and Robinson left, I was moved ahead. They had to have a 'he man.' Now they use Johnny Garfield and Bernie Zanville—what's his name? Dane Clark—to keep me in line.

"All the studios do it. They have to protect their investments. They can make anyone a star if they get behind him. That's why I don't kid myself, why I can't take myself—or the business—seriously."

In 1946, the first year of his contract and their marriage, Bogart's income according to the Treasury Department was $432,000. Taxes were much lower in those days, and the Bogarts' standard of living was not high when compared with their income; for example, rent at the Garden of Allah was less than $700 a month—about what Betty was earning monthly.

Bogart was a happy man at last. He had almost everything he wanted: financial security, a dependable profession, a loving wife, and a position of respect among his peers and in his community. He lacked only one thing, in his view, and that was the means to escape from Hollywood from time to time and be on his own. The sea was his therapy. So Betty was enthusiastic and encouraging when he told her Dick Powell was going to sell his boat, the *Santana*, and he wanted to buy it.

The *Santana* was to the Pacific Coast yachting fraternity what Whirlaway was to racetrack aficionados. She came in second in the Santa Monica–Honolulu race in 1934 and was the pride of the Pacific Coast.

After Bogie bought the boat for $55,000, Powell agreed to check him out on her in a shakedown cruise. But Bogart couldn't wait. He bundled Betty into the car and went down the night before so they could sleep on her and he could admire the sleekness and beauty of her lines. He even brought a can of brass polish for the brightwork (which was unnecessary since every inch of her was polished and gleaming). Early in the morning Powell appeared out of the fog in his dinghy.

There was trouble getting the motor started, and for an hour the old owner apologized to the new for the problem while they were down in the engine room cursing at the fuel pumps.

Finally the engine got going and, with Powell at the helm, they ran out of the harbor and past the jetty. There was no wind and the haze was too great to see Catalina, but they decided to hoist the sails anyway, so Bogie could find out where things were.

The amateur crew, friends of Powell's, went to work efficiently and within minutes she was dressed in full rigging. Although the sails were luffing, they decided to go to Catalina under sail anyway.

At dusk the rough outline of Catalina rose up out of the mist and they moored for the night in a quiet cove. Betty, who had been alternating between the helm and the galley, produced dinner and they listened to the radio afterward; it was the day that Tilden beat Stoefen at Wimbledon and everyone cheered.

The next day they caught a good wind. The *Santana*

heeled over and her lean bow split the waves into neat slices. Bogie was filled to bursting with the pride of ownership, and Powell looked sad because he had loved her, too, and was now parting with her.

Betty, looking at her husband's joyful face under the two-day growth of beard, said, "He's the ugliest handsome man I have ever seen."

The *Santana* soon became a major part of Bogart's life, so much so that Betty was to tell a reporter that she not only "married a character named Bogie, I also married a boat named the *Santana.*"

The Bogarts lived aboard the *Santana* for three and four months at a time and took her out alone for two and three week excursions. Betty, who had been raised in Manhattan and was familiar only with the Atlantic Ocean as seen from the beach, adjusted to life aboard quickly, although not happily. As a woman, she had the responsibility to prepare food for Bogie and whomever he could talk into crewing with him.

During their "courtship" days, Betty had made an attempt to like the sea and had even learned to sail a small boat to please Bogie, but the truth was she disliked the confinement, frequently got seasick, and hated her chores below deck.

Soon Betty began to stay home on weekends, letting Bogie go on the boat with any friends he could get to crew for him, a group including: his make-up man, Schiffler, photographer John Swope, actor Jeff Richards and Bob Millotte. The Bogarts had a tacit understanding that Bogie was to be home Sunday evening by six for dinner but he telephoned Betty on the ship-to-shore telephone at least twice a day to tell her that everything was all right and that he loved her.

His tremendous income gave Bogart the financial security he wanted and considered important for just one reason: to enable him to tell the studio to go to hell. "Nobody can be a good actor without a sense of truth, of right and wrong. If you want to be an actor, be honest with yourself. Don't let them push you around. When you believe in something, you fight for it, even though you may suffer for it. We actors are better judges than any studio as to what is good for us. As soon as your name gets known and you feel you can say, 'I won't do this'—if you think the part isn't right—go ahead and say it. In the long run it will pay off. Just remember to put some dough aside for the times you are suspended."

In those days, as today, even a top star under contract to a studio had to accept any role offered or go on suspension. This meant that the star did not receive any salary and could not work for any other employer or studio until the suspension was lifted, which usually happened when star and studio—often after months of negotiation—agreed on a property.

Many stars lived up to or beyond their incomes, which meant they had to accept all roles offered to them because they could not afford to be without an income. From the beginning of his career, Bogie had made it a point to live below his income and put money aside so he could refuse roles he did not consider worthy of his talent.

Betty agreed with his philosophy. She had just been suspended for refusing to do a film which she thought was not right for her. Bogie, who had had his share of suspensions, enthusiastically supported her determination to hold out for the right roles.

Betty was beginning to change from an inexperienced young girl into a female counterpart of her husband, but by this time, she was no longer role-playing. She was becoming in real life the woman she had played so effectively on screen in *To Have and Have Not*.

CHAPTER 9

"It's better when you help."
—TO HAVE AND HAVE NOT

Although the *Santana* was Bogie's therapy, it was not a home, and Betty wanted more than anything else to have a real home where she and Bogart could settle down and start raising the family she was determined to have. Soon after their marriage she got in touch with a Hollywood realtor and told him she wanted a house, "in or near Beverly Hills, not too expensive, but large enough for us to grow into."

One night, Dave Chasen, owner of Chasen's Restaurant, told them that Hedy Lamarr wanted to sell her house, Hedgerow Farms, completely furnished, and with Frigidaire, stove, washing machine and other items not easily available because of wartime shortages. The fourteen-room, three-level ranch house sat on a hillside in Benedict Canyon, had a tennis court and swimming pool, plus a separate house built over the garage which would accommodate their staff: Bogie's cook, May Smith, and Aurilio Salazar, his handyman-gardener. There were also three and a half acres for Harvey, their boxer dog, to run loose. Harvey, a wedding gift from Louis Bromfield, was the son of Prince, the boxer who had almost interrupted their wedding. Droopy, Betty's cocker spaniel, had gone to New York to live with Mrs. Bacal, who in 1948 would marry Leo Goldberg, City Marshal of Brooklyn.

The house was comfortably furnished in Early American style, but Betty planned to discard much of the furniture and replace it with new items in keeping with the period. She intended to keep the carpeting intact, however. "Nuts to thirty-five-dollar-a-yard carpeting," she said.

One of the first items Betty purchased was a 7' x 6½' bed which, in those days, had to be specially built. Although she intended to shop for most of the furniture herself, she soon despaired of the magnitude of the project and hired an interior decorator to help out. But she kept a firm control on all purchases and carefully comparison-shopped to be certain she was getting the best prices. Having grown up poor, she was extremely conscious of the value of a dollar, a trait that delighted Bogart, who trusted her completely with the furnishings and decorations.

They moved into the new house in May 1946, and I met Bogie and Betty soon after that. I had just arrived in Hollywood from New York as a feature writer for the *New York Herald Tribune*, and Bogart's press agent, the late Bill Blowitz, arranged for me to interview Bogie in the new house.

On that first meeting with Bogie he asked me what I wanted to drink.

"A Coke, please," I said.

"You don't drink?" Bogart asked, adding hopefully, "You A.A.?"

"Nope," I said. "I never drank."

Bogart, who was behind the bar in his den, accepted this news without comment for a moment. But when he stepped out with a glass of Scotch in his hand he said, "I don't trust any bastard who doesn't drink—especially a pipe-smoking newspaperman. You must have something to hide. People who don't drink are afraid of revealing themselves.

131

"Furthermore," he said, "I don't trust any man who has more hair than I have."

Having delivered himself of a pronouncement I was to hear many times in the coming years, he turned again to the bar. I picked up my pad and pencil and started for the door.

"Where are you going?" Bogart asked.

"How are we going to do an interview if we start out with your not trusting me?" I asked. "I don't drink and I certainly have more hair on my head than you do, but then so do most men."

Bogart thought that over for a moment. "You're just going to have to work that much harder to make me trust you," he said. Shooing a couple of boxer dogs off a seat, he gestured for me to sit down.

That was our introduction, and the routine of insult followed by wary acceptance became our standard every time I saw him over the next decade. He finally trusted me, but it took a long time. Even then, when I went to visit him at his home where he was dying, he called me a "freeloader like all the rest of the press."

But that was Bogart, and, as the late Peter Lorre once said, "I like Bogie because he is one hundred percent what he is, and that is very rich if you know him. So you take all the disadvantages with the advantages."

I found it the same with Betty. Although we were contemporaries, she had, even in those early days, an aura of glamor that made me always aware that she was a star.

Some months after that first interview with Bogie I returned to the house to interview Betty, who, in a revealing interview, told me why the new house was so important to her.

"I always wanted a career," she said, "but I also always wanted a home of my own, a husband and children. I made up my mind long ago that when I did find them they would come first. If my career interferes with our domestic life, it's best that I give it

132

up. Bogie loves a home. He likes to come home to his meals, stay home and share it with his friends. I feel that a wife should be in a home. She should be there to see that it is run properly—not leave it in the hands of strangers. When I have children I want to raise them myself—not force them to get used to a strange nurse who takes the place of their mother.

"Ours is my very first home—the first time I have ever lived anywhere but in an apartment. It's a wonderful feeling to wander from room to room, to feel that it is ours. It's gratifying and comforting to know there is someone there to share it. For the first time in my life I have a safe feeling. When I look around at some of the career girls I have met in Hollywood, I don't envy them. They make lots of money. They are famous. But they are the loneliest people in the world. Not all, but some. Big mansions and empty hearts. I don't want to end up the same way. If it's possible to combine a career and home, that's for me. The minute I see that it isn't working out, home I go and home I stay."

Betty meant what she said. She had again refused a picture at Warners and had gone on suspension rather than work just for the sake of working. She was putting as much thought and energy into her career of being Mrs. Humphrey Bogart as she had into acting, but she was finding her way in this new role with difficulty.

Soon after moving into the new house the Bogart's acquired a butler named Fred, reportedly Oxford-educated, who called Betty "Milady." Soon after Fred joined them the Bogart's gave their first party.

Mary Baker, who was present at that first dinner party, recalls that Betty, who was wearing an elegant hostess gown, was trying to be very much the lady. "Fred had planned an elaborate dinner," Mrs. Baker said. "There was a great deal of silver on the table. Betty took one look and obviously didn't know where to begin. Bogie noticed her fumbling and said, 'Ask Fred. He'll tell you.' "

The color drained from Betty's face and her skin blotched as it always did when she was nervous and angry, but she held her peace and said nothing. She finally picked up the fish fork that Mary already had in hand.

The next day Betty had Fred explain each one of the eating utensils in the elaborate silver service she had received as a wedding present. She also had him demonstrate for her how to use the various other items such as the cake knife, cheese parer and various serving forks.

Warners soon scheduled another Bogart–Bacall (or B & B film, as the fan magazines designated it) to take advantage of the popularity of their two previous films, which had been so successful. Women all over America were beginning to imitate Betty's husky voice, and men were lighting cigarettes with four fingers cupping the flame, as was Bogie's habit.

Their third picture together was to be *Dark Passage*, written and directed by Delmer Daves, who had known Bogie since *Petrified Forest*, which he had adapted for the screen. *Dark Passage* was the story of an accused killer (Bogart) who escapes from jail; with the help of a girl (Betty) whose father had been unjustifiably jailed, he finds the murderer who actually committed the crime.

Although Betty was considered a star by the public, Warners still had some reservations about her ability as an actress, and, in October 1946, Betty was asked to test for the role opposite Bogie in *Dark Passage*, rather than just being cast outright.

But by this time Betty was, as Hollywoodians say, beginning to believe her own publicity. She was punctual and always prepared with her lines, but she was not averse to expressing opinions on various facets of film-making, even though still only a neophyte.

One day she hurt the feelings of a cameraman, Sid Hickox, who had been on her two previous pictures, and Daves, the director, had to "chop her down." The incident happened when Hickox was asked to shoot a cold dawn effect for a scene in Betty's apartment near the end of the film. "To shoot black and white dawn is one of the hardest assignments for a cameraman," said Daves. "Sid did a superb job of it, and Betty saw the scene at rushes the following morning. When I asked her what she thought of them she said, 'They stink. They're gray and flat.'

" 'That's how they're supposed to be,' I said. 'And God bless Sid for being able to get the right effect.'

" 'Shit, I don't like them at all.'

"Sid overheard the conversation. His mouth was drooping and he looked stricken.

"I decided to teach Betty a lesson. We lined up for her last scene in the film—one in which Bogie is supposed to telephone her from a bus depot and she gets the call in her apartment. Since it was an important scene, she was anticipating a big close-up, but I told her we were going to photograph her from the back so that the audience could imagine what was going on in her mind.

" 'With my back to the camera?' she said. Tears came into her eyes, but she was a great sport about it and rehearsed, even though her voice was trembling and she was fighting to hold back the tears. That broke me up and I relented.

" 'For God's sake, Betty, we're lit for the front,' I told her. 'I just wanted to teach you a lesson because you were so cruel to Sid.'

"She sniffed. 'I know I was.' Tears started to come into her eyes, which was just perfect, and that's how we shot the scene.

"A few minutes later Bogie came on the set. He saw her sobbing and followed her to her dressing room. When it was time for him to come on set, he had on his great Bogie face—no emotion. Usually, he was a one-take actor, but this time he kept blowing his lines and apologizing. We finally got the scene after eight takes and Bogie came over and said, 'I'm sorry about letting you down, but you know what was bothering me. Betty told me what happened, and

135

the kid can still break me up. But I think you did the right thing. Maybe she was getting a bit too big in the britches.' "

Bogie was too much of a professional to defend his wife against the director in such an untenable situation. It is likely that he felt such lessons were part of Betty's education as an actress. Betty still had a lot to learn and she would have to get some lessons the hard way.

During the film, Daves also learned that Bogart, who liked to come off as a tough brawler, was neither a fighter nor an athlete at all. "I never saw Bogie nude from the waist up," Daves said. "Actually he was quite spindly and didn't have an athletic build. I remember for one scene in *Dark Passage* we had staged a knock-down-drag-out fight with the murderer on a cliff under the Golden Gate Bridge. I choreographed the fight and then told Bogie what to do.

" 'Hold it, Del, old man,' Bogie told me. 'I have bad news for you. I have absolutely no coordination as an athlete, which is why I stay out of brawls. I'm no good as a fighter and you can only tell me to do one thing at a time.'

"So we rehearsed the scene and did it blow by blow with constant cutting. And it worked."

Daves, one of the most erudite men in Hollywood, was an occasional guest at the Bogart home. He was especially in demand when they had some of Bogart's more prominent writer friends as guests. Bogie told Daves, "You'd be surprised how few guys I can invite to my house who can carry on a civilized conversation about any subject that comes along with some of my friends."

Most of the Bogarts' circle were his old friends, people who had known him during his marriage to Mayo. This is not surprising when one considers that he was older than Betty and had been in Hollywood for so many years that it was only natural that she should acquire his friends as hers. Also, Betty had always been pretty much of a loner and the few friends she had were in New York. And like most loners Betty had very few female confidantes, preferring instead to concentrate her time on her husband.

Among their closest friends in the film colony were Mel and Mary Baker, Raymond and Dorothy Massey, Betty and John Reinhardt, Patrick O'Moore and his wife, Zelda O'Neil. Bogie admired and liked Spencer Tracy, Peter Lorre, Clifton Webb and Charles Butterworth. But by and large, his best friends were writing people like Louis Bromfield, Nunnally Johnson, Harry Kurnitz, Robert and Nathaniel Benchley, Noel Coward, Mark Hellinger and John Huston, the writer-director, who directed him as Sam Spade in the *Maltese Falcon.*

In 1942 Bogie had worked with Huston again in *Across the Pacific,* the story of an Army officer "dismissed" so he could work for Army Intelligence. It was the first of Bogie's "man in the trenchcoat" roles. Near the end of the film Huston was called up into the Army.

After Huston was discharged he returned to Warners, where his first film was to be *The Treasure of Sierra Madre,* with a cast including his father, Walter Huston, Bogie, Bruce Bennett and Tim Holt.

Huston still recalls his initial reaction to Betty, whom he met just before the picture started. "Mayo had made an indelible impression on me," he said. "The knives and shotgun came out almost instantly and there was hell to pay on almost every occasion. Betty was just the opposite. She was adorable to Bogie and his friends and she was always warm, charming and dear. She was anything but a fighter, not that she catered to Bogie, but she was supportive to his ego. She was in love with him and he with her, and anyone who liked Bogie liked her. They were a joy to behold together."

Treasure of Sierra Madre was to be made on location in San Jose de Perua, then an isolated village about 140 miles north of Mexico City.

Huston, who had scouted the location, reported that

life would be rugged for the actors, with burning sun, tropical downpours, assorted insects and reptiles. "It's no place for a woman," he warned Bogie, who was determined to have Betty accompany him or he wouldn't do the picture. "Without her I'll be miserable," he said. Bogie had no intention of attempting a "modern marriage" with Betty, such as he'd had with three previous wives. "We got married to be together," he told Betty, "and that's how it's going to be."

Betty was equally determined to be with him and turned down a film at Warners so she could go on the location. "A wife belongs with her husband," she told Huston, who agreed that she could come along.

"Actually, Betty was a godsend on location," Huston was to say later. "She wasn't in the picture but she arranged lunches for everyone and made regular trips to the kitchen to prepare ham and eggs for Bogie. She'd sometimes show up on location with champagne when that was in order. She did all kinds of helpful things for everyone."

Huston, who was a stickler for authenticity, soon earned the nickname "Hard-way Huston." "John wanted everything perfect," Bogart said. "If he saw a nearby mountain that could serve for photographic purposes, that mountain was no good: too easy to reach. If we could get to a location site without fording a couple of streams and walking through snake-infested areas in the scorching sun, then it wasn't quite right."

Bogart and John Huston got along wonderfully well until the end of the picture. Then Huston decreed some extra scenes, which lengthened the schedule, causing Bogie to miss taking part in the Honolulu race with his new yacht, *Santana*. "We had a terrible row and were sore as hell at each other for days," recalled Huston. "Betty was responsible for smoothing things out. She'd say to me, 'John, for God's sake, don't be silly,' and she'd say the same thing to Bogie. Finally she arranged for us to get together for a few drinks of an ancient tequila laced with Scotch, and anger melted into understanding and everything was fine again."

The Hustons, father and son, were to get Oscars for their work, and Bogie's performance as a trigger-happy prospector in the Mexican hills would receive excellent notices.

The Treasure of Sierra Madre was so successful that Warners immediately cast Bogie in *Key Largo,* with Betty as his leading lady. Again, Huston was to direct a cast that also included Edward G. Robinson, Lionel Barrymore and Claire Trevor. The Maxwell Anderson melodrama of a disillusioned veteran facing gangsterism on a Florida key was a compact and exciting film that suffered little from the fact that it was all filmed on the sets at Warner Brothers. Even the storm scenes were done at the studio.

"Bogie helped Betty on the set," recalls Huston. "He'd help her with her part, not as the master and the pupil, but he'd give her little clues, such as the time he told her, 'The audience is always a little ahead of you. If a guy points a gun at you, the audience knows you're afraid. You don't have to make faces. You just have to believe that you are the person you are playing and what is happening is happening to you.'

"Betty only comes into her own as an actress when she is expanding her character, taking it off the leash, and in our film she had a conventional role which gave her some difficulties, and Bogie was a help to her."

Claire Trevor got an Oscar for her brief role as the gangster's ex-mistress, and Bogie's reviews were good. But the two films Betty made with Bogie since their marriage had not added much luster to her reputation as an actress.

Howard Hawks, who still followed Betty's career with interest, saw *Dark Passage* and *Key Largo,* and told Bogie, "You're a good enough actor to know that Betty is no damn good if she forgets the stuff I taught her; you followed along with it and you know what it is. Everything she has been doing in her most recent films is utterly wrong for her. Now it's up to you to see that she does it right, otherwise she's going to be messed up."

Hawks then chided Betty. "For Chrissakes, Betty, why don't you do scenes the way I taught you? You're losing your attitude in films. You're no actress, you're a personality."

Hawks' points were well taken and Betty realized it. Her career had flowered with Hawks because he had not demanded too much of her and he tailored his films especially for her limited abilities. Betty still was not an experienced actress and needed special handling and parts, but Warners, which owned half her contract, was determined to put her in rather stereotypical, slinky roles opposite established leading men rather than train her.

During the first two years of their marriage Betty was not overly concerned with her career and had refused two films, preferring to go on suspension so she could be with Bogie. Perhaps she sensed Bogie didn't want her to be very successful. He had often said he married a woman and not an actress. If he thought about it at all he undoubtedly considered his career more important than hers. After all, he was the man in the house and the breadwinner. Betty also believed that a good lasting marriage was more important than a fleeting career.

Betty was willing to follow where Bogie led, and during the summer of 1947 he was to lead her into politics with a disastrous result. That summer, J. Parnell Thomas, a Republican congressman from New Hampshire, began an attempt to "prove" that the communists had been spreading propaganda by infiltrating the film industry and "taking it over." Ten writers, known as "The Hollywood Ten," refused to tell Thomas and his interrogators whether or not they had ever been communists. The writers all went to jail.

Bogart, who was unquestionably a liberal in politics,

was so incensed over what was happening to The Ten that he organized a protest committee in Hollywood. An article in the October 24, 1947, edition of the *New York Herald Tribune* summed up the facts and factions succinctly:

The Committee for the First Amendment, a group of three-hundred independent movie producers, directors, writers and actors, formed in the last ten days, today chartered a plane to take fifty members to Washington to combat what they feel is an unfavorable picture of the film industry arising from testimony before the House Committee on un-American Activities. The plane will go to the capital on Sunday, with stopovers in Kansas City, St. Louis, and Chicago. Press conferences will be held at those cities and in Washington. Humphrey Bogart and Lauren Bacall will be among those aboard.

The testimony of Louis B. Mayer, vice-president in charge of production for Metro-Goldwyn-Mayer; Sam Wood, independent producer; and Jack Warner, vice-president of Warner Brothers, was the focal point of the resentment. The chief concern here is the effect of a split between the employee groups and the top-rank producers. Others on the Committee include David O. Selznick, Lionel Barrymore, George Stevens, John Ford, Ira Gershwin, Katharine Hepburn, Paul Draper, Arthur Hornblow, Jr., Anatole Litvak, Burgess Meredith, Gregory Peck, Irwin Shaw, Billy Wilder, Larry Adler, John Huston, William Wyler and Philip Dunne.

The local papers have played up the investigation with daily pictures and front-page headlines. Editorial comment has been sparse, a local newspaper referring to it as "a witch-hunt."

"We went in there [Washington] green and they beat our brains out," Bogart told a *Newsweek* reporter, explaining that he thought he was defending the Bill of Rights. "But in the shuffle we became adopted by the communists, and I ended up with my picture on the front page of the *Daily Worker*. . . . That the

141

trip was ill-advised, even foolish, I am ready to admit. I am an American and very likely, like a good many of the rest of you, sometimes a foolish and impetuous American."

Not only did the junket turn out to be ill-advised, it had little political impact. But it was responsible for a schism between Bogart and Jack L. Warner, and the two men would never be good friends again.

Many years later Bogart was to tell the late Richard Gehman that he felt Warner and others in the industry wanted to show the government they were willing to cooperate and offered up scapegoats in the form of a blacklist of stars, writers, producers and all the rest.

"Warner was one of the worst, if you ask me," Bogart said. "Sure, I worked for him a long time, and you might say I owe my career to him. . . . But he and a good many of the rest of the stuffed shirts who control this town decided they had to do something to take the heat off the industry, and so for a long time there have been people who can't get work. There's been a blacklist. Nobody's ever proved these people on the blacklist are or ever were communists, but there it is, that list and their names on it, and nobody hires them.

". . . If I'd been less valuable to the studio, I probably would have had to make [a retraction] or I'd have been dropped from the list of contract players over there. I'm sure of that. . . ."

Although Betty was with Bogie during the trip to Washington, not much was made of her participation by the studio. It was assumed, rightfully, that she sided with her husband and went with him. But within a few years their positions would change and Betty would lead Humphrey into the political field, and this time the studio would place the onus on her.

CHAPTER 10

"I'm not the orchid-bearing type."
—THE BIG SLEEP

Bogie had never wanted children in his first three marriages. Then, when he married Betty, he felt he was too old. Also he believed that a husband and wife are one unit until there is a child. He was afraid that when Betty became a mother she would be preoccupied with the child and have too little time for him, and he had a very real dependence upon her. But he felt that if Betty wanted a child he didn't have the right to penalize her because he was too old. So he had been taking hormone treatments during the three years they had been married.

One night in April 1948 Betty told Bogie over dinner that she was going to visit an obstetrician the next day. "I think I may be pregnant," she said quietly. Bogie, who then was forty-nine years old, said nothing, but, that night, before they went to sleep he asked her to please call him on the set the next day as soon as she heard, one way or the other.

At the time he was working at Columbia Pictures in an independent film venture for his own company, Santana, named after his boat. The film was *Tokyo Joe*, the story of an ex-flyer who, to prevent his daughter's death, smuggles war criminals into Japan. During the day Bogie tried several times to reach Betty by telephone from the set, but she was not at home.

"He told me Betty had gone to the doctor, but that's all he said," recalls producer-writer Robert Lord, Bogie's partner with writer Mark Hellinger in Santana. "But I noticed he was more tense than usual and anxious to get the last scene finished. He left the set without even taking off his make-up."

When Bogie arrived home he found Betty waiting outside the house for him. He kissed her on the cheek and casually asked, "What's new?"

"We're going to have a baby, Humphrey," she said softly.

"He didn't jump up or down or even act excited," Betty said. "He just got kind of quiet and emotional and put an arm around me as we walked into the house. Nothing else was said about the baby all through dinner and the rest of the evening.

"That night we had one of our biggest arguments. I don't remember what it was about now, and not once did the word 'baby' ever get mentioned, but I knew that was what had brought the argument on. Bogie was just expressing his resentment that he— like most other married men—was about to become a father."

When the news that the Bogarts were about to become parents reached their friends, there was unrestrained glee.

Someone suggested a baby shower for Betty. "I wouldn't give one for Betty, but I would give one for Bogie," said Harry Kurnitz.

The fact that Kurnitz suggested a "stag" shower was unusual, but Bogie was the celebrity in their marriage and although his friends undoubtedly liked Betty, he was the focus of attention in their group.

Kurnitz' idea met with instant acclaim, and the shower was arranged on a stag basis at the upstairs room of Romanoff's.

After dinner everybody took turns toasting Bogie.

Mike Romanoff, who owned the restaurant, got up, and in his cultured Guardsman voice started out by saying he wanted to pay tribute to his dear friend who was not like the other chicken-pluckers in town. He then went into a thirty-minute discussion of Howard Hughes, eventually shifted to comments on Linda Darnell and never mentioned Bogie again.

The other speeches were equally irrelevant to the occasion. By 9:00 P.M. Collier Young and John Huston had Bogart on the floor while Huston delivered the "Baby" with fireplace tongs.

Then Bogart sat on a couch and received the gifts: layettes, silver mugs and other baby presents. "By the third gift Bogie was so choked up about the fact that he was going to have a genuine baby that he was in tears," recalled Kurnitz. "He made a speech but he was too confused with emotion and booze to make sense. He wanted to make a square speech, but it wasn't in him to do it."

One night while Betty was pregnant, the Bogarts had dinner with Harry Truman, who then was in Los Angeles campaigning for re-election. Bogie made a $20 bet with Truman that the child would be a girl. Truman bet it would be a boy.

During Betty's pregnancy Bogie said little about her condition but he watched over her diet carefully. He insisted she cut down on cigarettes and get enough sleep. They agreed that if the infant was a boy it would be named Stephen. A girl was to be named Leslie Howard after the English actor who had given Bogart his first big break on stage and in the film of *Petrified Forest*. They decided against naming a boy Leslie because, by then, the name had effeminate overtones, and Bogie remembered too well the problems he'd had growing up with the name Humphrey.

Betty designed her own maternity suits, which were featured in a *Life* article. As she got larger and her time drew nearer, Bogie, like any other father-to-be, would sometimes place his hand on her stomach to feel the baby kick.

Christmas that year in the new house was festive, with a big tree and presents scattered around the living room; it was also Bogie's birthday, and Betty, who knew that he had rarely had a birthday of his own, was determined that he should have a real celebration. "Next year we'll be three," she said, her thoughts already on Christmases to come when they would have a family.

Bogie gave Betty a gorgeous gold cigarette case for Christmas with the gruff comment, "Here, I'm tired of seeing all that tobacco in your bag."

"The crack was meant to take the sentiment away from it," Betty said, but she knew that the gift was not only for Christmas but also because he wanted to express his happiness that within a week they were going to be parents.

On January 6, 1949, the day that Stephen was born, Bogie went to the studio. Betty timed the pains herself in the morning, called the doctor and drove herself to the office. After the examination, he called Bogie who rushed to the doctor's office looking absolutely pale. Bogart drove Betty to the Cedars of Lebanon Hospital and went into the labor room with her. "He stayed as long as he could take it," Betty said, "but his face got whiter and whiter, and finally he said he would have to leave."

Jaik Rosenstein, Hedda Hopper's "leg man," went to the hospital at 11:00 A.M. to keep Bogart company. "When I got off the elevator on the fourth floor, I saw Bogie in the waiting room, white as a sheet," said Rosenstein.

Dr. Myron Prinzemetal, Betty's obstetrician, emerged from the delivery room to say it would be a while yet.

"What's happening in there?" Bogie asked, jerking his thumb toward the delivery room.

"Nothing yet," said the doctor. "Your wife just told me to come out and take care of you, because you're so nervous and upset."

"I'm not upset at all," snapped Bogie.

An hour later the doctor returned, and Bogie said, "Is it all right if I have a drink?" He took a pint from his overcoat pocket and put two glasses on the table.

"None for you," he told the doctor. "You've got work to do."

A baby boy was born in the afternoon and weighed six pounds, six ounces. When a nurse brought the baby for Bogie to see, his first reaction—like so many parents'—was, "My God, he's ugly." But the nurse, Carole Sweetnam, recalls that there were tears in his eyes. "He insisted on being allowed to see his wife, and even though we told him she was still sedated he went into her room, looked down at her until she must have sensed him there because she looked up and smiled. 'It's a boy, honey,' he said, and kissed her."

When Betty awakened, Bogie was still by her bedside, in a room that looked like a florist's shop—many of the blooms came from friends, but two-dozen long-stemmed roses bore only a card with the legend, "I Love You." The card was not signed, but it was from Bogie.

The day following Stephen's birth, Bogie sent President Truman a twenty-dollar bill with the request that he return it autographed so Bogie could keep it as a memento.

The autographed twenty-dollar bill came back to Bogie in February 1949 with a note from Truman saying, "I need it more than you do." With the bill was a newspaper article saying that Bette Davis was listed by the United States Treasury Department as the highest paid actress in films for the fiscal year which ended in 1947. She collected $328,000 from Warner Brothers, displacing Betty Grable, who had been the first the previous year with $299,333 paid by 20th-Century Fox. "Both were eclipsed by Humphrey Bogart," the news story reported, "who earned more than anyone on the acting side of the movies. Mr. Bogart got $467,361."

The birth of his first child seemed to have little

impact on Bogie. He was content to let the nurse and Betty, who had taken another suspension from the studio, take care of him. But almost every morning he went into the kitchen to check on the preparation of the baby's formula: evaporated milk, Dextro-Maltose, cod liver oil and ascorbic acid.

His daily routine did not change. He went to work in the morning at the studio, came home promptly at night so he could spend a few hours playing with Stephen before the baby was put to bed. Then he had dinner and, if he was working, retired early. As usual, whenever possible he spent the weekends on the *Santana*, but called Betty often from the boat to be sure that everything was all right.

Seven months after the birth of Stephen, Betty was back at work again at Warners in a picture called *Young Man with a Horn*. Her co-star was Kirk Douglas, who had been one of her classmates at the New York Academy of Dramatic Arts.

When her picture ended, Bogie, who had some business to accomplish in New York, suggested they take a vacation together.

They checked into the Gotham Hotel, and while Bogie was away, Betty spent the morning shopping at Saks Fifth Avenue, Bonwit's and Bergdorf Goodman. During the evening they usually went to the theater together, catching up on the hit shows.

One Saturday night, after the theater, Betty went back to the hotel early, leaving Bogie to do the town with a friend. Shortly before three o'clock on Sunday morning, September 15, 1949, Bogie and friend arrived at El Morocco, an elegant nightclub on 54th Street. Both men were carrying stuffed pandas that Bogie had bought for Steve.

Noticing a friend across the room, the men put the stuffed animals on a table and went to the bar for a drink. They returned a few minutes later in time to surprise two girls in the act of making off with the pandas. Bogart tackled one of the young ladies and in the ensuing scuffle, a flying plate hit the other one on the hip.

Bogie was back at the Gotham by 5:00 A.M. and found he had forgot his room key. "I was awakened by a loud pounding at the bedroom door," recalled Betty. "I got up, cursing faintly, and went to see what loathsome creature would be awakening me at that hour. It was Bogie, and what an idiotic picture he presented. His face wore a catlike grin, and his clothes showed signs of an evening of merriment. In each arm he clutched a life-sized panda doll. 'I thought I had better tell you all about it before you read it in the papers,' he said.

It could have been an expensive evening, as the girl, a model named Robin Roberts, later brought a physical assault suit for $25,000 against Bogart. Although Bogie refused to take the suit seriously, Betty insisted on attending the trial with him. When Bogie was asked in court if he were drunk, he cracked back, "Isn't everybody at three A.M.?"

When the judge told the girl, who lost her case, "That was his personal property, you know, and you shouldn't have tried to take it away from him," Betty nodded agreement.

The crowd outside the court mobbed the Bogarts when they came out, and booed the girl. Bogart was delighted, but was sportsman enough to shake hands with the girl later.

The incident, spread over the national press, might have harmed any other actor, but as a Bogart gesture it seemed wry and funny and nobody minded.

When the Bogarts returned to Hollywood the celebrated pandas were placed in the entry hall where they greeted all visitors.

Years later Betty was to say of this time in their lives, "I think when he married me Bogie thought I would be like his other three wives—a companion for his semibachelor existence. In a sense I don't suppose he's ever forgiven me for not being like them, because

149

I don't think he knew what he was getting into until Stephen was a year old. Then without my doing or saying anything, Mr. Bogart began to realize he was not the carefree roustabout he always thought he was. He was the head of a family—a man of many and numerous responsibilities."

Lauren Bacall, date unknown.

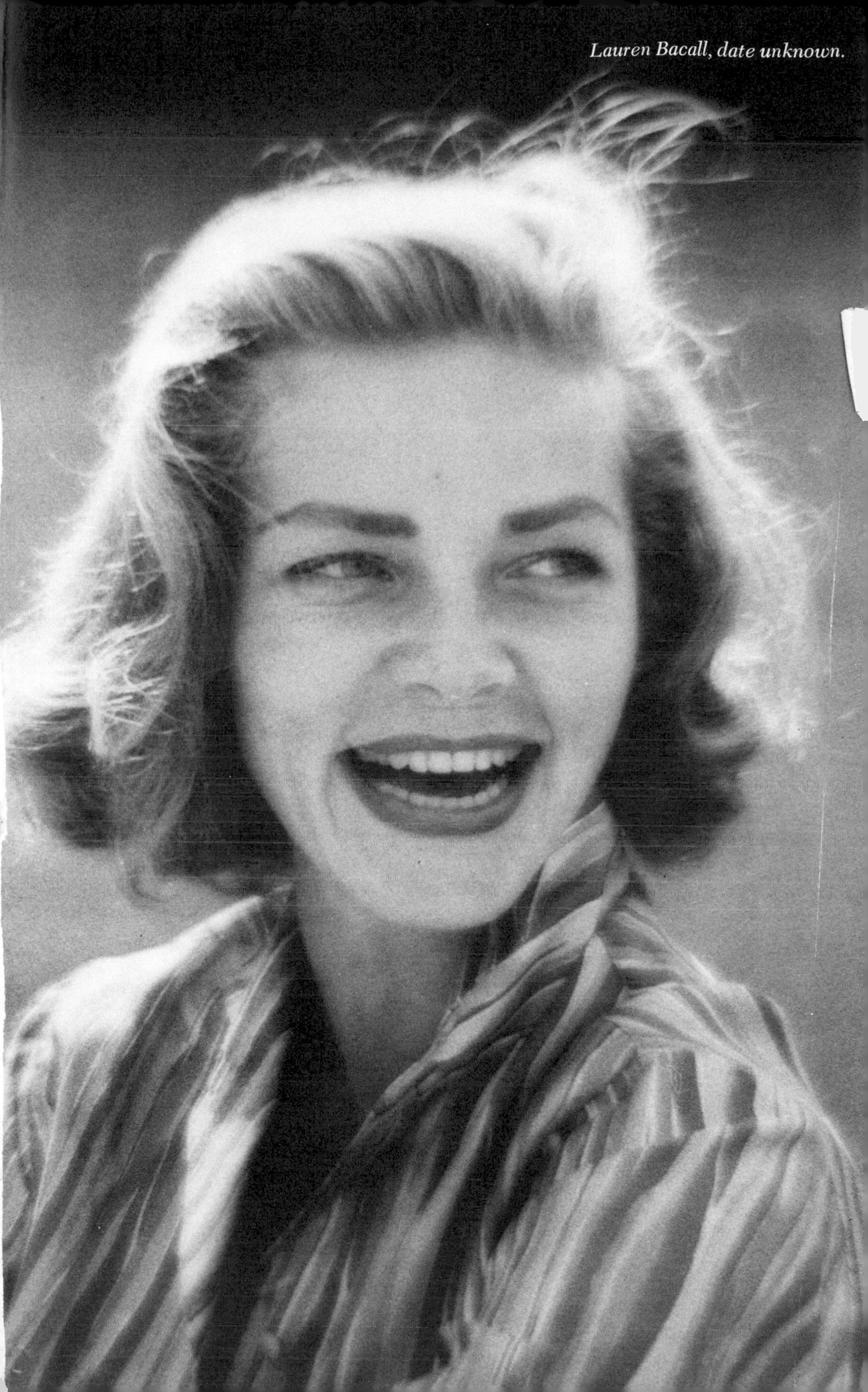

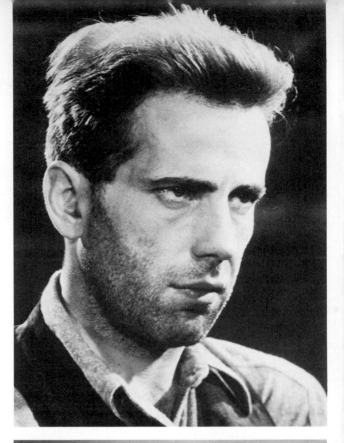

RIGHT: *Humphrey Bogart as Duke Mantee in* THE PETRIFIED FOREST, *1936.*

FAR RIGHT: *In line with a new production technique, director John Huston held week-long preproduction rehearsals and story conferences for Warner Brothers'* KEY LARGO, *1948.* L TO R: *Lionel Barrymore, Bogart, Dan Seymour, Lauren Bacall, Frank Stevens (Mr. Barrymore's stand-in), and Thomas Gomez. (Mac Julian— Warner Brothers)*

RIGHT: *Bogie as Sam Spade in* THE MALTESE FALCON, *1941.*

FAR RIGHT: *leaving the story conference,* L TO R, *Lauren Bacall, Bogart, writer Richard Brooks, director John Huston, and Dan Seymour (Mac Julian— Warner Brothers)*

OPPOSITE: *Bogie and Betty at the helm of the* SANTANA.

ABOVE: *Bogie and Betty in the front yard of their Benedict Canyon home with Harvey, their wedding gift from Bromfield.*

Bogie and Betty at home together.

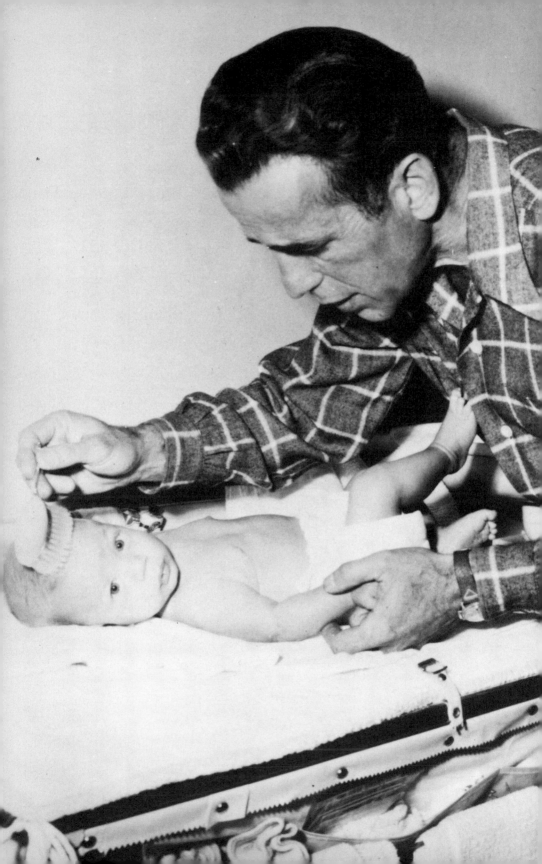

OPPOSITE: *Fatherhood was Bogie's most difficult role.*
A 1949 snapshot reveals him brushing Stephen's hair.

ABOVE: *Lauren Bacall in the den of her*
Holmby Hills home with her son, Stephen Humphrey Bogart,
aged 10 weeks.

ABOVE: *Christmas 1950. Stephen, almost 2, helps decorate the tree.*

BELOW: *The Bogarts and their staff.* L TO R: *Unknown, Betty, Aurilio Salazar (butler-handyman), Bogie, May Smith (the Bogarts' cook), with Baby, one of Harvey's sons.*

OPPOSITE: *In 1952, a few months before Leslie's birth. (Phil Stern Photo)*

OPPOSITE TOP: *Betty and Droopy.*

OPPOSITE BOTTOM: *Betty at the wheel of a
1953 Mercedes Benz 220-A cabriolet, a Christmas present from Bogie.
Admiring the car were Judy Garland
and her daughter, Liza Minelli. (Phil Stern Photo)*

BELOW: *Birthday party for Leslie and the kids on "our block." (Phil Stern Photo)*

OPPOSITE TOP: *At home in 1956, the last year of Bogie's life. (Phil Stern Photo)*

OPPOSITE BOTTOM: *In the backyard of the Bogart's Holmby Hills home, a month before Bogie died. The little girl is Leslie. (Phil Stern Photo)*

ABOVE: *Lauren Bacall and Leslie (about 14) at Malibu.*

OVERLEAF: *Photo taken on location for* BLOOD ALLEY *in San Francisco in 1956 during Bogie's visit there to see Betty, who was co-starring in the film with Robert Mitchum. (Phil Stern Photo)*

CHAPTER 11

"They don't come no better'n you."
—THE AFRICAN QUEEN

One day in 1950 John Huston called Bogie on the telephone at home. "I have a great story," Huston said. "The hero is a low life. You are the biggest low life in town and therefore most suitable for the part."

Enchanted by Huston's novel pitch, Bogart suggested they drink lunch at Mike Romanoff's new restaurant, in which Bogie was an investor. Huston told Bogie of a book he was interested in directing called *The African Queen*. The novel, written by C. S. Forester and published in 1935, was about an English missionary who persuades a river-rat boatman to take her out of German territory at the beginning of World War I. It had been owned by both Warners and 20th-Century Fox, but the big studios were averse to producing the film because of the high cost of the location. The property had finally been bought by Sam Spiegel, a classic prototype of the Hollywood producer. Spiegel chomped cigars, called everybody "baby," except babies, and spoke nine languages, all of them, except his native German, with a heavy accent.

Although a talented producer, Spiegel was such a

151

hustler that the verb "Spiegeled" had become part of the Hollywood vocabulary. It meant to soothe, cajole or con, and the producer had "Spiegeled" Huston into taking over *The African Queen.*

Huston and Bogie continued lunch until the wee hours of the morning, and early the following morning went to visit Miss Hepburn, who was living in a big, hidden house on a hill cluttered with the orange crates and Salvation Army furniture with which Miss Hepburn furnished all her rented houses.

In ten minutes and several thousand words, Miss Hepburn convinced Bogie and Huston of their wisdom in seeking her out. She liked the part in *The African Queen* and would also be happy to invest in the film. "But she regarded us as a couple of disgusting old men who were badly in need of her guidance," Bogie wrote in a *Coronet* article.

Finally it was decided to go ahead, and Bogie, accompanied by Betty, started off for Africa via New York, leaving Stephen at home with a nurse. One night when Betty went to bed early, Bogie, accompanied by Quentin Reynolds, stopped in at the Stork Club for a nightcap. Sherman Billingsley, the proprietor, asked Bogie to appear on his television program.

Bogart said, "I'm sorry. I wear a wig for professional appearances and I haven't got it with me."

Billingsley persisted. He said it didn't matter—after all, he wore one himself. "Look," said Bogart, "I can't go on a TV screen like this. I'm known as a screen lover. That sort of type," and he added with a straight face, "not like you."

That did it. Billingsley flushed angrily. Bogie, enjoying the effect of the needling, then told Billingsley straight out that he didn't want to appear in the show, that he considered it a bore anyway, and wouldn't appear on it under any circumstances.

"Then you'd better get out of my restaurant," said Billingsley.

"You mean I'm barred," said Bogart, his reaction

somewhat less penitent than might have been expected.

"The challengers will never overtake me now," he announced happily to writer George Frazier. "I still have several more days to go in New York and feel, with a little effort on my part, I can probably get barred from Central Park and Ebbets Field. As a matter of fact, the only places I am really socially acceptable now are "21" and Grand Central Station. Put it down to natural charm. I'm loaded with it. And experienced, too. You don't get to be the Boris Karloff of the supper clubs overnight. You've got to work at it."

A few days later the Bogarts arrived in London only to discover there were complications with the film. Spiegel's backers had withdrawn their financial support on almost the same day that Huston had left for Africa to scout locations. Meanwhile, the Bogarts and Katharine Hepburn had been put up in Claridge's, one of the most expensive hotels in London, and there was some doubt that Spiegel had enough money to pay the bill.

The forthright Miss Hepburn nailed Spiegel in the hotel lobby. "I've lived a lot of other places than Claridge's, Sam," she said. "I wouldn't have lived here on my own because I'm too tight and I don't want to get stuck with the bill, so if you don't have the money, say so."

Spiegel murmured something about having "a plan."

Spiegel's plan was novel to say the least. He persuaded Bogart to invest in the film himself and convinced Bogie, Huston and Hepburn to defer their salaries in order to get the picture made. Miss Hepburn had only one condition: that Spiegel pay their hotel bills as he had agreed. "I didn't mind doing the film for nothing but I didn't intend to pay money for the privilege of doing it," said Miss Hepburn later.

It was the first time that Betty Bacall had met

Katharine Hepburn, who was one of her childhood idols. The women soon became friends, although it would take some time before the frosty and proper New England-born star would take to Bogie.

Bogie started to win her over on the trip to Africa, soon after the flight started. "I was alone and had settled down for the night when he came by and asked me if I had everything I wanted," Miss Hepburn recalled. "I said, 'yes,' and he said, 'Okay.' During the flight he constantly asked me if I was all right, which was terribly nice of him. Most people wouldn't have cared less as long as they got what they wanted. But Bogie was a real gentleman."

The film was shot almost entirely in the most inaccessible spots Huston could find in the Belgian Congo and Uganda. Betty was with Bogie on much of the rugged location filming for the picture.

"She supported him and everybody else," said Huston. "She practically carried a standard. And it was, to some extent, a difficult location. The food was very bad at one time and Betty herself reorganized it and sent away for food and had it flown in, to the delight of everyone."

Cameraman Ted Scaife recalls the Misses Hepburn and Bacall as "a couple of Florence Nightingales who made sure that members of the unit had their anti-malaria tablets."

Miss Hepburn, who was convinced that Bogie and Huston were profligates, lectured them on the evils of drinking and, in an attempt to shame them, drank water in their presence at meal times. As a result she got dysentery and was in bed for several weeks. Bogie and Huston continued drinking hard liquor and avoided getting sick.

Bogart used to take a siesta on a hammock set up on a raft in the river. He boasted that after the mosquitoes bit him, they rolled over either dead or drunk. "His strength was in Scotch," Huston said. "He even brushed his teeth with Scotch. I think all of us were ill in some way or another, but not Bogie."

The humidity was so extreme in the Congo that it mildewed all the costumes, covering them with a green mold. The waters were infested with crocodiles, and one night the camp was attacked by an army of huge soldier ants. Bogie, with drink in hand, sallied out to cheer on the crew who were burning oil and yelling, trying to divert the column. Miss Hepburn, who, with Betty, had discovered the ants earlier in the day, came out on the balcony of her bungalow and verbally lambasted Bogart in ringing tones for staging a drunken brawl in the middle of the night.

"Bogie was wonderful," recalled Huston. "With simple dignity he explained to her, 'Katie, old girl. Ants.'"

"Damn Hepburn! Damn her, she's so goddamn cheerful," Bogie exploded one afternoon. "She's got ants in her pants, mildew in her shoes, and she's still cheerful. I build a solid wall of whiskey between me and the bugs. She doesn't drink, and she breezes through it all as though it were weekend in Connecticut!"

The old boat they used in the picture sprung a leak one day and settled to the bottom of the river deep in the African jungle. It took five days to raise it. Meanwhile, the English engineer who had kept the temperamental boiler perking had packed up and left the movie troupe. "John was delighted," said Bogie. "He had a real crisis. My only crisis was the time the party ran out of Scotch for two days."

There were, however, other crises in the film which Bogart, with characteristic modesty, neglected to tell since he was the actual hero of one of them. But Peter Viertel, the screenwriter, still remembers vividly a time when he saw Bogart reveal the truth about himself under pressure.

The incident took place during an excursion to Stanleyville, Africa, where Betty wanted to buy some African art. "Bogie, Betty and I hired a boat to go up the river to have a look at some art in a village," Viertel said. "As we cast off from the dock, the guide went below to start the engine. When it didn't catch, he lit

155

a match. The fumes inside the hold exploded. The man leaped into the water and threw himself on the sand in agony. Meanwhile, the burning boat started to float down the river toward a river steamer.

"Bogie acted like a trained fireman. 'Pete, there's a fire extinguisher on the forward bulkhead. Get it.' I did, but it was empty. Bogie meanwhile managed to get to the wheel and steer us near enough to the steamer to throw them a line. We unloaded the women, then he stayed aboard to help put out the fire. In the moment of truth he had guts like Manolete."

Although in the retelling, Bogart's adventures seemed mostly concerned with his favorite beverage, he assured me once that the entire picture was a labor of love. "We loved those two silly people on that boat," he said. "And Katie, of course, was absolutely perfect."

Perfect as Miss Hepburn was, it was Bogart who got the Oscar this time. On the night he was announced as Best Actor for 1951, Bogart kissed Betty and jauntily walked up to the stage of the Pantages Theater. Once in front of the imposing audience of his peers, however, he fluffed his carefully prepared ad lib and stammered a polite thanks. Backstage in the press tent where Oscar winners are photographed and interviewed, he recovered his composure in time to proclaim that it was all bunk, that the only true test of ability would be to have all the actors don black tights and recite Hamlet. But there was a happy gleam in his eyes as he hefted the seven-pound, gold-plated $64 statuette which purports to prove that the recipient is the best film actor of the year.

That night at a party in Romanoff's upstairs Crown Room, Bogart was square again as he modestly acknowledged the toasts. "He was terribly pleased because he didn't think he would win," said Adolph Green, recalling that that was the year that saw Marlon Brando and Montgomery Clift set the two basic styles for modern acting in *A Streetcar Named Desire* and *A Place in the Sun.*

The next morning son Steve, then almost three years old, brought Bogie back to earth when he seized the Oscar and hurled it at his parent. Bogart spent the day relishing a spate of telegrams from such friends as Spencer Tracy, John O'Hara, Louis Bromfield, Henry Blanke, and Miss Hepburn. All the messages were properly derogatory.

"The way to survive an Oscar," Bogart told columnist Erskine Johnson a few days later, "is to never try to win another one. You've seen what happens to some Oscar winners. They spend the rest of their lives turning down scripts while searching for the great role to win another one. Hell, I hope I'm never even nominated again. It's meat-and-potatoes roles for me from now on."

The year 1951 was one of Bogie's most successful, but it was marred for him by the death of Mayo, at the age of forty-seven. According to the obituary notices of June 11, 1951, she died "after a lengthy illness."

The "lengthy illness" was a steady bout with alcoholism. When news of Mayo's death reached Bogart he was despondent for several days and sent his sister Pat to Oregon to console Mayo's mother, Evelyn Methot, a police reporter on a newspaper. Pat was to remain in Oregon for six months before returning to Hollywood.

CHAPTER 12

"Mine's bigger than yours."
—THE MALTESE FALCON

When Stephen Bogart was three years old the doctor came to examine him for a hernia. He had to probe to see whether an operation would be needed. He had Betty hold the boy's hands and Bogie his feet. Bogie winced with every probe, got pale, and said, "Better hurry, doctor, or I'll have to leave."

"He nearly passed out," recalled Betty, who said that Bogie never mentioned the incident to her again, but the next day she heard him on the telephone telling Nunnally Johnson that he should have seen Stephen, braver than a soldier. "His voice rang with pride that I had never imagined Bogie would feel. That night he went in while Steve was sleeping in his bed and looked at him for a long time saying nothing. Later, when the question of having another child came up, Bogie said he wanted one if I could guarantee another like Stephen."

Betty understood her husband well enough to know that in his own way he was saying he was agreeable to their having another baby. Later that year, when Bogie was fifty-four, Betty became pregnant again.

By then they had been married seven years, and

the balance of power in their relationship had begun to shift. In the beginning Bogie led and Betty followed. But as time went by and she gained assurance, she established her position as a wife as well as an individual in her own right.

During the 1952 election, Bogie was strong for Eisenhower, as was Betty. Together they went to Madison Square Garden to greet Ike on his return from Europe. Then when Adlai Stevenson was nominated for President, Betty saw him on television.

"I fell in love with him when I saw him make his acceptance speech at the convention," Betty remembers, "but I fell even more in love with him when I met him."

Betty first met Stevenson at a cocktail party in his honor at producer Dore Schary's house in Brentwood, attended by all the stars at MGM, where she was working. She asked screenwriter Allen Rivkin, director of the Hollywood for Stevenson Committee and an old friend of Bogie's, what she could do to help.

Rivkin told her that, for a beginning, he would like her to lend her name and support and appear at occasional rallies. And he asked about Bogart. "Leave him to me," said Betty, who began to win her husband over to Stevenson. She kept leaving Stevenson literature around the house where Bogie would come on it. She was careful never to knock Ike but kept quoting Stevenson. Soon, Bogie started to watch Stevenson on TV and study his speeches carefully, explaining, "I just want to know what the opposition is up to."

It was not to be an easy victory for Betty, however. One night Allen Rivkin and Mark Brandell, the novelist, drove to the Bogart house to pick up Betty and take her to a public appearance downtown. Brandell went to the door and told the butler he was there to pick up Mrs. Bogart and immediately returned to the car. "They are screaming and yelling in there," he reported. Twenty minutes later Betty came out of the house, furious. "That SOB," she said. "He didn't want me to go."

They arrived late at the stadium and the police had to escort Betty through the crowd. They found that Stevenson hadn't been introduced yet. "I wouldn't have started without you," he told Betty.

Finally, Bogie became interested in Stevenson. The changeover came the night Betty was going to greet Stevenson at the Cow Palace in San Francisco. Betty didn't ask Bogie for permission to go, which annoyed him. While she was getting packed he went into the bedroom and said, "You can tell them if they want me, I will go, too." Betty relayed the welcome information to the Stevenson forces and they went together, despite unofficial word circulating around Warner Brothers that any contract player coming out publicly for Stevenson was in danger of having his contract cancelled.

On the morning that the stars were to make their first appearance in San Francisco, Allen Rivkin went knocking at hotel room doors to be certain they all showed up for a nine o'clock breakfast with some influential people.

"I went around to the Bogart room and knocked on the door at about eight," he said. "No answer. I knocked again. Then Betty came to the door in the flimsiest of nightgowns. I said, 'Betty, it's time to get up and go.' She opened the door for me and Bogie came out of the bathroom holding a half tumbler full of Scotch. He shouted to her, 'What the hell are you exposing yourself to him for?' It was not an auspicious beginning for the day.

"Then we all had to go to a rally being held in an open space in front of the St. Francis Hotel, where there was a mob of people. As soon as they saw Bogart they started rushing him. He grabbed me and said, 'You gotta protect me, otherwise they'll kill me.'

" 'You're here to be seen and I'm not here to protect you,' I said. 'You protect yourself.' Bogie clung to me as we started to the platform, but after a few minutes he began to relax and enjoy himself.

"Afterwards, Bogie said to me, 'Let's go to lunch.

160

I've got a date with Herb Caen and I want you there.' I showed up at lunch with Betty and found there were twelve for lunch. It was a fine meal and afterwards Bogie handed the check to me."

Despite his recalcitrant behavior, Bogie became an ardent supporter of Stevenson, and soon he and Betty dropped everything else and went touring about the country on the Stevenson campaign train, taking bows at whistle stops in order to help draw larger crowds for his speeches.

The Bogarts were very influential in getting Stevenson support from their group of friends. Bogart never contributed money to the Stevenson campaign because, Rivkin believes, he probably figured rightly that he was giving his time and that was more than money could buy. They gave only one small dinner party at their home for some of Stevenson's Hollywood supporters.

"Bogie never seemed to give a damn for what people said or thought," Adlai Stevenson later told reporter (now director) Peter Bogdanovich. "And it was quite perilous in those days to be a Democrat, especially one partisan to me."

Alistair Cooke met the Bogarts on the Stevenson train. "Of course, Stevenson won't win," he said.

"What?" said Bogie.

"Not a prayer, I'm afraid," said Cooke.

"Why, you son of a bitch," said Betty, "that's a fine thing to say."

"Look," said Cooke, "I'm a reporter. You're the lieutenants."

The Bogarts bet Cooke $10 that Stevenson would win. When they lost, Bogart paid up, though he grumbled that he didn't think Cooke should take the money. "It's a hell of a guy who bets against his own principles," he said.

Betty thought that some of her propaganda about what a great man Stevenson was may have induced Bogie to change. "But," she said, "he was always his own man, and he made up his own mind long before

161

most other Hollywood people dared to come out for Stevenson."

"Betty was Bogie's political conscience," claims Rivkin. "If it hadn't been for her he probably wouldn't have done a thing other than go to Romanoff's for lunch and hold court."

Betty had not only become Bogie's political conscience, as Rivkin observed, but she also became strong enough intellectually so that he could trust her judgment and he came to depend on her more and more.

It would be easy to say that she had become the dominant one in their relationship, but although often described as ballsy, Betty was entirely feminine in adjusting to Bogie's needs. He needed her in a particular way and she fulfilled that need. He never had any real mothering and she had never had a father. So she became his mother and he became her father. The symbiotic relationship had a sound psychological foundation, and it worked.

Betty had changed in many other ways. As a model in New York when she didn't have money enough to buy originals she often bought showroom samples which she had worn and liked. Now that she had money enough to indulge her taste and elegant figure, she became a clothes horse. When *The African Queen* was completed she had Bogie stop in Paris enroute home long enough to see the fashion openings. It was there that she met Givenchy and Pierre Cardin. Most of her clothing in the 1950s came from those eminent houses although her taste was beginning to shift to the more simple lines of Norman Norell, who would become her favorite couturier. By 1952 she had already been on some "best-dressed woman" lists, and Bogie was proud of her taste, although he often complained that he could dress for a year on what she spent on one outfit.

Always a quick learner, she was beginning to mature into a woman of style in every direction. As Mrs. Humphrey Bogart she knew her social power, enjoyed it, and used it. Hollywood, in the Fifties, was populated by many of the most glamorous public figures in the world, either residents or passing through while making films.

The Bogarts were among the film community's social leaders, and rarely a day passed that their home was not crowded with celebrated guests. Among the frequent visitors were: Spencer Tracy and Katharine Hepburn, who had become their friends since *The African Queen*; actor David Niven and his wife, Hjordis; writer-director Nunnally Johnson; Adlai Stevenson, whom they had campaigned for, directors John Huston and Billy Wilder; agent Swifty Lazar, restaurateur Mike Romanoff and his wife, Alona; songwriter Jimmy Van Heusen; Frank Sinatra and writer-wit, Harry Kurnitz. Again, most of their friends were his friends.

But Betty was beginning to come into her own and had already developed a dramatic flair as a hostess. For example, the Bogarts frequently gave black-tie parties and served hot dogs and hamburgers, in contrast to most Hollywood parties which were dull, sit-down affairs. Soon theirs were the "in" parties among the Hollywood set because they were unusual and fun, and other hostesses began to emulate them.

With the advent of another child, as well as their increased social life, Betty decided it was time for them to move to a larger and more elegant home more suited to their position as social arbiters of the community. But Bogart was bitterly opposed to moving to a more elaborate establishment. He hated any kind of change, domestic or otherwise. To get her husband to do the things she wanted, Betty had developed a technique he admiringly called "the art of misdirection"—a refinement of the system she had used to interest him in Stevenson.

"The art of misdirection works like this," Betty said. "I knew that getting Bogie to move would be a long, hard battle, so I started asking him for a stainless steel stove. Some women want pickles, avocados or imported nuts when they're pregnant. I wanted a stainless steel stove, I told him. I couldn't cook on anything but a stainless steel stove; I couldn't eat meals that weren't cooked on one; the food tasted better on stainless stoves; they were easier to clean; and if I got one I would shut up.

"I got it. The next step was obvious. The kitchen was too small for the stove.

"Bogie needs a full-time secretary, and what with her, two kids, nurse, cook and steel stove, our kitchen was too small. Added to this, it didn't have enough closet space, and every woman knows how necessary that is.

"I started to leave brooms and pans lying around the kitchen. Bogie is a very neat and orderly person and when he'd ask why they weren't put away, I'd go into the closet routine.

"Slowly, I went through the rest of the house, room by room, pointing out flaws. Meanwhile, I started house-hunting on the sly. I looked at every available house and turned them all down for one reason or another. I knew if I was to get Bogie to move I'd have to have the perfect place—one without defects he could pounce upon.

"Everytime we'd visit friends who had lovely homes with nurseries I'd drag Bogie there and talk about the baby we were expecting and how it was going to need room to grow up.

" 'You grew up in a crowded New York apartment, two rooms and bath,' he'd say. 'There's nothing wrong with you.'

"At that point I'd say nothing and drop the subject. Later in the evening I'd get the conversation going about schools in the neighborhood. I'd mention, just in passing, of course, that there were no good private schools in our neighborhood and the children would probably have to grow up as morons.

Then one day, Betty found the house she was looking for. A fourteen-room, white-washed French Colonial-style mansion with a four-car garage, pool and a tennis court, on an acre of land—situated on Mapleton Drive in Holmby Hills, a narrow and exclusive strip of land between Beverly Hills and Bel Air. The price was $170,000 and the yearly taxes were higher than the average gross income.

Lana Turner lived on the street, as did Art Linkletter, Mr. and Mrs. (Judy Garland) Sid Luft and songwriter Sammy Cahn. Bogie had often said he would rather be caught dead than live there because ever since he had come to Hollywood he had consistently fought against "going Hollywood," which, to him, meant living up to one's income. He still believed it necessary to have F.Y. money in order to maintain his independence.

Betty knew it would be a tough fight to get him to move there, so she plotted a careful campaign. First, she started calling the Cahns and Lufts and other friends in the neighborhood—some of whom must have been surprised to hear from her since she hadn't called them in years. She wangled invitations to their home, and each time she and Bogie visited them she'd bring the subject around to the neighborhood and let them do the selling.

Meanwhile she was getting bigger daily. "I started bickering about where would we go from our present house. It was too small for more kids. Bogie said there would be no more. At the same time the rental agent began to breathe down my neck.

"I put some of my own money down on the house and decided to take Bogart by the horns. I cajoled him into going out to see it. He wasn't interested. It was too expensive and he was perfectly happy where he was.

"I finally pinned him down to admitting it was the cost of the house that bothered him most. Then I dropped my trump card. I had made out a list of things I could deprive myself of to get the house. I showed him how the rugs we had bought for the old house (which I had never let them lay because I knew we were going to move) could be cut to fit the new house. I promised to furnish very slowly and told him this was the house we could grow old in. We'd never have to move again.

"I began to clean up his argument about it being too expensive. When I had it washed dry, he was licked."

The stainless steel stove was the first item of furniture moved into the Holmby Hills house. One of the principal rooms downstairs was a white marble solarium with a glass façade opening onto the terrace overlooking the pool. The other was a huge, pine-paneled study with a bar and a huge fireplace and bookshelves up to the ceiling; for entertaining, this was to become the Bogart's favorite room.

They moved into the house in May 1952, and Betty, who was determined to slowly furnish the house herself, started with the den. Most of the Early American-style furniture worth saving from the old house was in this room. The tennis-court-size living room was the last room of the house she planned to furnish because she intended to take her time and make it a showplace.

The Bogarts' bedroom suite on the second floor had two rooms—a bedroom and a dressing room—all decorated in her favorite shade of blue. The curtains were white with blue fringe and the oversized bed they had built for the old house occupied a prominent place in the room. Betty liked the feel of luxury, and the sheets were of blue silk, with blue pillows and comforters. Their initials, "B & B," were on all the towels in theirs and the guest baths. Around the room were half a dozen photos of Betty, most taken since she had come to Hollywood, and several of her and Bogie.

Stephen's room was on the same floor, and adjacent to it was a room which was soon to be used as a nursery for their second child.

CHAPTER 13

"You can insult me just as well face to face. I don't bite much."
—THE BIG SLEEP

On August 23, 1952, after being in labor two hours, Betty gave birth to a six-pound five-ounce daughter, christened Leslie Howard Bogart. The first time Betty got up from bed after giving birth to Leslie, Bogie sent her some flowers and a wire reading, "I like Ike and I love you."

The birth of a daughter was something very special to Bogie, as it is to most men. He was afraid of her at first, even nervous about holding her in his arms, but gradually he realized that although she was a female, she was also his.

"I've finally begun to understand why men carry pictures of their children with them," he told a reporter at Romanoff's, adding needlessly, "They're proud of them."

"After the birth of the children you could see Bogart beginning to mellow," said Mary Baker, a frequent visitor to the house.

Before marrying Betty, Bogie had been standoffish with people because, Betty discovered, he feared he would offer affection and be rejected; a throwback to his childhood. Betty worked on him patiently, telling

167

him that he was making the same mistake with his children that his parents had made with him. "You only get back from children as much love as you give them," she said.

Bogie began to realize that not only did Stephen need him but he loved him. And Bogie began to give love in return, first to Stephen who was then five and, later, to Leslie was still an infant.

It was not unusual to go to the Bogart home and see him in the backyard in the children's play area pushing five-year-old Stephen on a swing or teaching him how to catch and throw a ball, complaining all the while that he was too old for such nonsense, but doing it and enjoying it.

"Bogie rarely cried," Betty told me. "But on the morning he first drove Stephen to nursery school and left him there he came home with tears in his eyes. The impact of fatherhood and the awareness that Stephen was growing up got to him all at once."

Meanwhile, Betty, who had never been trained to run a large household staff, was busy most of the time at home. Not only did she have the children and Leslie's nurse to be concerned with but she also had five other people on her regular house-staff payroll, including Kathleen Sloan, Bogie's secretary, who handled their fan mail and Bogie's voluminous correspondence. His contacts around the world were extraordinary, and he corresponded regularly with Harold Laski and Justice Holmes. Betty also had to be concerned with extra help such as gardeners and handymen.

Every morning after feeding Leslie herself she organized breakfast for Stephen, who was going to a local nursery school. Then she laid out a work sheet so that everyone in the house was usefully occupied. Although Bogie liked simple meals, she went to pains to be certain that he had the best cuts of steak and often went to the meat market herself. Most of the other shopping was done by the cook over the telephone.

Betty's goal was to run the house so efficiently that Bogie was never bothered with household problems.

He left it up to her to run the house and manage the children, and he expected things to go smoothly. When faced with a household crisis such as a trouble with the plumbing his standard retort was, "I never wanted this house. You did. You take care of it."

Betty had more than the house to cope with. She also had to cope with Bogie, who, when he was not working and the children were away at school, was bored. He didn't know what to do with himself. "Unfortunately, I got him at a bad time," Betty was to tell a friend. "He had already gone through the golf stage and other pastimes that men acquire, then give up. He had discarded them all and was left with nothing except the boat, but it was a long drive to the marina and a hassle to get a crew together so he finally hired a captain to live aboard and be ready to shove off at a moment's notice."

When he was at home and not working, Bogie gave the appearance of being prepared to take off for the boat at any moment. His uniform was a white jump suit made of terrycloth, topped off by his weatherbeaten captain's cap. His feet were invariably encased in tassled moccasins.

But he rarely went out on the boat during the week. He felt that, as a family man, he belonged at home, a concession he modified when not working by spending two or three hours at lunch at Romanoff's gabbing with his cronies. "This is my recreation," he told reporter David Hanna. "I like to sit around and gab, enjoy my drinks and my family. That's what a man wants when he gets over fifty. Drinking never caused me any harm and I think I'm a damn good father." After leaving Romanoff's Bogie would return home and take a nap, leaving it up to Betty to keep the children occupied and quiet. By the time he woke up it was the hour to have a before-dinner drink and get ready to eat.

Bogie disliked dressing up, even for guests, and was almost totally uninterested in clothing. Although he had his suits made, he left it up to Betty as another one of her chores to pick out the colors and fabrics. She also bought his shirts, ties, socks, pajamas and other furnishings.

Betty thrived on her domestic life and preferred her role as contented mother and wife to her role as an actress. Just before Stephen was born she made *Bright Leaf* opposite Gary Cooper. During the three years between Stephen's birth and Leslie's she had turned down six films.

Most evenings when Bogie wasn't working and the children were asleep the Bogarts had a kind of endless open house. There was a light above the front door visible from the street. When it was switched on, it meant they were staying up, drinking, and not averse to having friends join them. Sometimes, for five nights in a row, they'd have a crowd in, people like Judy Garland and husband Sid Luft, who were neighbors, the songwriting-composing team of Betty Comden and Adolph Green, the Romanoffs, the Nivens, writer Nunnally Johnson, songwriter Jimmy Van Heusen, Swifty Lazar, Frank Sinatra and John Huston, who would recall that "their hospitality went far beyond food and drink. They fed a guest's spirit as well as his body, plied him with good will until he became drunk in the heart as well as the legs."

Although much of their social life was involved with drinking, Bogie had cut down considerably his consumption of Scotch thanks to Betty's influence.

"His insecurity was what made Bogie a big drinker," Betty was to say at this time. "Now that he has realized that he has security—emotional as well as professional—he confines his drinking to social amenities and has found he can be without a drink in hand for a prop."

Her secret for keeping him from drinking too much was never to nag at him. "Instead I used to ignore him, a trick he soon discovered, and for a while he'd do everything but fall flat on his face to get me to pay him some attention.

170

"I knew better than to try and outdrink him or stay up with him. That would have been a physical impossibility for most men, let alone a woman.

"Also, I never tried to bawl him out that night or the next morning. When he is hungover it's a waste of time to talk with him because he just doesn't hear. I'd wait until he was dead sober, then go about telling him what an ass he made of himself the night before. He didn't like to hear such things when he was sober, and gradually the sober intervals became more frequent."

Despite the fact that he had cut down his drinking, Bogie still liked to give people the impression he was a boozer. Nunnally Johnson was with Bogie many times at his home when the doorbell rang and Bogie would pick up a glass just to answer the door. "He couldn't have been as good at his job if he drank as much as he was supposed to have," Johnson said.

Although Betty had had a restraining influence on most of Bogie's behavior, she could never get him out of his habit of needling Hollywood people at parties.

To Bogie, needling was an exercise of the mind as well as of the spirit. And if practice makes perfect, he was expert at it. Most of his friends agree that his pattern of insulting and needling both friends and foes began when he arrived in Hollywood, because he felt Hollywood people were, for the most part, pompous phonies. "Bigwigs have been known to stay away from the brilliant Hollywood occasions rather than expose their swelling neck muscles to Bogart's banderillas," said John Huston.

"Bogie could be pretty exasperating at times," Nunnally Johnson said. "He never stopped thinking how he could stir things up a little. I don't think it was an act—it was natural in Bogie. He was an ingrained mischief-maker like Scaramouche, the mischievious scamp who sets off the fireworks, then nips out."

In Johnson's opinion, Bogie demonstrated social brinkmanship on its highest level. "He had dozens of

171

ingenious ways of avoiding disaster," Johnson said. "It really was an art. His psychological timing was perfect."

One day when Johnson was with Bogie and Betty, she gave Bogart a fierce bawling out for his behavior at a party the previous night. He had needled Rock Hudson about his first name, suggesting that a new star would come along named Dung Heap and knock Rock on his Butt End—". . . and there's another name you might adopt."

"Who the hell do you think you are, Bogart?" Betty said. "You might have had your neck broken."

"Easy, easy, old girl," he said soothingly. "I wish you would realize that there is a real art in getting this close to calamity."

Certainly Bogie knew when his needling would precipitate violence, and he almost always pulled up just short of it. But, if things got rough, he had ways of handling that, too. "I have two rules for fighting," he once told me over lunch at Romanoff's. "First, any time a guy wants to start a fight in a club, be sure there's a big head waiter around. Hit the guy first, then get near the waiter who will stop the fight.

"Second, and equally important: never step outside."

Harry Kurnitz, who was present at many of Bogart's near brawls, agreed that he followed his rules closely. "Bogie's animosity and arrogance ranged in direct ratio to the number of people holding him back," Kurnitz said. "The truth is, I believe, that Bogart lived his whole life without ever having been in a fight."

Bogie always seemed able to avoid a real, knock-down fight, and often referred to himself as a physical coward—which he wasn't—and once said he hated the sight of blood. "My father was a doctor, and I saw too much of it in his office when I was a child."

A typical Bogart brawl, illustrating both his debating style and his sense of self-preservation, occurred one night at a party at actor Louis Calhern's house.

Bogie overheard an argument director Norman Panama was having with agent Paul Small—who was not aptly named: he was big.

Panama was saying that he thought Danny Kaye was the greatest talent in show business. Small said he wasn't, that comic Lenny Kent was the greatest.

At this point Bogart entered the conversation. "What would you know about it, you tub of lard?" he asked Small.

The agent angrily grabbed Bogart's wrist.

Bogart looked around the room and saw that the host was coming to the rescue. He snarled, "Let go of that wrist or I'll let you have this glass in the face."

Small held on. Just as Calhern, a big man, reached the group, Bogart heaved the glassful of liquor at Small, who ducked. The liquor splashed on Mrs. Small, Dore Schary's sister. Betty screamed, as did Mrs. Small, Calhern separated the combatants. Once again Bogie had looked tough, as fearless as any screen hero—and had gotten away with it.

Another time Bogart figured a great excuse for following his rule number two. At a party at the home of Milton Bren and his actress wife, Claire Trevor, he was almost falling down drunk and was enlivening things by needling the host and other guests with too much vulgarity to suit Bren, who finally said, "Cut it out, Bogie."

Bogie kept it up. "I'm damn sick of your vulgarity," Milton said. "Step outside with me—I'm going to knock the hell out of you."

"Sure, I will," said Bogart. "Just help me up, please." Everybody broke up—Bogart's superb brinkmanship had won the day as it did on the afternoon Sid Luft and Judy Garland came to his house to pour out their family troubles.

Richard Burton recalled the afternoon. "Bogie told Sid and Judy to get out, stay out and never come back, that he was fed up with their problems. He added a few choice epithets and ended by admonishing Sid 'to take that dull wife of yours with you.'

173

" 'I've got a good mind to bust your face in,' growled Luft, a husky man who once had been a test pilot.

"Bogart backed off a few steps, grinned and said, 'Sid, you won't lay a hand on me.'

"Nonplussed, Luft stopped a haymaker in midair to ask, 'Why not?'

" 'Because, Sid, you're my friend,' Bogart said gently.

"It was a magnificent moment," Burton reported.

Arms around each other, Bogart and Luft strolled over to his bar, raised glasses, and the incident was closed.

Swifty Lazar recalls a night when Bogie's needling was for real: he was jealous. The incident took place at a party in honor of the Shah of Iran given at writer Charles Lederer's home. The Shah, an extremely handsome man, had danced three times with Betty, who was staring up at him, almost enraptured.

Bogie watched from the sidelines, absolutely glowering, suddenly he brushed past the Shah's body guards and halted the dance. "Shah, baby," Bogie said. "You just can't keep dancing with my wife, because she's going to be overimpressed. You want some broads, tell me, I can handle your action. What kind of broads do you want?"

The Shah was rigid. "Sir?" he asked, not believing what he had heard.

But Bogie did not let up. "Shah, baby, this is the third dance and my wife is going to get home tired. You want broads, speak up."

"The whole party cleared out after that," said Lazar.

Betty never gave Bogie any real cause for jealousy, however. "She was a one-man woman," a close friend of hers said. "If Bogie was ever jealous of anything, it was of the time she spent away from him. But he kept that to himself. He was wise enough to give her her freedom so that even though she was tied down much of the time with the children she still had the feeling she could do what she wanted to do."

Considering the difference in their ages, it is

174

remarkable that Betty was never interested in another man from the age of nineteen when she first met Bogie. But, as she was to say in a *Look* article, she never liked young men and was always attracted to older men because they knew how to treat and appreciate a woman.

Betty also knew that Bogie would not tolerate her going out on him because, in his view, that was tantamount to lying. "The one thing he could never forgive was a lie," she was to say. "He said if you tell a lie your character has been damaged and if you lose character you have nothing. He always felt that no matter how much he loved me, if I had ever done anything wrong, that would have been the end. He said to me always, 'If you ever meet anyone and want to take off, don't do it behind my back. Come to me and tell me. If you did anything dishonest, I'd never like you again and I never want to stop liking you.' He believed liking somebody is much more important than loving them."

Betty allowed Bogie the same freedom that he permitted her. One night while they were in Rome enroute to the location of *The African Queen* they met Howard Hawks, who was also in Italy making a film. "We had a few drinks and walked home on the Via Veneto where there were always a bunch of good-looking prostitutes hanging around," said Hawks. "Some of the girls recognized Bogie and started to talk to him. Betty and I kept on walking to the hotel and, when he came in fifteen minutes later, instead of being angry with him she asked, 'Did you have a good time?'

"I couldn't help contrasting her attitude with what Mayo's would have been in the same situation. Mayo would have torn into him and accused him of going off with one of the girls."

Occasionally at parties when Bogie had had too much to drink Betty would step in and, as she put it, "make myself known." She even told certain ladies off if they were persistent in their attentions, making it plain she was not above making a scene if necessary. "Bogie dislikes scenes and he has no heart for the chase anyway, so the problem of other women doesn't exist," she said.

Swifty Lazar believes that Bogie had no ambivalence about his affection for Betty. "He was married and he didn't know about that other nonsense," Lazar said. "He'd kid around and be outrageous, but he never flirted.

"Actually he would run for the hills if a girl made a pass at him. I've been with Bogie in Las Vegas when girls came up and said to him, 'I'll meet you later,' and he was petrified. I don't think Bogie ever had an affair with a woman other than the women he was married to or was going to marry."

CHAPTER 14

*"How long do you suppose since we've
said or done anything about ourselves
that hasn't been said or done before? Or
thought a new thought?"*
—THE BAREFOOT CONTESSA

In 1952 the Bogarts were Hollywood's royalty, which
is tantamount to saying they were world royalty.
Movies were at the peak of their influence and popularity and the appellation "star" implied glamor,
excitement and romance, unlike today, when it is
applied to any actor whose name comes before the
title of a film. Men cupped their cigarettes with four
fingers as Bogart did. Women tried to emulate Betty's
deep voice. Crowds followed them on Fifth Avenue
during their visits to New York. Police had to rope off
the entrance of the Gotham Hotel to hold back the
surging, swooning fans who literally camped on the
streets just to catch a glimpse of the world-famous
couple.

In Hollywood, which was really like a small one-
industry community in which everyone is involved in
the same business, the Bogarts, like royalty, had
knights, court jesters, footmen, servants and their own
games to while away boredom when they weren't
involved in pageantry; film-making. The moat which
separated them from the populace was composed of
press agents, unlisted phones and their celebrity

status. They even had a Round Table and a castle where they foregathered most every day belonging to Prince Michael Romanoff, proprietor of a restaurant he had named after himself in Beverly Hills.

The late Michael Romanoff was one of the most colorful figures in Hollywood. He was neither a prince, nor was his real name Romanoff. His antecedents were vague, but certainly not royal, and it is hard to believe that in his younger days he made a successful career of posing as His Imperial Highness, the Prince Michael Alexandrovitch Dmitri Obolensky Romanoff, nephew of the last of the czars. Phony prince or not, Mike was beloved by the ultra-snobbish film crowd which actually accepted him as its social arbiter.

"I like Romanoff's because it's the only place to go," Bogart told reporter Ezra Goodman. "I like Mike very, very much. He is a very entertaining, interesting and kind man, a civilized citizen. I can meet my friends here. It's kind of like a club."

A gag of which Bogie never tired was to sit at Romanoff's and con one of his friends into picking up a big luncheon check. This was not meanness or avarice on his part. It was part of a game to drive away the boredom when he was not working. And it was a game Betty often joined.

From many interviews with the Bogarts there, marinated with nostalgia and with the help of screenwriter Peter Viertel's ear for dialogue, it is possible to reconstruct one of these Romanoff luncheon sessions which were so much a part of the Bogarts' Hollywood life.

On this day the Bogarts arrived together at the entrance to the main dining room where they are greeted by maître d' Kurt Nicklas, who exchanges a joke with Bogie and kisses Betty on both cheeks. Kurt leads them to the first booth to the left of the entrance, a booth reserved for the Bogarts, comedian Robert Benchley or English actors Herbert Marshall and Sir Cedric Hardwicke. Of the group, only the Bogarts were ever in Hollywood for any length of time so the booth was virtually theirs. A plaque had been put on the wall over the booth with the names of the people allowed to sit there.

The Bogarts' arrival caused a stir among the tourists who were selected discriminately by Kurt and placed against the far wall where they could see but not be heard. The lunch regulars—Jack Benny, Peter Lawford, Frank Sinatra, Gary Cooper and Groucho Marx —acknowledged the Bogarts' arrival with smiles and waves but continued with their eating.

Because Betty is with him, Bogart is well dressed in gray flannels and a black cashmere jacket with a neat checked bow tie. Betty is wearing the latest in elegant Paris fashion.

Once they settled into the booth Bogie announces to Betty, "Swifty will pay for lunch today," referring to Irving Paul Lazar, the literary agent who has a lunch date with the Bogarts but is, as yet, unaware that it will be his treat.

When the Bogarts are seated, Romanoff comes over to greet them, moving as he speaks, slowly and carefully. He is a small man with an incongruous "butch" haircut which gives his genial face a military look, and his clothes are frantically dapper—a very English blazer, flannels and bench-made shoes.

"Hello, my darling Betty," Romanoff says in a faultless, cultivated Oxford accent as he kisses her proffered cheeks, one after the other. "I see you're still with the same aging actor."

"I can't live without him," says Betty.

"Good morning, your royal phoniness," says Bogart with obvious affection.

"It may be morning to you, but it's afternoon to working people," says Romanoff who starts to move off.

"Join us in a drink, Mike?" asks Bogart.

Romanoff, who will not sit down unless invited, settles next to Bogart. "I should be most honored to do so," he says, in the formal manner he affects.

At that moment Swifty, who is also known as "Ipl"

179

(as in "ripple"), has entered the restaurant and is talking with Kurt. Swifty is as short as Romanoff but built like a miniature fullback. He has a smooth, cherubic face. The late Richard Gehman once wrote that Swifty was destined to go down in history as the most preposterously successful Hollywood literary agent of all time, and one of the most delightfully preposterous characters in a community where preposterousness is well-nigh obligatory. (Gehman's prophecy was accurate: in 1974 Lazar would ask for $2,000,000 for President Richard Nixon's memoirs.)

Swifty follows the Hollywood practice of kissing Betty on both cheeks, a greeting once reserved by European royalty for equals. A less important person than Betty would have been kissed on one cheek only.

"Hello, my love," says Betty.

"Here's our host! Hya, Swifty," says Bogart.

"I thought you asked me for lunch," says Swifty, as he shakes hands with Romanoff, exposes his shirt cuffs, and neatly adjusts the creases on his trousers prior to sitting down.

"Did I?" asks Bogart with surprise. "Well, then, it's Mike's check. He should pay anyway, after what he's been saying about you . . . that you wouldn't have been at this table if you weren't dining with us even though you are one of the best customers this joint has. What do you think of that?"

"That's a lie," says Romanoff calmly, carefully selecting a filtered cigarette from a solid gold cigarette case with his "family" crest which matches his solid gold Dunhill lighter.

"I don't care if it's a lie or not, I shall be delighted to pay," says Swifty cheerfully.

Bogart, who has been listening carefully for just these words but has been pretending to be unconcerned, suddenly excuses himself to go say hello to Judy Garland and her husband, Sid Luft, who had just come in.

Bogart halts the Lufts enroute to their own table.

"Hiya, Bogie, what's new?" says Luft, who has spent the previous evening getting drunk with Bogart.

"Good afternoon," says Bogie, bowing formally to Miss Garland. (He does not favor the double cheek kissing routine.) "I wondered if you would join us for lunch?"

The Lufts look toward the Bogart table and see Swifty, who waves rather painfully. "Swifty's buying again," says Sid Luft.

"That's right," says Bogart.

"I don't think the joke's funny anymore," says Judy. "It's getting too old."

"Sure it is," says Bogart, "but it's the only joke we've got."

Back at the table Mrs. Bogart watches the Lufts and Bogie threading their way around tables, pausing to shake hands and acknowledge greetings, but obviously making a course for the Bogart booth.

"He's asked them over," she says.

"And I'm astonished to see they've accepted," says Romanoff.

"Well, what difference does it make," says Swifty. "Let him have his fun. When the check comes I'll sign his name."

This news does not please Mike, who says in a somewhat hollow voice, "Let's not have a row, that's all I ask."

"I'll not have a row with Bogie," Swifty promises. "He's my pal. Anyway, he doesn't believe in fighting anymore. He's a new man since he married Betty." Swifty follows his compliment with a slight bow but gives away the fact that he is irritated by exchanging the Ben Franklin-type half-glasses on his nose for an identical pair which he takes from an inner coat pocket.

Betty acknowledges the compliment with a smile, then sighs at the sight of her husband with the Lufts in tow. "What a charmer," she says. "He doesn't remember we have an interview here in half an hour."

As the Lufts settle themselves into the booth, Bogart explains to Swifty, "I told them that you insisted we all have lunch together."

"We really didn't want to barge in," says Luft, "but Bogie said you'd be sore if we said no."

"Delighted," says Swifty, trying to be genial. "Be my guests."

"The table is too small, Bogie," complains Betty.

"That's Mike's fault. Don't blame me," says Bogart.

Kurt, whose professional gaze has taken in the entire incident, unhappily asks if everyone is dining at one booth.

"That's right," said Bogart, grinning as he meets the angry gaze of his spouse.

Everyone squeezes right around the circular table, but it is not large enough. Kurt brings a chair for the host who now has to sit in the traffic outside of the crowded booth.

"Somehow we never manage to have a quiet lunch with you, Swifty," says Bogart cheerfully. "I don't know what it is. You don't plan ahead."

Romanoff, who is being edged out of the booth, rises. "If you'll excuse me," he says stiffly, "someone important has just come into the pub."

"Have them join us," says Bogart.

Kurt tries to make order of the chaos and finally manages to distribute the menus.

Swifty has been stiffed: Bogart has managed to fill the booth and the bill will be large. Swifty's face is angry, but Bogart is chuckling happily as he surveys his little kingdom.

At 1:30, when I arrived for my interview, Bogart and Bacall were alone. "It's too peaceful around here," Bogie complained. "Can't get in a good fight anymore. There's no more controversy."

Miss Bacall smiled and rolled her eyes ceilingward. "You came just a little too late, Joe," she said. "Bogie was doing his best to liven things up for you."

Bogie, who was looking thoughtfully at his Drambuic, turned to me and said tentatively, "You know, motion picture directing is a highly overrated job. It's not difficult. Anyone could do it."

"Oh, no," said Betty. She foresaw how many friends this line would make.

"Go on," I said.

"It takes no talent to direct a film," continued Bogart. "The popular notion that directors rehearse lines and tell actors how to read them is nonsense. For example, while we were filming *We're No Angels* at Paramount, I heard Mike Curtiz go up to Aldo Ray and say, 'When you smile you're a good actor. When you don't smile, you stink.' Is that directing?"

I took my note pad out and started to scribble. "I'm with you," I said.

Bogart pushed his drink aside. "The trouble is most critics can't tell the difference between a bad script, a bad actor and a bad director. What burns me up is that when the actor is good, the director gets the credit, and when the actor is bad it's the actor who stinks. If he's bad, why not blame the director?

"Take Marlon Brando, for example. He was good in *Streetcar* and *Waterfront* and Elia Kazan got the credit. Brando's been good in other things, too. He's bad only with a bad director."

"What do you think of producers?" I asked.

"In twenty years in Hollywood I've never been able to figure out what they do. I suppose they give the Green Light. After they flash it they ought to go on a fishing trip until the picture is over. Everything would still end up fine."

Bogart paused to watch me scribble. "How're we doing?" he asked.

"We need a little more about directors," I said. "We can end with the quote about producers."

"There are only ten good directors in Hollywood," said Bogart. "There's John Huston, William Wyler, William Wilder, Edward Dmytryk and John Ford, who's an in-and-outer. Wyler isn't sure of what he wants but invariably he gets it. Dmytryk and the others know what they want and go after it. But most directors don't know what they want and wouldn't know if it was good anyway."

"Who are the other five good directors?" I asked.

"I can't think of them at the moment," Bogart retorted. "Anyway, why let five more men get swelled heads? Besides, I have to have someone to talk to at Romanoff's."

I made a mental calculation of the words I needed for a column and estimated that I had enough. "I think it'll work," I said to Bogart, who went back to his drink, a pleased grin on his face.

"Now it's your turn, Betty," Bogie said. Nudging me under the table, he added, "Betty's going to be immortalized—she's putting her footprints in Grauman's Chinese Theater next week."

"Congratulations," I said.

"Thank you," said Betty.

Bogart ignored the polite exchange and continued, "It used to be an honor—it was at least back in 1946 when I did it—but it doesn't mean a thing anymore. It's just a publicity stunt for every starlet. It's no honor."

Betty looked a trifle pained but bravely picked up the thread of her husband's conversation. "You're right, I guess," she said. "They ask most everyone."

Bogie looked triumphant. "It's time someone spoke out about this phony practice," he said, his meaning all too clear.

"This is a very tricky area you're steering Betty into," I said. "Grauman's is an institution."

"Well, I don't know about that," said Betty, warming to the subject. "Before I came to Hollywood, Grauman's Chinese was something very special to me. It meant not only achievement but it was the hall of fame of the motion picture industry, and the people in it were unforgettables and irreplaceables. I don't think of myself as either."

Bogart smiled on his spouse proudly and shoved my

note pad under my nose. "You're not taking it down," he said.

Needled to the point of action, Betty, at Bogie's suggestion, went into Romanoff's accounting room and, borrowing a typewriter, wrote out a statement explaining why she would not put her footprints in the cement forecourt of Grauman's Chinese Theater.

She returned fifteen minutes later and read the statement to us. Bogie nodded approvingly, suggested a few minor changes, and gave it to me.

"I guess I've blown my chance at immortality," Betty said as I pocketed her statement.

"It's time someone spoke out," said Bogie happily.

The joint interview was over. Typical of all my interviews with the Bogarts, either alone or together, it was fun to do as well as fun to read.

None of the Bogarts' friends stopped by our table to kid around or say good-bye. Bogart would not have tolerated any interruption. When he gave an interview he was as coolly professional as on the set. "If I'm going to spend my time talking to someone for publication, it's as much my job as standing in front of the cameras," he told me. "And I work just as hard at it."

It was 3:30 in the afternoon and the main dining room was empty when Mike came by the table to show Bogie the luncheon bill. It was for $96.00.

"Note here," said Mike, pointing to the signature.

Swifty had signed: "Humphrey Bogart."

Bogie laughed. "It's a forgery, Mike, and you know it," he said.

"All I know is that it says 'Humphrey Bogart,' and that's who is going to get the bill," said Mike.

"Anyone can come in here and sign my name and I get the bill, is that what you're saying?" said Bogie.

Mike said nothing but there was an amused gleam in his eyes.

"Then I'll sign Swifty's name to the tab next time," said Bogie gleefully—as he initialed the bill: "O.K. H.B."

It was all pretty childish stuff, of course, and Bogart knew it, but it was an activity of the mind. That and the fact that he and Betty had done interviews at the same time made it an enjoyable tax-deductible afternoon.

CHAPTER 15

"When the head says one thing and a lifetime says another, the head always loses."

—KEY LARGO

One night in 1953, Bogie, John Huston and some other friends were shooting the breeze rather tipsily about life and its meaning and the question arose as to whether there was any time of their lives they'd like to live over again. All of them except Bogie came up with cynical answers. Somebody said, "God forbid." Somebody else: that he'd only like to cancel out a couple of times. Then Bogie spoke. "Yes," he said. "There's a time I'd like to relive—the years that I have had with Betty."

After nearly eight years of marriage Bogie was more in love with Betty than he had ever thought possible. Over those few years they had almost blended into a single human being. They had the same outlook, liked the same people, and laughed at the same things. Furthermore, they were on the same wavelength and each could sense what the other was thinking even before the thought was given voice.

They had overcome one of the biggest hurdles of a marriage between two people with such a vast age difference. The older spouse generally remains the same while the younger one changes. But Betty had kept Bogie young. "It would have been a big mistake for me to have tried to become old to catch up with him. It was much wiser and better for him to adjust in the direction of youth."

That was the secret of their marriage: she constantly made him feel as if he were still a young man in love with a young girl.

The Bogarts at home and in public behaved much like the sophisticated couple in *The Thin Man* books, but beneath their dry, tart repartee with one another lay the fact that they refused to take themselves too seriously. Undoubtedly they developed some murderous tensions. Bogie still had a hairtrigger temper, but almost never exercised it on Betty. She had a quick temper, too, but learned to control it. There were exceptions.

One afternoon he was showing Mary Baker some new construction work that had been done in the bedroom when he opened a sliding door in Betty's closet, a place he rarely entered. There, in the closet, he saw sweaters of all kinds wrapped neatly and filed in order of color in a stack that reached from floor to ceiling.

"My God, look at what the bitch has here," he said to Mary. "She must have one of each sweater Saks sells."

He rushed downstairs for a confrontation with Betty, who quietly explained that she had had some of the sweaters since before they were married. Bogie began to calm down. "And I bought a lot of these with my own money," she continued. Bogie gave her a pained smile. Then Betty followed up with the clincher. "And you do like me in sweaters, don't you, darling?"

Bogie left the room and the subject was closed.

On another occasion I sat in Romanoff's with Bogie waiting for Betty, who was due at 12:30 and was always prompt. At 12:35, I sensed that Bogie was getting edgy. By 12:45 the line of his jaw was taut and he was nervously glancing from his watch to the entrance. By the time Betty arrived at 12:50 he was in a fury. As she started to come toward our table he got up and walked right past her without saying a word.

Betty turned around and went after him. She found Bogie standing alone in Mike Romanoff's office. "What's the matter?" she asked.

"Where the hell were you?"

"I'm sorry, honey," she said. "I know I'm late but we couldn't get the car started. Something was wrong with the battery and Aurilio had to drive me here."

"You could have called."

"I know I could have and should have but I thought we'd get going at any moment. Now what's really the matter?"

"I thought something had happened to you," Bogie admitted and took her in his arms.

Bogart was equally tender with his children but less demonstrative, possibly because he was still somewhat in awe of them or, possibly, because they were still too young for him to feel able to communicate with them. In any event, Leslie was still an infant tended by nurses and watched over carefully by Betty. Most often when he was working, he returned home after her bedtime and tiptoed carefully into the nursery, where he kissed her good night.

He was reticent about showing outward affection toward Steve, probably a throwback to his own childhood with undemonstrative parents. I was with him one day when he was with Steve. "I don't know," Bogie told me. "I guess maybe I had the kid too late in life. I just don't know what to do about him." Then, kind of shamefacedly, he said, "But I love him. I hope he knows that."

As Steve began to grow up, Bogie found it easier to display the affection and pride he felt for his son.

Soon after Leslie was born, Bogie announced to Betty that it was time for Stephen to "take his place among men. He's grown up enough now."

Although Betty feared that Stephen who was only five would probably be bored she was delighted that her husband wanted to take their son on an outing.

189

So she dressed Stephen in a new suit, with long pants, shirt and tie.

When he was neat as an Eton soprano, she brought him downstairs to see Bogie, who gave him a critical once-over, straightened the knot in his tie, and gave him a firm pat on the head and then led him by the hand out the door to his gray Jaguar XK 140 convertible which Aurilio, the houseman, had parked in the driveway.

Bogie got in on the driver's side, then waited impatiently for Stephen to fumble with the doorknob on the other side.

When they arrived at Romanoff's, Bogie proudly introduced Stephen to everyone he knew and then took his usual booth to the left of the entrance, Stephen next to him.

"Be a good boy," he said, and went about the business of preparing for lunch, a prescribed ritual which included a martini with everyone who came by to admire Stephen.

Stephen, undoubtedly happy and proud to be with his parent, who knew everyone and was obviously liked and respected by everyone, manfully sat straight and quiet until the eighth martini when he began to get restless and Bogie was ready for lunch. To the boy's credit he had waited patiently for some time but, by then, he began stamping on the seat and pounding the glassware with a fork.

Bogie tried in vain to calm Stephen down, first trying cajolery and then threats. Now that Stephen had his father's full attention, however, he became even crankier. Bogie soon realized that the boy was not only bored, he was probably tired.

By the time they returned home, father and son were not speaking to each other and Bogie stormed into the house announcing to Betty, "Never again."

But the excursion was to be repeated again until Stephen, finally, got to look forward to it just as he did weekends with Bogie on the *Santana*. Stephen liked to sail with his father, and Bogie liked having him aboard. His dream was that one day Stephen would have as much respect and affection for the sea as he had. Bogie was training his son as his own father had trained him at the same age. By the time he was five Stephen could handle a small sailboat skillfully.

Bogie was delighted by Stephen's skill, but, at the same time, he was saddened by the fact that there was so much he wanted to teach his son and so little time to do it. Although only fifty-four years old, Bogie had always feared that he would die early; his father had died at fifty-five. As a result he seemed to have an obsession about leaving an estate behind for Betty and the children.

"He had the occupational insecurity of most actors," Betty told me. "He was always talking about 'something to leave' for me and the kids. For that reason nearly all the picture deals he made were negotiated with that in mind. He felt he must amass a legacy."

With the passing years Bogie had become increasingly aware of the dignity of his profession. Actor, not star. Actor. He never took himself too seriously, but he always took his work most seriously. He regarded the somewhat gaudy figure of Bogart, the star, with an amused cynicism. Bogart, the actor, he held in deep respect.

His professionalism and sense of what was real and what was phony had rubbed off on Betty, who, during eight years, made only five pictures at Warners and turned down twelve because she felt they were wrong for her. It was more important for her to be with her family than to just work, and, in 1950, she had bought her contract from Warners.

While Betty's career was almost at a standstill, Bogie's was at its zenith. In September 1953, Bogie asked Warners to set him free of the fifteen year, one picture annually contract he had signed just after marrying Betty in 1946. Although he was paid $200,000 a picture and had the right of script approval, he and the studio had not been able to come to terms on a story since *The Enforcer*, a routine melodrama made in 1950, and he didn't want to hold himself available to Warners for six months a year for the following eight years.

Those were the days when many top stars had gotten into independent production because, that way, they owned a share of the picture's profits which could be spread out over a period of years thus lessening the income tax bite.

Bogie had made four pictures for his own company, Santana: *Knock on Any Door, Tokyo Joe, In a Lonely Place* and *Sirocco*. After Warners agreed to the parting, Bogie decided to make *Beat the Devil* for Santana. The film about the leader of a gang of scoundrels who are trying to get hold of some uranium money in Africa was to be made in Rome and directed by John Huston.

At almost the same time Betty was approached by writer-director Nunnally Johnson to star in *How to Marry a Millionaire*, a 20th-Century Fox comedy with a cast which included Betty Grable and Marilyn Monroe.

Bogart was distraught. He wanted Betty with him on location in Italy but he felt it would be selfish of him to ask her to give up the best role she had been offered in years. When she promised to visit him on location when her picture ended he agreed that she should do it.

On the day Bogart was to leave for Europe the chauffeur didn't arrive to take him to the plane. He telephoned Betty, who was at Fox doing wardrobe fittings, and she rushed home, picked him and Stephen up in her car and dashed to the airport. Bogie called her from New York to say good-bye before leaving for Europe and to thank her for taking him to the airport. "It never occurred to me to think that taking him to the airport was such a big deal, but he thought it was," Betty said.

When he arrived in Paris to change planes, Bogie cabled to tell Betty how much he missed her and to give his love to the children. He cabled her again to say he had arrived safely in Rome and he was waiting for her.

From the moment he arrived in Rome, Bogie was miserable and lonely without Betty. It was not just that he was used to her, he needed her. He was a man full of private fears and one of them was a fear of going anywhere alone, particularly to Europe where he did not speak the language and was embarrassed at being caught helpless in a restaurant.

Bogart viewed most everyone, not just the Italians, with suspicion. As a world-famous star he was always being hustled by producers and directors who, if they could get him, would have a picture assured; no matter where he went he was always conscious of eyes staring at him. He could never relax and be himself.

Betty was his buffer against the world. She took care of all the domestic details when they were traveling; she checked the tickets, confirmed reservations, and transportation arrangements, supervised the packing, organized his meals. Most important, he could be himself when he was with her. He could relax.

Although he disliked writing letters, he wrote to Betty every other day, filling her in on how things were going with the movie, telling her how much he missed her and wanted her with him.

At least once a week after Betty's picture started he sent hot cables to Darryl F. Zanuck, the head of 20th-Century Fox. One of them read: "You've had her long enough. I demand you release her."

After Betty's picture ended the studio insisted that she remain in Hollywood another month until there was assurance that retakes on the picture, made in the new Cinemascope process, would not be required.

They were to be separated for four and a half months, the longest separation of their life together, and Bogie was despondent. Being a convivial man who hated to eat meals alone, he began to invite some of the cast and crew whom he knew to have meals with him. By the time Betty finally arrived he had managed to acquire a retinue that equalled the cast of a DeMille epic. These hangers-on, who are part of the cortège of any star who permits it, laughed at his sallies, took his needling with great good humor, and, of course, allowed him to pick up the tab.

When Betty arrived, she disposed of them all at once by confronting Bogart with the fact that he hated to be alone and had to have company. To prove she was all wrong he refused to have anything more to do with them. In any event, he didn't need them. He had Betty.

CHAPTER 16

"I could have been a good captain but
they fought me at every turn."
—THE CAINE MUTINY

When they came back from Rome, the first thing
Bogie did was rush to the yacht harbor and the
Santana.

His life on the *Santana* was completely divorced
from his life in Hollywood. The only members of the
film crowd who went on the *Santana* regularly were
David and Hjordis Niven, who loved sailing as much
as he did. The other Hollywoodians were more like
Frank Sinatra, whose idea of a sail to Catalina was to
hire a power yacht with a dance band and booze and
broads for action.

Bogie frequently used the boat as a testing ground
for people. If he didn't like someone, he would take
him on the boat for a day's sail to find out why: Bogie's
theory was that in the confinement of the *Santana* a
person's true character would become apparent, just
as it would when he was drunk.

I asked him once why he liked sailing so much. "An
actor needs something to stabilize his personality,
something to nail down what he really is, not what he
is currently pretending to be," he replied.

195

Whether he had a good picture coming up or whether the critics liked his current picture never mattered on the ocean, which was one of the few places where he could get away from acting.

Since acquiring the *Santana*, Bogie had added as much to the *Santana*'s luster as she added to his. He had won the four Channel Island races, and he'd earned the respect of the sailing fraternity up and down the coast. Many of the old salts didn't even know he was an actor. An anecdote he liked to tell—probably apocryphal—concerned the day an old character accosted him on the wharf as he was tying up the *Santana* and asked him what he did for a living. "I act in pictures," Bogie said. There was a long pause while the old fellow shifted the tobacco plug to the other side of his mouth. "Talkies?" he asked.

Bogie's greatest pride was that, to the yachting fraternity, he was considered a sailor who acted rather than an actor who sailed. He was accepted by the rugged and sophisticated sailing fraternity as a sailor only because of his excellence at the helm. He had retired the Channel Island race cup and it was on the mantel next to his Oscar—"The only two awards I really cherish," he once told me.

By then, Stephen, who was eight, loved to sail with his father and Bogie liked having him. But he was most happy when Betty was aboard, too, although he knew that Betty disliked sailing and was jealous of the *Santana* because of the time it took him away from her. But every time he went sailing, he asked her to come along.

I went sailing with Bogie occasionally, sometimes with my own son, Jay, who was Stephen's age. It was tacitly understood that since I was useless as a deckhand my function was that of babysitter. One day in 1954 Bogie told me that he, Betty and Stephen were going to spend the weekend in Catalina. He asked me if I would care to join them with Jay.

The weather was beautiful that weekend, and even though my son had other plans, I decided to fly over to Catalina by myself. I looked forward to the excursion. As a reporter, I knew it would give me an opportunity to see the Bogart family in a light that most people never saw.

I arrived at Catalina early in the morning just as the bright sun beating down on the blue water was reflected brilliantly on the glistening hull of the *Santana*, which lay straining gently against her mooring at White's Landing. In the galley, breakfast was being prepared by the rugged sunburned Swedish sailor named Peter whom Bogie had hired as captain.

I came aboard just in time to hear Pete bellow, "Chow down, Mr. Bogart." Since I had had breakfast on the plane, I settled down forward where I had a good view of the activity taking place below me on deck.

Bogie appeared from the stateroom wearing his old yachting cap and terry jump suit. "Chow up, you mean," he countered.

Betty, dressed in white linen slacks and the top of a blue bathing suit, was next to arrive from the stateroom, followed by Stephen, a blond, almond-eyed replica of the skipper. "Mommy, can I have bacon and eggs?" he asked in a surprisingly deep voice.

"I've told you three times—yes," Betty replied.

"You can have anything you want on this boat," said Pete.

The Bogart family took their places in the small cockpit while Pete disappeared into the galley and returned quickly, carrying eggs, bacon and toast on a silver platter and coffee in a white thermos. There was a glass of milk for Stephen.

"It's easier to eat below," grumbled Bogie.

"If you don't get sick," snapped Betty.

"I wouldn't get sick," said Stephen.

Bogie nodded his head in agreement. "Of course you wouldn't. Seasickness is mental, that's all. It's based on fear. If you make up your mind not to be sick, you never are."

"It doesn't work that way with me," said Betty with

a smile. "I make up my mind not to be sick and I always am."

"Like I said, it's mental," said Bogie, giving his son a generous helping of eggs and toast. Then he poured a cup of coffee for himself and one for Betty.

"You like this, Steve?" he asked.

"Yeah." Steve nodded. "When do we sail?"

"Set sail," Bogie corrected his son. "That's what we say on board. We set sail right after breakfast. This is living, isn't it, Steve, boy?"

"Yeah," Steve said solemnly, chewing his toast. "As long as we *set* sail pretty soon."

"You got ants in your pants?" Betty asks. "This is nice, isn't it? Sitting here quietly without the boat standing on its ear. Why not leave well enough alone?"

"Because I want to sail," Steve said doggedly.

Bogie grinned. "Attaboy, Steve. Stick to your guns. We'll put up our canvas and sail along the island to a nice beach they got there."

Betty groaned. "Take your time with breakfast, Steve."

After Pete expertly cleared the table, Bogie took his place at the helm. Pete slipped the moorings, unfurled the sails, and in a few minutes the *Santana* was slipping through the water and was soon heeled over at a sharp angle. Steve, wearing a bulky yellow life jacket, held tightly to his mother's leg. Bogie, happy to be under way, watched with narrowed eyes, a cigarette stuck between his teeth as Pete trimmed the jib.

Spray blew over the cockpit, and Betty clutched her son close to her.

"In a couple of years," Bogie said to Steve, "you'll be coming with me every weekend. No more hanging around the house. I'm going to make a sailor out of you."

"You lucky boy," his mother murmured.

Bogie failed to hear her because he was shouting to Pete. "When you're all secure, the skipper would like a little liquid refreshment."

198

Pete nodded and padded aft on sun-browned feet, returning in a moment with "one for the skipper and one for the crew."

The two men toasted each other.

"How much farther do we have to go, daddy," Steve asked. "I'm cold."

"Not too much farther," Bogie replied gently. "The beach is about a mile away. You'll like it there, Steve. We'll drop anchor and loaf. That ought to suit all hands." Bogie flashed a grin at Betty, who was staring rigidly straight ahead.

Betty tightened the life jacket around Stephen. Bogie watched her for a moment and glanced off to the left where another boat had taken the same tack and was racing alongside next to him. The *Santana* pulled away leaving the other yachtsmen in her wake. Bogie lit a cigarette, cupping his hands against the wind, then turned the helm over to Pete and came over to me.

"This is what it's all about, Joe," he said. "All the hours spent in make-up under hot lights, all the lines you have to learn, all the deals and the talk that goes with them. So once a week I can have this."

In that moment Bogie was not just a yachtsman to me, or a sailor, or a star or the father of a family, or the owner of a movie company. He was just a truly happy man.

In the distance was a small inlet, protected from the deep, wild sea. It was our destination. Betty saw it, too, and relaxed.

"You know, once in a while, I find myself liking the boat," she said bravely.

"That makes three of us in the Bogart family who like the boat," said Bogie. "Next year Leslie will be old enough to come along, too."

"Heaven forbid," murmured Betty, whose farewell to the *Santana* was to come soon after that day, following an Ensenada race which Bogie won. She was aboard as a passenger, cook and barkeep. "I was below decks with the food all the time," she told me. "I must have been mad to do it."

CHAPTER 17

"I kid you not."
—THE CAINE MUTINY

Betty's role as one of three models in search of rich husbands in *How to Marry a Millionaire* had revitalized her career, which had been almost at a standstill. She had graduated from a slinky sexpot to a comedienne and, at the age of thirty, seemed to be finding her niche in films. No one was happier for her than Bogie.

"I always knew that if she got the right part, she'd be great," he told me. "I just hope she doesn't have too much of a career. I married her because I want her with me."

During the next eighteen months Bogie was to go from picture to picture and turn in some of his best performances. When a young actor asked him why he worked so much Bogart answered, "I have a charming wife, two beautiful kids, a gorgeous home, a yacht—and I've had the applause. But I'll be damned if I know why I work so hard. Sinatra and I were talking about it the other day. Working is therapy, I guess. It keeps us on the wagon. This is a very bad town to be out of work in. After a week or so of not working, you're so bored you don't know what the hell to do."

Acting was, as Truman Capote said, almost the sum total of Bogart's life. "He was really an artist and a very selective one. All the gestures and expressions were pruned down, and pruned down."

Nowhere was this professionalism and maturation as an actor to be more evident than in Bogie's creation of the role of Captain Queeg in *The Caine Mutiny*, a film based on the best-selling book which had also been a hit play.

Much of the film was to be made in Hawaii, and the entire Bogart family journeyed there by plane for the location shooting. They stayed in a suite at the Royal Hawaiian Hotel, an elegant pink palace situated directly on the beach at Waikiki.

One day Bogie, Stephen and Betty lunched on the palm-tree-shrouded lanai overlooking the Pacific. The tourists were gawking at the film family and hanging onto their every move and word. Suddenly Stephen left his chair and discreetly whispered in his father's ear that he had to go to the rest room.

"Go pee in the ocean," said Bogie in a loud voice.

The tourists were shocked, but Stephen took it all in stride. He found the men's room alone.

The Bogart family was back in Beverly Hills by Labor Day weekend 1954, when Ed Murrow and his TV crew came by to do a "Person to Person" TV show. Murrow was one of America's most distinguished newsmen and his interview show telecast from the homes of his subjects had a wide viewing audience. Part of the show's appeal was that it was live. No editing or cutting was possible.

I dropped by to see how the show was going and found Betty and Bogie having a family conference in the center of what appeared to be a snake pit of TV cables. Suddenly, Bogie broke out laughing. He told me: "Betty's afraid that when Stephen looks into the cameras he's going to say to Mr. Murrow, 'Hello,

Blubberhead.' He calls everyone Blubberhead. Worse, he might use one of his other pet names like Mr. Dog-Do-in-the-Pants."

Luckily, Stephen was already a pro and he carried off a greeting to Mr. Murrow with aplomb.

The show was memorable for three-year-old Leslie, however. It was the first time she had seen her father wearing the toupee he hated but always sported for public appearances. At first, she thought it was a hair hat.

For his next picture, *Sabrina*, Bogie played a worldly Wall Street type, complete with Homburg, furled black umbrella, Brooks Brothers suit and briefcase. And he got the girl, Audrey Hepburn, edging out Bill Holden. While he was working in *Sabrina*, Betty was signed to do *The Cobweb*, an MGM picture co-starring Richard Widmark.

Although Bogie was pleased that Betty was working, he was his usual irascible self. He knew that when Betty went to work she felt guilty about leaving the children all day; her studio calls were at 6:00 A.M., before they breakfasted, so she didn't see them until evening.

Although Bogie was working, too, she often left before he was up or was not around when he came home.

Like many husbands with working wives, he would needle her: "You giving up your children for your career? Who do you think you are, another Duse or Bernhardt? [Those two famous stars of another era were the only actresses of note in his book.] Your career comes before your kids, eh? Just like any other actress."

If Betty already felt guilty about going to work, she usually let him leave the field a victor. Occasionally she snapped back, saying they could bank the money she made. He dismissed this notion by claiming her money only put them in another tax bracket and it was costing him money to have her work.

Betty understood what was underneath Bogie's carping. He wanted her around when he was home, and when she was away he was miserable. "They were closer than any two married people I ever saw," said a good friend. "He was the complete professional on the set, but off the set and away from her he was lost."

For his next picture, *The Barefoot Contessa*, Bogie's company was to receive a percentage of the profits and he was paid a salary as well. *Contessa* was directed by writer-director Joseph L. Mankiewicz and co-starred Ava Gardner.

The character Bogie played in *The Barefoot Contessa* was a thorough summation of Bogart's own nature and attitude in those years. Bogie's Harry Dawes, the old Hollywood director and philosophical observer in this film, has no illusions about the sanctity of movies or the rewards of life. "How long," he asks, "do you suppose since we've said or done anything about ourselves that hasn't been said or done before? Or thought a new thought?"

Some of the picture was made in Italy, and for most of that time, while Betty was still working in Hollywood, he was alone. But the shadow of Betty followed him. He wrote, called or cabled almost daily. Before leaving he had promised Betty he would cut down on booze and cigarettes—he had a hacking cough every morning when he woke up that distressed her. He trimmed his cigarette consumption to less than a pack a day and confined his drinking only to after working hours.

David Hanna, who was a press agent on the film, said he was chagrined to discover that Bogie was not living up to his reputation as a drinker. "He invariably ordered English gin, considerably weaker than American, and no man could murder a Scotch so unmercifully with water. Moreover, he drank very slowly; so slowly that it often embarrassed me when I'd order two to his one."

Bogart's next film was *We're No Angels*, a comedy based on a Broadway play about three convicts who are moved by the troubles of the family they meant to rob, and end up playing Santa Claus. Peter Ustinov, one of the three convicts, was much impressed with Bogart. "His great basic quality," said Ustinov, "was a splendid roughness. Even when he was perfectly groomed I felt I could have lit a match on his jaw. He knew his job inside out, and yet it was impossible not to feel that his real soul was elsewhere, a mysterious, searching instrument knocking at doors unknown even to himself."

Bogart was in full presence on the set, however. "He carried the light of battle in his eyes," Ustinov said. "He wished to be matched, to be challenged, to be teased. I could see a jocular and quarrelsome eye staring out of the character he was playing into the character I was playing—rather as an experienced bull fighter might stare a hot-headed bull into precipitate action."

Bogie worked hard and played hard. During a brief hiatus in Hollywood before Bogie was to do his next picture, *The Desperate Hours*, he and Betty resumed their position as leaders of Hollywood's inner circle.

Shortly after Christmas 1955 the Bogarts and some of their carousing friends met for a festive occasion in the upstairs banquet room at Romanoff's. Betty looked around at the group of adults, who acted, much of the time, like overprivileged delinquents, and cracked, "I see the rat pack is all here."

Something about the casual in-joke name, Rat Pack, intrigued the group. After a few hours of drinking they formed an organization with a platform of iconoclasm—they were against everything and everyone, including themselves.

I got wind of the meeting and called Bogie for the details.

First official notice of the Rat Pack appeared the next day in my column in the *New York Herald Tribune*.

204

The Holmby Hills Rat Pack held its first annual meeting last night at Romanoff's restaurant in Beverly Hills and elected officers for the coming year. Named to executive positions were: Frank Sinatra, pack master; Judy Garland, first vice president; Lauren Bacall, den mother; Sid Luft, cage master; Humphrey Bogart, rat in charge of public relations; Irving Lazar, recording secretary and treasurer; Nathaniel Benchley, historian.

The only members of the organization not voted into office are David Niven, Michael Romanoff and James Van Heusen. Mr. Niven, an Englishman, Mr. Romanoff, a Russian, and Mr. Van Heusen, an American, protested that they were discriminated against because of their national origins. Mr. Sinatra, who was acting chairman of the meeting, refused to enter their protests on the minutes.

A coat of arms designed by Mr. Benchley was unanimously approved as the official insignia of the Holmby Hills Rat Pack for use on letterheads and membership pins. The escutcheon features a rat gnawing on a human hand with a legend, "Never Rat on a Rat."

Mr. Bogart, who was spokesman, said the organization has no specific function other than "the relief of boredom and the perpetuation of independence. We admire ourselves and don't care for anyone else."

He said that membership is open to free-minded, successful individuals who don't care what anyone thinks about them.

A motion concerning the admittance of Claudette Colbert was tabled at the insistence of Miss Bacall who said that Miss Colbert "is a nice person but not a rat."

Betty, whose official title was den mother, was actually a very busy hostess when the Pack met at her home. She kept things going, keeping the drinks filled, the ashtrays emptied, and the fights to a minimum. Usually the group just sat around and talked; sometimes Judy Garland or Frank Sinatra would sing, with composers James Van Heusen or Sammy Cahn at the piano. They all stayed up late and drank a good deal when not working. Sometimes there were loud arguments, mainly political, which delighted Bogart.

Although Bogart was officially only the director of public relations, as the driving force in Hollywood society in those days, he was the Pack's acknowledged leader and Betty was his consort.

CHAPTER 18

*"Life every now and then behaves as if
it had seen too many bad movies, when
it winds up in a pattern that's too pat,
too neat. As it was in the beginning, you
fade out where you faded in."*
—THE BAREFOOT CONTESSA

Early in 1955 Betty was signed to co-star with Robert
Mitchum in *Blood Alley,* a film to be made in San
Francisco. Bogie, who had just completed *The Left
Hand of God* at Fox and had some time off, decided
to visit her on location. He asked if I wanted to go
with him.

"We'll go to Frisco on the evening train to see Betty,
and then maybe on Saturday we can go to the zoo,"
he said, rather more quietly than usual.

"Who's going to the zoo?" I asked.

"We are—you, me, Stephen and Betty," he said.

"You want me along as babysitter for Stephen?" I
asked.

"Hell, no," said Bogie. "I want you along for company." He paused, then admitted, "You've got kids, I
figure maybe you'll know what to do when Steve acts
up."

Before meeting Bogie and Steve at the train I took
the precaution of stopping at a five-and-dime and

buying some crayons, coloring books and little toys that I thought might amuse a six-year-old boy.

Bogart was waiting at the gate for me, standing hand-in-hand with his son. There was a worried frown on Bogie's face. "First time I've been alone with the kid this long," he said. "I hope it works out all right."

Noticing the paper bag I was carrying he asked me what was in it. I told him.

"You're a genius, kid, and I knew it," he said.

It was 8:30 before the train got started and we found our compartment. Bogart was for "bedding down the kid" and going in to the dining car for some liquid refreshment for himself and a Coke for me. But Steve, who was lolling comfortably in an upper bunk, insisted on a fairy tale. "I don't know any fairy tales," said Bogart. "Uncle Joe will tell you one."

"No," said Steve firmly. "I want you to tell it to me. Mother always tells me a fairy tale before I go to sleep."

Bogart looked to me for a suggestion. "Spin it out," I said, kicking off my shoes and climbing into a lower on the other side of the compartment. Bogart took off his shoes, too, and climbed in next to me. "You tell me what to say and I'll repeat it," he said. So I started to improvise a story about a six-year-old boy on a train trip, with Bogart echoing the words after me. Twenty minutes later Steve was quiet. So was his father.

I stopped when I heard snoring. Then I noticed that Stephen was wide awake. It was Bogie who had fallen asleep.

In the morning when the porter knocked on the door to wake us Bogie went over to Stephen, who was sleeping soundly, and kissed him tenderly on the forehead.

While Stephen was washing up with the parental admonition to "clean behind the ears" Bogie had a terrible coughing fit which lasted for several minutes.

I knew nothing about coughs, but I was worried at how long and violently they racked his body.

"You ought to go see a doctor," I told him, carefully keeping concern out of my voice.

He shrugged. "All they'll tell me is to give up smoking, which I'm going to do anyway."

Like most people Bogie smoked not only because it was a habit but because he felt smoking relaxed him. Always tense before starting a film, he had just signed to do a new picture, *The Harder They Fall*, a raw, brutally realistic film about a ruthless fight promoter played by Rod Steiger and an out-of-work sportscaster (Bogart) who finagled a simple-minded giant into the big-time fight game.

The Harder They Fall was the last film Humphrey Bogart was to make. "I feel tired all the time," he told Betty one night when he returned from the studio. "I don't know what's the matter with me. I don't seem to have any pep at all any more. Old age is catching up with me, I guess."

Between Christmas and New Years, 1956, Bogie had a bad coughing spell while lunching at Romanoff's with Buddy Fogelson, Greer Garson's husband. When he also complained that he had pain when swallowing, Romanoff, who had commented before on Bogie's coughing spells, pointed out that Buddy was going to the Beverly Hills Clinic to see a dentist after lunch. "There is a lung specialist in the building." Romanoff said. "Why don't you go along and have him check out your cough."

Without an appointment Bogie went to the office of Dr. Maynard Brandsma, a specialist in malignancies of the lung and throat. The doctor heard Bogie's symptoms, put him on a diet and told him to cut down on smoking and drinking. Bogie laughed and said he'd see what he could do.

"Come back in three weeks," Dr. Brandsma said.

Three weeks later Bogie returned, complaining of the same pain.

"Did you stay on the diet?" the doctor asked.

"No," said Bogie.

"I can't help you without your cooperation," the doctor said, but arranged to have Bogie's chest and esophagus x-rayed. Nothing showed up. Brandsma asked him to stick to the diet this time and report again in a few weeks.

Meanwhile Bogie and Betty were planning to make a movie together, *Melville Goodwin, U.S.A.* They had already done the wardrobe tests and signed the contracts. Although Bogart was not terribly concerned about the pain in his throat, it continued to get worse, so at Betty's insistence, he went back to see the doctor.

This time Dr. Brandsma arranged to have Bogie bring in some of the mucus he coughed up in the morning during his coughing spells, which sometimes lasted as long as thirty minutes. The mucus was sent to a laboratory to be checked for malignant cells. The lab man reported that three of the five criteria for cancer were positive.

Another specimen, sent to the lab a week later, showed that four of the five criteria were positive. Dr. Brandsma called Bogie into his office and told him he didn't know what was going on in his esophagus, but recommended he be fluoroscoped. Bogie went to Good Samaritan Hospital in Los Angeles where Dr. Michael Flynn found an ulcer immediately. He performed a biopsy. It was cancerous.

Dr. Brandsma told Bogie he had a malignant ulcer in the esophagus and would have to be operated on. "It's small and early enough in the game so I think we have time to get it," the doctor said.

"Can't we make the movie first, then the operation?" asked Bogie, who was scheduled to go before the cameras the following Monday.

"You can make the movie first—and you'll be a big hero at Forest Lawn," said Dr. Brandsma.

On a Friday morning in March Bogie called Mary Baker to say he had just come from the clinic and that he had a polyp on the esophagus which was supposed to be malignant. He had to have it taken out. Would Mary please call Milton Sperling, producer of the picture, and tell him it would have to be postponed a few weeks?

Dr. John Jones, a prominent Los Angeles surgeon, removed the ulcer but found, when he cut into the chest, that the cancer had spread to the lymph glands. They, too, were removed.

"I told Bogie that we had taken all the cancer out, which we hoped was true," Dr. Brandsma said later. "In cancer you never know. He was in great pain, though, and he smoked like a chimney, so he had chemical bronchitis plus that terrible cough. Once, while in the hospital, his coughing ruptured all his stitches."

Betty who had been with him all the time, sleeping on a cot in his room at the hospital, was told the same thing: that the doctors thought all the cancer had been removed. "She believed what the doctors wanted her to believe and what they probably thought at the time was true," insisted one of her close friends who was with her some of that time. "And if Bogie was frightened, he didn't let her in on it, so they played a beautiful game with each one bolstering the other's spirits."

When he got home Bogie was not reluctant to admit he had been operated on for cancer. "Hell, I was in the operating room eight hours. I knew it wasn't tonsilitis," he told me. "Anyway, why shouldn't I say I had cancer. It's a respectable disease. It's nothing to be ashamed of. It's no worse than gall stones or appendicitis. They'll all kill you if you don't do something about them soon enough."

Bogie was fascinated by the details of his operation. One afternoon when Dr. Brandsma came for a visit he had the doctor draw a complete diagram of the operation for Adolph Green, who had dropped in.

Raymond Massey, who had come to Hollywood at the time to do a television show, was another guest

211

taken along the gory route. Mr. Massey told me he went to visit Bogie armed with a fund of small talk and reminiscences, hoping to cheer him up. "I didn't know what to expect when I was ushered into the sick room, but there was Bogart, sitting in a chair, looking as good as ever, sipping a Scotch and soda, waiting for me. I was just beginning on the small talk when he cut in, 'I'll tell you what happened to me down there,' he said. 'It was awful!' "

Bogie went into great detail about the operation. "The sicker I got from his story, the healthier he became," said Mr. Massey. "Then we spent a marvelous afternoon reminiscing about our adventures together."

Another who got the grisly treatment was Swifty Lazar, who brought a date to the house. "Spencer Tracy was there, too," said Swifty. "Both of them knew I can't stand talk about operations, so they started to discuss them, but the girl stayed. She was fascinated but getting greener and greener as they made the stories gorier and gorier. Finally she went over in a dead faint. Bogie couldn't have been happier."

Ill as he was, Bogie was still being Bogieish, using the details of the operation as a grisly gag. Or, perhaps, as John Huston suggested, "He didn't believe he was going to die, not that he refused to consider the thought—it simply never occurred to him. He loved life. Life meant his family, his friends, his work, his boat and he could not imagine leaving any of them."

By June, Bogie was aware that it was going to be a long fight. Alistair Cooke remembers going to see him on a day that Bogie was signing his will. "He spoke of it and of his illness and the sudden uselessness of money with an entirely unforced humor and an equally unforced seriousness; neither with complaint nor with a too-brave absence of complaint."

Although frequently in pain, Bogie refused to admit it or give in to it, although he did make some concessions. Clutching and shifting his four-speed Jaguar—

a Christmas present from Betty—became too tiring for him, so he traded it in on a Ford Thunderbird with automatic drive. He also tried to eat more, even going to the length of having breakfast, which he had never done before, but he still could not gain weight.

"I've got this goddamned pain across my shoulders," he told me one day. "Otherwise I feel fine."

Despite the pain and discomfort, Bogie was still master of his house. One afternoon writer Richard Gehman dropped by to visit Bogie in the paneled den for a drink and a talk. A series of startling sounds came from the kitchen at the opposite end of the house. First there was a loud scream, then a slap, followed by derisive laughter. Bogie tensed in his chair and leaned forward. Another scream followed the first, then more laughter.

"Excuse me," Bogart said, "I got to go and belt somebody."

He stalked toward the kitchen, looking exactly like a Humphrey Bogart film character heading into the villain's hideout to clean things up.

Gehman could hear Bogie say in that menacing voice of his, "What's going on in here, anyhow?"

"Steve," said Leslie in a whimpering little four-year-old voice, "was shooting me with rubber bands."

"Is that true?" Bogie demanded.

"Aw," said Steve, aged seven, "I wasn't shooting her much."

"You were, too," Leslie charged indignantly.

"I was not!"

"Wait a minute," Bogie said. "Steve, you shut up. I don't want to have to rap you. Listen, you got no right shooting your sister with rubber bands. She's littler than you, and besides she's female. They cause us a lot of trouble, but we got to endure it. They're not as strong as we are."

"She was teasing me and she was teasing Jim [a white mouse]," said Steve.

"I don't care what she was doing to you or Jim,"

213

Bogie said. "You're in the wrong. Come on, now. Be a good boy. Be a gentleman. It sounds like a ratfight in here."

Bogie came back to the den and sat down, his mouth grim but not enough to conceal his amusement at the scene he had just played with his children, who had been told only that their father was ill and needed quiet so he could rest.

Presently the pain became so unendurable that Bogie implored his physicians to put him back in the hospital to see if they could find some way of giving him relief.

He was still full of fire, however, and determined to keep his problems to himself, although he knew that all over Hollywood there were rumors—as yet unpublished—that he was dying of cancer. On October 8, 1956, he telephoned me and asked me to come over and do him a favor.

When I arrived at the Bogart house I found him in the den, slumped in his favorite easy chair. He waved a typewritten letter at me. "Will you promise to print this exactly as written?" he asked me, and then read it aloud in a hoarse voice, pausing occasionally to cough.

An open letter to the working press:

I have been greatly disturbed lately at the many unchecked and baseless rumors being tossed among you regarding the state of my health. Just to set the record straight, as they say in Washington (and I have as much right to say this as anybody in Washington has), a great deal of what has been printed has had nothing to do with the true facts. It may even be necessary for me to send out a truth team to follow you all around.

I have read that both lungs have been removed, that I couldn't live for another half hour, that I was fighting for my life in some hospital which doesn't exist out here, that my heart had been removed and replaced by an old gasoline pump salvaged from a defunct Standard Oil station. I have been on the way to practically every cemetery, you name 'em, from here to the Mississippi including several where I'm certain they only accept dogs. All the above upsets my friends, not to mention the insurance companies—so, as they also say in Washington, let's get the facts to the American people—and here they are.

I had a slight malignancy in the esophagus. So that some of you won't have to go to the research department, it's the pipe that runs from your throat to your stomach. The operation for the removal of the malignancy was successful, although it was touch-and-go for a while whether the malignancy or I would survive.

As they also say in Washington, I'm a better man than I ever was and all I need now is about thirty pounds in weight, which I'm sure some of you could spare. Possibly we could start something like a Weight Bank for Bogart, and believe me, I'm not particular from which part of your anatomies it comes from.

In closing, any time you want to run a little medical bulletin on me, just pick up the phone and as they say in the old country, I'm in the book.

After he'd finished reading the letter aloud, Bogie got up from his chair and jabbed a finger at me.

"Remember, you promised to print it exactly as written. Now keep your word."

He walked slowly over to the bar and mixed himself a stiff drink. "Here's to Mark Twain. Reports of his death were exaggerated, too."

On November 25th, he called me again. "Come on over, Joe, and I'll give you another story."

This time Betty greeted me at the door. Although her face showed signs of strain, she was gay as always. When I asked her how Bogie was feeling she said she'd let him tell me.

Bogie was in the den, as usual, a glass of sherry in one hand and an unlit cigarette in the other. His voice was casual. "I am going back into the hospital in a week or so. They're going to give me some treatments, and I'll have physiotherapy."

For the first time, I thought Bogie looked terrible. Yet he acted as though the hospitalization was a routine matter.

"I called you over so that people in the East won't think I'm going to have a leg amputated or my head cut off. Most of my friends are either on the wagon or have joined Alcoholics Anonymous. The shock of hearing that anything serious is happening to me might lead them away from the straight and narrow."

Dr. Jones, the surgeon, was in the room, too, and explained smoothly to me that "the purpose of this hospital visit was to reduce the pain brought about by a pinched nerve in Bogie's shoulder." I had a sinking feeling, despite the doctor's easy manner and Bogie's confident smile, but Betty seemed unconcerned and acted as though it was, indeed, routine so I tried to slant my story on the hospitalization in the way Bogie would have liked, concentrating on minutiae and personal anecdotes. I mentioned, for example, that his personal luggage for the hospital visit included seven mysteries, a book about chess, a portable chess set and two bottles of Scotch. I also wrote that although Bogie was still underweight, he still appeared to be pound for pound his usual irascible self. He and Betty (I wrote) had a dispute over his Thunderbird as I was leaving that day. He insisted she have his car tuned while he was away, and made her promise not to drive it. The last line of my article quoted him:

"Can't trust a woman at the wheel of a good car. They not only fix everything with a hairpin, they leave the things every place they go."

When Bogie returned from the hospital, even thinner than before, his voice was firm and strong as ever. And his spirits seemed up, although he said he was going to have to keep going to the hospital several times a week for cobalt treatments. He told me how frightened he was, not of the treatment itself, but at

216

what it represented. "I know it's the last resort in cancer treatment," he said. That was as close as he came to admitting to me that he thought he might not make it.

After the first treatment Bogie felt sick to his stomach. Later in the day, however, he felt a little better; the pain seemed to have diminished. And his doctor was encouraging. He said they were making progress.

So Bogie accepted the treatments, and for a while it appeared as though he was holding his own. "I'm going to beat it," he told Swifty enthusiastically after the first week of treatment. "I feel in my heart I'm going to make it."

If Bogie was brave, Betty was gallant. Although he never voiced his fear of imminent death at that time, I believe she knew it was there, every hour of the day and night—a dreadful shape slowly materializing. John Huston is certain that Betty knew that from the time he was operated on that at best he had a year or two to live. "But out of the power of her love she was able to hide her grief and to go on being her own familiar self to Bogie and his friends. She could not even afford to let others know what she suspected because in that way the knowledge might get back to Bogie. So, she not only had to play a role for him, but the world. And it was a flawless performance. She attended to his every single want most often before he himself knew what his want was. She never missed a trick."

Betty was at her best and brightest every afternoon when friends came to visit him in the den. Their conversation was directed at him and made for him. If he couldn't go out, most of his world came to him, and it had been that way since the beginning of his illness. The list Betty kept of the people who had phoned or came to see him during the time he was sick would fill a small notebook.

Only a few were conspicuous by their absences. But Bogie understood. "They're afraid of sickness and

217

they don't want to be reminded of it," he explained to Betty.

Later, John Huston would say: "From the day of her marriage to him until the hour that death parted them, she was true—truly true. It can only be put down to class—class and love."

Meanwhile, the tradition of wonderful hospitality the Bogarts had established was to continue on to the last hour he was able to sit upright. I will never forget a day during the last month of his life when he was being prepared to receive company at the cocktail hour. He was little more than a genial skeleton by then, lying most of the time in the upstairs bedroom.

He lay on the bed, head propped on pillows, and helplessly submitted to the nurses who attended him around the clock. On that afternoon a fat nurse cushioned his head gently and began to lather his face.

"There now, Mr. Bogart," she said, drawing back for a better look at her razor work. "We look just fine." She held a little vanity mirror of Betty's to his face. He nodded and rubbed his right hand over his jaw reflectively.

Betty came into the bedroom, carrying the old Daks slacks bought in London and the scarlet smoking jacket she had given him the prior Christmas-birthday. She put the trousers on, right leg first, then the left leg, and then pulled them over his waist. They were loose.

"Christ, I'm going to have to gain some weight," he said.

"Harry Cohn is having the script rewritten for you," Betty said, although I was certain she knew the film would never be made and Cohn was merely trying to keep Bogie's spirits up.

"I always claimed Cohn was a bastard," Bogie said. "Maybe I ought to start changing my mind."

"Why?" said Betty. "He just wants you in the picture. He figures you're worth waiting for, but he's still a bastard."

218

"The hell with that picture," he said. "What about the boat? How're they doing on the hull?"

"Pete says it'll be ready by the weekend," she said.

He nodded, then winced with pain as Aurilio, the handyman, and the nurse picked him out of the bed and lifted him into the wheelchair.

He pushed the wheelchair himself to the dumbwaiter shaft across the room, looking proud that he still had the strength to propel it. For a moment it looked as if he would try to get out of the chair and walk, but then he gave it up.

They lifted him out of the chair and sat him on a little stool in the dumbwaiter shaft. The top had been removed to give him headroom. "Are you all right, Mr. Bogart?" the nurse asked.

"Yeah, just dandy," he said, making the words sound cheerful and sarcastic at the same time. Down below in the kitchen Aurilio was pulling the ropes. The little elevator used to transport food from the kitchen to the bedroom started down.

It was dark in the shaft and the ride from bedroom to kitchen was less than twenty seconds, but from the look on Bogie's face when he arrived in the kitchen he obviously hated it.

They lifted him out of the dumbwaiter and back into the wheelchair, and transported him through the house. The marble floor of the patio facing the swimming pool was polished to a high gloss. He put his hands on the chair wheels and brought it to a halt, examining the recently built pool house intently. "It's off center," he said. "Fifteen thousand dollars and they can't even follow a plumb line."

The little group following him in the wheelchair looked like a tableau from the movie *Sunset Boulevard*. He rolled past the living room, which was rarely used. Everything in the room was expensive: from the Dufys and Picassos to the French Provincial furniture. They had spent a quarter of a million dollars on the room and it had just been furnished. He was to

219

sit in it only once. "It's the most beautiful room I've ever seen," he said. Betty was going to have the first big party in it when he was well.

Harvey, the boxer dog, came running in and almost jumped on his master's lap. "Get down, Harvey," Bogie said gruffly, meanwhile patting him gently on the head.

In the library he wheeled to his chair opposite the bar. They lifted him out of the wheelchair and into his favorite chair. They sat him down, smoothed out his trousers, and gave him his props—a glass of sherry for the left hand, a cigarette for the right. It was a few minutes after five, and he said his back already hurt like hell.

The telephone rang. Betty came quietly into the room moving like a leopard. She picked up the phone, listened a minute, then said, "Nonsense, Bogie is fine."

"Here, let me talk," he said and got on the extension phone on the table next to him. "I'm getting along well, just a little underweight," he said, putting his hand over the telephone while he coughed.

"This is an old rumor. Last time you people had me on the eighth floor of the Los Angeles Memorial Hospital. The fact that there is no such hospital doesn't bother me, but the eighth floor is what burned me up. That's pretty ominous sounding, isn't it. You can tell your bosses I'm fine, never felt better."

He banged the phone into its cradle. Another coughing spasm was interrupted by the phone again. He reached for it. The caller was an editor checking for himself on whether a reporter had really talked with Bogart.

Bogie was furious. "You don't trust your reporters, then fire them. What kind of newspaper are you running? I'm going to call my lawyer to see what legal action we can take against you people printing that I was in a coma. Then you'll know you talked with me."

This time when he hung up there was a thin smile on his face. "What's the matter with you newspapermen?" he said.

220

I recognized the familiar needling technique and started to fiddle with my pipe.

"Well, aren't you sometimes ashamed of your profession?" Bogie persisted.

"No," I snapped. "No more than you are when some actor turns in a lousy performance and then blames the script. All those reporters in New York have to work with is a few rumors, and they're doing their job and checking them. That's their job."

Bogie grinned and was still grinning, the light of battle in his eyes, when Betty came into the room bringing me a Coke and announcing that company was at the door.

Friends began to arrive: David Niven, Frank Sinatra, Spencer Tracy, George Cukor, Katharine Hepburn, Richard Burton. The group was limited now to those who had known him best and longest; and they stayed, two and three at a time, for a half hour or so until about eight o'clock, which was the time for him to go back upstairs by the same means he had descended.

"No one who sat in his presence during those final weeks would ever forget his display of sheer animal courage," said Huston. "After the first visit—it took that to get over the initial shock of his wasted appearance—one quickened to his grandeur, expanded under it, and felt strangely elated, proud to be there, proud to be his friend, the friend of such a brave man."

During the last month Bogie saw many of his old friends. "There was no strain of any kind, because [I believe] he knew the worst and was resolved to rouse himself for two hours a day to relax with his friends until the end came," claims Alistair Cooke. "Another of his triumphant deceptions was that he managed to convince everybody that he was intermittently uncomfortable but not in pain.

"It is hard for actors to avoid the dramatizing of their emotional life, whether grossly by 'living the part' or subtly by sentimental deprecation. Bogart was merely

221

himself, a brave man, who had come to terms, as we all may pray to do, with the certain approach of death."

The late Adlai Stevenson, who also saw Bogie during the last month, said, "He was very ill and very weak. But he made a most gallant effort to keep gay. He had an impatience for weakness, an impatience with illness."

Truman Capote visited him a few times. "He seemed to bring out the best in all of his friends," the writer said. "He looked so awful, so terribly thin. His eyes were huge and they looked so frightened. They got bigger and bigger. It was real fear and yet there was always that gay brave self."

Nunnally Johnson was to report, "He just seemed to get smaller and smaller."

George Cukor, the director, saw Bogie twenty-three days before he died. "He didn't come downstairs on that day and he was in bed heavily, heavily sedated. He kept closing his eyes. Still he'd be telling jokes and asking to hear the gossip. But his voice was the wonder. That marvelous voice. It was absolutely alive. It was the last thing that died."

The voice was one of Bogie's key attributes, the feature by which he was recognized throughout the world; and it was cruelly appropriate that when cancer singled him out, it went for his throat.

Fourteen days before the end, Bogie was still hopeful he would get well. He asked Aurilio Salazar to take his Thunderbird down and have it serviced. "I'm going to take Stephen to Newport for a cruise again," he said. "I want the car ready."

Then he began to weaken quickly. "He went through the worst and most agonizing pain any human can take," Dr. Brandsma said. "I knew this, but he never complained, never whimpered. I knew he was dying and, during the last week, I knew he knew it by the questions he would ask."

Five days before the end, Bogie was still entertaining guests downstairs at cocktail hour. It was a chilly

January day, and he was sitting in his old chair in a dressing gown and pajamas. A roaring fire was in the fireplace when I came in. On the table near him was a copy of *Compulsion*, the novel about the Loeb–Leopold murder case. He was holding a martini in one hand and a cigarette with a long ash in the other.

David Niven, still in make-up from a TV Western, had dropped by after work to show Bogie a letter he had received from Douglas Fairbanks, Jr. Someone —I think it was Katie Hepburn—admired a new portrait which Claire Trevor had painted of Betty and Leslie for a Christmas gift. Betty said she liked it but thought her nose and mouth needed repainting.

"That's the trouble with you actresses," needled Bogart. "You want all your pictures to be glamorous. Leave it the way it is. It's beautiful, just as you are."

I noticed the copy of *Compulsion* on the table and mentioned it was the book actress Marie McDonald had been reading before she was kidnapped. Bogie asked me how I knew and I told him I had been covering the story all week. "Well, go on," he demanded impatiently. "Let's hear the facts you aren't writing for the *Herald Tribune*."

When Betty decided that Bogie had had enough company he tried to act irritated, but it was apparent that he was tired.

Friday morning Bogie telephoned Jess Morgan in Morgan Maree's office to say that some of the press had been writing stories that he was dying of cancer. "Get me a lawyer, I'm going to sue them," he said. Jess called Martin Gang, a prominent Hollywood attorney, and explained the situation. The two men went to see Bogie, who was in bed.

"Bogie's voice faced in and out toward the end of the conversation, but he asked Martin to prepare a lawsuit," Morgan recalled. "He was full of fight even though he was obviously very sick." Morgan humored Bogie, saying he would attend to the lawsuit.

Friday afternoon Mary Baker went to the house. After a short visit Bogie took her hand and squeezed it. He usually said, "See you tomorrow," but this time he said, "Good-bye, Mary."

Saturday morning Morgan Maree dropped by on his way to northern California for some pheasant shooting. "I'll look in again when I get back Monday morning," he said. Bogie squeezed his old friend's hand and said, "Okay, kid."

Saturday afternoon Swifty Lazar came by the house as usual. "I used to go every day to see him because he knew how I hated sickness and death, and if I missed a night, he'd say to Betty, 'Swifty thinks I'm going to die.'"

Saturday night Spencer Tracy and Katharine Hepburn were leaving just as Dr. Brandsma arrived. Miss Hepburn kissed Bogie goodnight as she always did. Tracy, who was standing behind Bogie, put his hand on his shoulder and leaned forward. "Bogie looked up at him with a most rueful smile and said, 'Good-bye, Spence,' and you could tell he meant it," said Miss Hepburn. "He'd always said 'goodnight' before. When we were downstairs, Spence looked at me and said, 'Bogie's going to die.'"

When Dr. Brandsma finished his evening visit, Bogie said, "Good-bye" to him and thanked him for everything he had done. The doctor told me, "I am sure that night he knew he was going to die."

After Dr. Brandsma left, Pat Bogart, Bogie's sister and the only surviving member of his family, came in to see him. "Is it a man's privilege to take his own life?" he asked her. "Yes," she said. "He wouldn't have killed himself but he would have given up trying to live," Pat was to say later.

Later Betty went to kiss Bogie goodnight. "I don't know why, but that night I slept on the bed with him," Betty told me. "In the morning before I took the kids to Sunday School he woke up and said, 'Boy, I hope I never have another night like that again.'" He never did.

When Betty came back to the house fifteen minutes

224

later, Bogie was in a coma and the nurse had phoned Dr. Brandsma, who rushed to the house.

At 2:10 on the morning of January 14, 1957, Bogie took his last gulp of life—a deep one.

Betty telephoned me at 2:30. She was sobbing but her voice was firm. "Bogie died tonight, Joe," she said. "It was the last story he could give you and he wanted you to have it first."

EPILOGUE

After the death of Bogie, Betty found that at the age of thirty-three she was on her own for the first time in her life. She had lived with her mother until, at the age of twenty, she married Bogie, and during the eleven years of their marriage he had been husband, father, lover, manager and best friend. He helped her make decisions, solved most of her problems, and was an integral part of her life. "When Bogie died, the bottom dropped out of my life," she told a friend.

Bogart had been her anchor. Without him she was adrift. Worse, she and Bogie had been mirror images of each other. With him dead, one half of the mirror was shattered. The image she had of herself was fragmented. She no longer had a clear identity.

So she tried to hold on to as much of him as possible. She slept in the same bed she had shared with him, and every morning she passed his clothes closet. His favorite chair was still by the fireplace in the den, mute reminder of the room he once dominated. Photographs of old friends hung on the wall over the fireplace, but age had cut many of them down; almost everyone who had attended their wedding at Louis

Bromfield's farm eleven years earlier was dead. The photo gallery was only another painful reminder of the past.

The death of a husband always presents problems for the widow, but in Betty's case they were greatly exaggerated. For one thing the last year of Bogie's life had not been a pleasant one. But Bogie was a man of great dignity, so the secret heartache of those last few months could never be shared by his widow with anyone else, no matter how close.

Bogie was also world famous and dearly beloved by millions. The eyes of the world were on Betty's every move and word.

Another problem which troubled her, and gave her many painful hours of self-examination, was trying to learn whether the friends they had were his *and* hers. Even while he was sick, their home was crowded with some of the most famous people in the movie colony. But after his death, many of the people who used to visit the house stopped coming. Betty didn't know whether it was because they were embarrassed and didn't know how to face her grief, or whether it was because they were his friends, not hers. Her circle of confidantes had been narrowed to less than six good friends.

The fact was that she wanted nothing less than to be left alone. She wanted desperately to see friends. Most important she wanted to talk about Bogie with people who knew him. But friends insisted on talking around him, while she wanted to talk about him normally, as though he was still there.

For the first few weeks of her widowhood Betty kept herself busy answering correspondence, sending out thousands of thank-you cards for condolences and tying up business affairs. Although Bogie had made millions of dollars during his lifetime there was less than a million dollars in his estate, much of it in trust for the children's education. The remainder was sufficient to keep her and the children comfortable for a while, but not enough so that she did not have to be concerned about the future. So she began some belt-tightening. The *Santana* was too expensive to keep up so she sold it at less than market value to a yachtsman who knew Bogie and would cherish the boat.

Then she began to look for things to keep her busy, to keep her mind from dwelling on Bogie. She subscribed to a clipping service and collected stories of Bogie's death printed in newspapers all over the world. She pasted them herself into large leather scrapbooks and had them bound chronologically for the children.

She started to read scripts and think about returning to work, not only for the therapy work offered but so she could resume her career. But she was unable to get her thoughts off Bogie. She found it impossible to leave the house for any length of time because she couldn't shake off the belief that he would be there waiting for her.

At the insistence of friends she went to New York for a two-week visit. She registered at the Gotham Hotel where she and Bogie had always stayed in the past and where he had announced to the press that they were going to get married. There, too, there were constant reminders of him.

Although her eastern friends entertained her royally, she soon felt she had to return home, that for some inexplicable reason she was missing something there. So she went back to the pattern of spending her days moping about the big house on Mapleton Drive, the full impact of her loss finally being felt.

Morgan Maree, her good friend and business manager as well as Bogie's, visited her there one afternoon and gently tried to find out what was keeping her so blue. They sat in the den that Bogie was so content in. Betty hedged, trying to find the right words. Morgan finally admitted that it was impossible for him to feel cheerful in a room where so many memories stared down at him. "It's the pictures over the fireplace that depress me," he said. "Everything is exactly as it was. Why don't you make some changes, starting with taking the pictures down."

At first Betty thought this would be heresy, but finally she acted on his advice. She had made a first step toward realizing that she had been beginning to die piecemeal herself. She had to remain living and vital, if not for her sake then for the children's, the realization hit home sharply six months after Bogie's death. On Father's Day, eight-year-old Stephen stood in the driveway sobbing, "I want my daddy. I want my daddy." All of his friends were with their fathers and he was alone. It was the first time a special day had been altered for him.

Again she began to read scripts offered to her. She had finished *Designing Woman* for MGM only a few months before Bogie's death. Although he never saw it, from all she told him of it he thought it would be her best picture to date, and it was. Then 20th-Century Fox offered her a role in *The Gift of Love*, a sentimental story about a dying woman.

Eight months after Bogie's death she returned to work. Her face, which was always thin, was drawn. Her eyes looked raw from crying but she was still a beautiful young woman, attractive enough to cause stares anyplace she went. Once she started working again, Betty began to come outside of herself and begin life again.

She sold the big house and rented a smaller home in the same neighborhood. Immediately after the film was completed, she gave a Halloween party—a "moving out party" she called it—for her friends and Bogie's.

Only one thing spoiled the party. The den was crowded with people but no one would sit in Bogie's chair by the fireplace. "I knew then I was doing the right thing by moving," Betty told me. "I had to get away from the physical reminders of Bogie. I couldn't live in the past any longer."

Bogie's chair and all the rest of the furniture in the

house were given to the Good Will people. Only the new living room furniture was moved into the new house, in which she would live for less than a year.

During the early months of her mourning, Betty had stayed at home, seeing very few people and going out rarely, most often with Frank Sinatra, who had been her and Bogie's good friend. Sinatra was everything Bogie had not been. Bogie was an old-fashioned man, actually a prude. Sinatra was an exponent of the ring-a-ding-ding style of life. Unlike Bogie he was flirtatious, gay and care free, constantly seeking new varieties of action. Bogie had always been careful with money; Sinatra's generosity was legendary. He thought nothing of renting a yacht with a band if the mood was on him. Bogart found it difficult to express emotion outwardly, but Sinatra was affectionate and endearing when the mood was on him.

Bogie and Betty had enjoyed Sinatra and lived vicariously through his various exploits. Now Betty envied Sinatra's easy acceptance of life and found in him the therapy she needed; someone who would make her laugh and understand her need to talk about Bogie.

The press made much of their occasional outings, and then, in March 1958 Louella Parsons reported they would get married. According to her, several people overheard Frank asking Betty to marry him at a Japanese restaurant in Hollywood where they were having dinner. Miss Parsons cornered Betty at a party given for Noel Coward at Zsa Zsa Gabor's house. Betty admitted Sinatra had proposed.

"And you'll say, 'yes,'" the columnist persisted.

"Of course," Betty answered.

Once the story got into the press Sinatra left Hollywood and Betty became unavailable for comment. A few weeks later Betty and the children left Hollywood for London, where she had accepted a film offer to play opposite Kenneth More in *Flame Over India*, to be made on locations in India, Spain and London.

I went to interview her just before she left Hollywood. As we were at the door saying good-bye she asked me why I hadn't questioned her about what she wouldn't miss about Hollywood. For a moment, the sadness disappeared from her eyes and was replaced by the twinkle I recognized as the sign of a good quote to come.

"I won't miss the idle chitchat," she said, "the smiling 'hello' and 'good-bye' that happen simultaneously in a room; the faces that open and close the minute you walk in; the 'hello, how are you and that's the end of it' conversations; the kisses-in-the-air greetings wherever you go; and the constant scrutiny of one's private life."

It was her only comment to me about the romance with Sinatra.

The film had a therapeutic value because it offered Betty an opportunity to meet new people and visit new places. She was beginning to come out of her shell, and on her return to Hollywood a year and a half after the death of Bogie she told me the answer to her grief was work. "I'm used to work, it's my whole life. I've worked hard since I was a kid. You just don't stop. And I don't believe in a useless life."

She soon found out, however, that work was not the only answer. It made the days pass quicker, but there were the nights and those minutes when you are with a crowd of people and still lonely. "Just working is not being a woman," she said. "I used to think it was when I was first married. I chased ambition. I thought I had something special to offer. In those days Bogie used to say to me, 'It isn't all that important. You'll find out. I found out.'"

But work was the only thing she had left and in the summer of 1959 she decided that the time was right for a new direction in her career. George Axelrod, writer-husband of her high school chum Joan Stanton, had written a play for her called *Goodbye, Charlie* in which she portrayed Charlie, a playboy who dies and returns to earth in the guise of a woman and learns how painful it is to be rejected by a woman. Her co-

231

star was Sidney Chaplin, son of the famous comedian. When the comedy opened on Broadway the critics found it to be scarcely more than a gag, but, in general, they admired Betty's acting. The show ran for 109 performances.

During Christmas week 1959, while appearing in the play, Betty went one evening after the theater to a large party given by actor Roddy McDowall where she was introduced to Jason Robards, Jr., then starring on Broadway in Lillian Hellman's *Toys in the Attic*. They hit it off immediately, and, a few days later, met again at a New Year's Eve party.

Betty was charmed by Robard's caustic wit and impressed by his professional talent. As a friend said, "He was a New York version of Bogie, complete even to his fondness for Scotch. Even their last names were similar."

There were other similarities. Just as Bogie had been married when Betty met him, Robards, too, was married to his second wife, actress Rachel Taylor, his bride of only a few weeks.

Again Betty knew what she wanted and went after it. Ultimately Robards became free and he and Betty were married in Ensenada, Mexico, on July 4, 1961. A son named Sam was born to them the following November.

The newlyweds moved into a ten-room apartment in the Dakota, New York's oldest and perhaps most elegant cooperative apartment at Central Park West and 72nd Street. Their family included: Sam, Steve, Leslie, a beagle named Benjamin, plus a cook, nurse and maid.

Betty was soon to openly state that their marriage was not the idyll that her first marriage had been. For one thing, she was trying in vain to re-create the spirit of Bogie in Robards but the only thing the two men had in common was talent, a fondness for Scotch, and Betty.

Also Betty's career was in another lean period. After the closing of *Goodbye, Charlie* she turned down parts in about a dozen plays as being unsuitable but she committed herself to two unrewarding motion picture roles—*Shock Treatment,* in which she portrayed a mad psychiatrist, and *Sex and the Single Girl,* where she had to play a screaming, dish-throwing shrew in a supporting role.

Most of her problem with the Hollywood producers was that they thought her too old for certain lead parts, identifying her with Bogie and his contemporaries, who in fact were twenty-five years older than she. Realizing, however, that it was important for her career to be showcased, she was reluctant to refuse assignments even when she knew they were mediocre. Her only successful picture in years was *Harper* (made in 1965), in which she had a small role as the vindictive paraplegic wife of a millionaire. The star of the film was Paul Newman, who played a cynical private eye in the Bogart style.

The shadow of Bogart continued to dominate her career and new marriage. Ironically he was even more alive six years after his death than before. A Bogart cult was spreading throughout the world. The cult had begun in 1957 when the small but selective Brattle Theater in Cambridge, Massachusetts, booked *Beat the Devil,* and found it did something for the "hip" audience made up largely of the summer population at Harvard, Radcliffe and MIT. The film's wacky, slightly off beat comedy tickled sophisticated fancies much more so than it had appealed to audiences the first time around. Patrons dug Bogie's style, his manner of being hard-boiled and contemptuous in a nice, dry sardonic way.

Soon avant-garde theaters all over America were playing old Bogart films to packed houses while other theaters playing more contemporary films were losing money. It was not long before most of the films Bogart had made since 1935 were showing in theaters across the nation. And during this time more articles were written about him in America, France, Germany and England than when he was alive.

233

German youths idolized him because he was gallant even in defeat. English youths considered him the universal type of a rebellious age. The French considered him the archetype of the outsider, the true existentialist. "He is the modern anti-hero," said a *New York Times*' writer seeking to establish Bogie's increasing popularity in America after his death.

"What is the powerful fascination of this old, gravel-voiced movie star?" Bosley Crowther, the distinguished film critic, asked in an *Esquire* article. "Let's begin by observing bluntly that the fervor is for a myth that has accumulated around a character that is part fictitious and part historical. The fictitious part is the fellow Bogart plays in his favored films—the disillusioned, disenchanted individual moving through what is generally an alien world. And the historical part is the image of Bogie as a Hollywood personality of great independence, coolness, candor and disdain for the brass and all the manifestations of smugness and hypocrisy that are shown by the establishment. This latter image emerged from his behavior in later years—behavior that naturally attracted attention and got a great deal of unplanned and unplanted publicity.

"And this accumulation of the fictitious and the historical have merged so it is hard to tell where the screen character leaves off and the historical character begins."

There were also his films, which stood on their own, distant echoes of his romance with Betty, the haunting history of his slow death by cancer, which he endured with the kind of courage that was his wont. The total myth was far from a reflection of the man that Bogie was. Yet Bogie himself was not really the man he appeared to be—the man he ultimately acted in real life just as devotedly and sincerely as the one he acted on the screen.

As John Huston had said in his eulogy, "He is quite irreplaceable. There will never be another like him."

As Bogie's widow, Betty was keeper of the flame.

She was constantly sought out by the press for interviews about Bogie. Six books were written about him. The constant identification with him continued to keep her own name in the public eye, and Robards, an established star in his own right, was beginning to sweat under the label of Mrs. Bogart's second husband.

Betty was fiercely loyal to Bogie and equally loyal to Robards. At a New York party she was seated talking to Robards when she was approached by the editor of a highbrow monthly magazine who began extolling Bogie's acting abilities while never once mentioning Robards, who was at Betty's elbow. Betty listened stonily to the editor for some minutes and then, giving him a glowering look, snarled, "Bug off, buster."

Although Robards was working pretty steadily, Betty was not, and with the children away in school —Stephen at Milton Academy in Massachusetts and Leslie at the Lycée Français—she was in the doldrums. Then David Merrick chose her for the lead in his 1965 Broadway production of *Cactus Flower*, in which she played a spinsterish dental nurse. The play opened on December 8, 1965, at the Royale Theater, New York, and the following morning the New York critics fell all over themselves in praise of Betty, who, at last, had her childhood dream come true. She became the season's reigning Broadway star in the town's biggest hit.

Betty remained with the show for almost two years of its run, taking only one week's vacation and not a day off for illness. At last she was on her way to being her own woman, as Bogie had been his own man. She was finally established as a star, if not in films, then on Broadway, and the career she had sought so hard as a girl was now becoming a reality.

But although she had what seemed to be a secure career, she did not have a secure marriage. Acting had become her life, as it was Jason's, and their marriage suffered from the long separations. After eight years of marriage, Betty and Robards were divorced in Juarez, Mexico, September 10, 1969, on grounds of incompatibility.

On March 30, 1970, Betty opened on Broadway in *Applause*, for which Betty Comden and her old friend Adolph Green had written the book, an adaptation of the film *All About Eve*. Again Betty was a hit in a hit play, and she stayed with it on Broadway until July 17, 1971. Then she moved to an elegant furnished flat in Belgravia, an exclusive suburb of London, with Sam and a spaniel named Blenheim. She opened in *Applause* on London's West End on November 16, 1972, to raves and capacity audiences and remained with the play until its closing, October 6, 1973.

Meanwhile, she had become a grandmother. Stephen had gotten married in October 1969, moved to Torrington, Connecticut, where he works for an insurance company, and had a son named Jamie Humphrey Bogart. Leslie, who, like her mother, was a great beauty, decided to become a nurse and enrolled at Boston University.

Four months after finishing *Applause*, Betty went into her first film in eight years—*Murder on the Orient Express*—based on Agatha Christie's thriller, with an all-star cast.

Now, in the winter of 1974–75, after two years of living in London, she is back in New York with Sam, who is twelve years old. At fifty—almost seventeen years after Bogie's death—she is virtually on her own again, but no longer adrift. She is firmly anchored to her stage career. She said recently that although she was brought up to believe in marriage as a way of life, she now believes it has become less and less important for a woman to be married.

"I like many aspects of my life alone," she said. "I've become more selfish and I feel I could live anywhere so long as there was a reason. I never felt that way before, even though I've been alone for a long, long time."

INDEX

238

244